Jan Muntermann

Event-Driven Mobile Financial Information Services

GABLER EDITION WISSENSCHAFT

Jan Muntermann

Event-Driven Mobile Financial Information Services

Design of an Intraday
Decision Support System

With a foreword by Prof. Dr. Kai Rannenberg

Deutscher Universitäts-Verlag

Bibliographic information published by Die Deutsche Nationalbibliothek
Die Deutsche Nationalbibliothek lists this publication in the Deutsche Nationalbibliografie;
detailed bibliographic data is available in the Internet at <http://dnb.d-nb.de>.

Dissertation Universität Frankfurt am Main, 2007

1st Edition October 2007

Readers: Frauke Schindler / Nicole Schweitzer

Deutscher Universitäts-Verlag is a company of Springer Science+Business Media.
www.duv.de

Cover design: Regine Zimmer, Dipl.-Designerin, Frankfurt/Main
Printed on acid-free paper
Printed in Germany

ISBN 978-3-8350-0888-5

Foreword

While Mobile Communications continues to be a very successful industry, the number of successful mobile applications still seems to be limited. Certainly, mobile voice and email are attractive to more and more customers. However especially during the boom around the UMTS license auctions much more fancy mobile applications were discussed, sometimes seen implemented – but never really widely used.

Often high costs, especially compared to the costs of the "fixed" Internet, were given as reasons for this. But considering the prices businesses, and more and more private people, pay for mobile voice and email connectivity, other reasons must exist for the reluctance to use mobile applications. One reason seems to be that quite a few people are not convinced, that mobile access or receiving information on a mobile device adds value. More formally speaking, usefulness or a relative advantage are not perceived, especially when the ones receiving the information are busy decision makers, who have other things to do. Especially when confronted with the still existing weaknesses of mobile devices, e.g. their limited I/O-capabilities they may see mobile work as mobile stress with no sustainable use.

In this situation, Jan Muntermann has thought about possible contributions that Business Informatics can bring to the table, and decided to aim for an example of presenting decision-relevant information and to show its use as well as its technical feasibility: He analyses the use of immediately receiving selected ad hoc messages to be able to buy and sell affected stocks quicker than other market participants. While this is a promising and innovative approach, Jan's contribution is just starting with it. He looks what non-institutional investors can gain from using a mobile information push service and how the design of this should look like. Then he implements his design in a prototypical IT artifact and evaluates it.

In addition to its core assets, this work contributes to computerized decision support, also to methods for analyzing the stock market and its long-term trends. Jan Muntermann has written a first class thesis in Business Informatics, which is already influencing neighboring disciplines.

Given this, I am more than happy to wish this to book all the best, especially many interested readers.

Prof. Dr. Kai Rannenberg

Preface

Timely information provision is a critical success factor for investment management of volatile assets. Previous research has shown that improved IT infrastructure can provide competitive advantages since traders with longer information processing often realize lower profits per trade. This work focuses on the design and evaluation of an event-driven mobile financial information system that supports private investors in making time-critical intraday investment decisions.

The empirical event study presented in this work provides an analysis of intraday stock price effects following the publication of ad hoc disclosures and proves the existence of abnormal intraday stock price effects. This intraday event study was conducted on the German capital market and provides evidence that investors could exploit these price effects when supported appropriately. Therefore, this thesis presents corresponding decision support models that assist investors in identifying those events after which abnormal price effects can be expected within an estimated period of time. Based on the design science research paradigm, these models are applied to the design of a mobile decision support system, which provides ubiquitous information access to private investors. This work concludes with an evaluation of the proposed IT artifact utilizing a novel customers' value simulation approach. The results illustrate that the identification of most relevant market events and a reduction of reaction time can produce significantly higher profits per trade.

When I started this thesis at the faculty of business administration and economics at the Johann Wolfgang Goethe-University in 2002, the dot-com bubble had just burst. Especially at that time, writing a doctoral thesis in the field of mobile financial services was a challenging idea that required broad academic and industry support.

Without the extensive support received from industry partners, it would not have been possible to complete this thesis. I would like to thank those partners, especially T-Mobile International AG, Interactive Data Managed Solutions AG and NOW Wireless Limited for providing invaluable support.

I am very grateful to my colleagues at the Chair of Mobile Business and Multilateral Security for the fruitful discussions and for the joint research paper projects. Here, I thank my colleagues Andreas Albers, Stefan Figge, Lothar Fritsch and Heiko Roßnagel for their support and their inspiring comments. Special thanks go to my adviser Prof. Dr. Kai Rannenberg for providing a stimulating and interdisciplinary research environment that made this work possible. The T-Mobile Chair of Mobile Business and Multilateral Security at the J.W. Goethe-University Frankfurt is providing the basis for many exceptional research outcomes.

Further thanks go to Prof. Dr. Wolfgang König and Prof. Dr. Peter Gomber for their instructive advice and to Jun.-Prof. Dr. Günter W. Beck, all members of the board of examiners. Moreover, the many fruitful discussions with Prof. Dr. Reinhardt A. Botha contributed significantly to this work. Michael Gellings has done a great job as editor and has enhanced the readability of the manuscript immensely.

I owe special thanks to my dear friend Cornelia Gellings who has given me unwavering support and encouragement during the years of my PhD phase and who has made, in many different ways, significant contributions to this thesis.

                                                                                    Dr. Jan Muntermann

Table of Contents

Figures

Tables

Variables and Symbols

Variables and Symbols in Section 2.1

μ_0	Hypothesized population mean
b_i	Binary variable
d_i	Median difference with index i
i	Event index
I	Sample size
m_0	Hypothesized population median
$rank_i$	Rank of absolute median difference with index i
s	Sample standard deviation
t	t-value
t_0	Event date
t_E	End date of the event window
t_S	Start date of the event window
t_{-E}	End date of the estimation window
t_{-S}	Start date of the estimation window
W^+	Wilcoxon signed rank test statistic
$\bar{x}$	Sample mean
x_i	Sample value with index i

Variables and Symbols in Section 2.2

$\mu(CAAR_t)$	Mean corrected absolute abnormal return with index t
$\mu(CCAAR_{t1,t2})$	Mean cumulated corrected absolute abnormal return with indices i and t
$AR_{i,t}$	Abnormal return with indices i and t
$\left| AR_{i,t} \right|$	Absolute abnormal return with indices i and t
$CAAR_{i,t}$	Corrected absolute abnormal return with indices i and t
$CCAAR_{i,t1,t2}$	Cumulated corrected absolute abnormal return with indices i, $t1$ and $t2$
H_0	Null hypothesis
H_A	Alternative hypothesis
i	Event index
I	Sample size
$MAAR_i$	Mean absolute abnormal return with index i
$median(CAAR_t)$	Median corrected absolute abnormal return with index t
$median(CCAAR_{t1,t2})$	Median cumulated corrected absolute abnormal return with indices i and $t1$ and $t2$
$P_{i,t}$	Stock price with indices i and t

$P_{CDAX,t}$	CDAX price with index t
$R_{i,t}$	Logarithmic stock return with indices i and t
$R_{CDAX,t}$	Logarithmic CDAX return with index t
t, $t1$, and $t2$	Price fixing index
T	Number of price fixings

Variables and Symbols in Section 3.3

$\Delta t_{i,1,2}$	Period of time (in minutes) in which the first two price fixings can be observed following the event date (with index i)
$\Delta t_{i,3,10}$	Price effect duration (in minutes) with index i
β_j	Forecasting model parameter with index j
ε_i	Error term (forecasting function) with index i
$\mu(\Delta t_{i,3,10})$	Mean of $\Delta t_{i,3,10}$ with index i
$\mu(CCAAR_{i,3,10})$	Mean of $CCAAR_{i,3,10}$ with index i
Ψ	Primary dataset (price effect duration)
Ψ^F	Forecasting dataset (price effect duration)
Ψ^I	Information dataset (price effect duration)
Ω	Primary dataset (price effect magnitude)
Ω^F	Forecasting dataset (price effect magnitude)
Ω^I	Information dataset (price effect magnitude)
$\#Analysts_i$	Number of analysts covering the company with index i
$CAAR_{i,t}$	Corrected absolute abnormal return
$CCAAR_{i,t1,t2}$	Cumulated corrected absolute abnormal return
df	Degrees of freedom
i	Event index
$Index_i$	Index membership (binary variable) with index i
$F(\Delta t_{i,3,10})$	Forecasted value of $\Delta t_{i,3,10}$ with index i
$F(CCAAR_{i,3,10})$	Forecasted value of $CCAAR_{i,3,10}$ with index i
R^2	Coefficient of determination (of a linear regression)
t	Price fixing index
$TVol_{i,1,2}$	Trading value during the first two price fixings following the event date (with index i)
Z_i	Observed category
$\hat{Z}_i$	Forecasted category

Variables and Symbols in Section 5.1

μ_0^{pd}	Hypothesized paired difference
μ_0^{sm}	Hypothesized difference between sample means
df	Degrees of freedom
I	Sample size
I_s	Size of sample s
pd	Paired difference
$\overline{pd}$	Mean of pd
s	Sample index
s_{pd}	Standard deviation of pd
s_s^2	Variance of sample s
x_s	Value from sample s
$\overline{x}_s$	Mean of sample s

Variables and Symbols in Section 5.2

c_i	Total trading costs of the transaction with index i
c_{Fi}	Fixed trading costs
c_v	Variable trading costs
c_{Max}	Maximum trading costs
c_{Min}	Minimum trading costs
d	Delay level
i	Event index
p_{i,t_c}	Closing price at the event date
p_{i,t_d}	First observable price fixing d minutes subsequent to the announcement date
$\left|r_{i,d}\right|$	Realizable return of stock affected by event i at delay level d
$\left|tr_{i,d}\right|$	Realizable trading return with indices i and d
v	Trading volume
v_{Max}	Maximum trading volume
v_{Min}	Minimum trading volume
$\overline{y}_d$	Mean realizable yield at delay level d

Variables and Symbols in Section 5.3

$\mu\left(pd_{d1d2}\right)$	Mean of $pd_{i,d1,d2}$
$\mu\left(\overline{\left|r_{1,d}\right|}-\overline{\left|r_{2,d}\right|}\right)$	Mean of $\overline{\left|r_{1,d}\right|}-\overline{\left|r_{2,d}\right|}$
df	Degrees of freedom
d	Delay level
i	Event index
I	Sample size
$pd_{i,d1,d2}$	Paired difference of realizable returns between delay levels $d1$ and $d2$
$\left|r_{i,d}\right|$	Realizable return with indices i and d
$\overline{\left|r_{s,d}\right|}$	Mean of realizable returns of sample s with index d
$\left|R_d\right|$	Realizable return population with index d
s	Sample index
s^2	Variance
$\overline{y}_d$	Mean realizable yield with index d

Equations

1 Introduction

We should help create the future, not just study the past.
Gray (2002), Communications of the AIS (8:23)

Information technology and the impact of the Internet have changed dramatically the banking industry in the last decades (Chowdhury 2003; Crane and Bodie 1996; Holland et al. 1997; McKenney et al. 1997; Nehmzow 1997; Parsons et al. 1993). This development has affected processes and communication within and between the banks but also customer relations and services (Awad 2000; Beck et al. 2003; Holland and Westwood 2001).

Especially in the retail-banking sector, online banking and brokerage services have become a necessity due to customers' demand for convenient, secure, and flexible banking services (Pikkarainen et al. 2004). The success story of online banking has become a challenge for the IT infrastructures of banks, not least because of the necessary investments. On the other hand, various studies show that these segments are highly profitable to banks because of realizable cost savings (Sheshunoff 2000; Southard and Siau 2004).

By contrast, the diffusion of mobile banking services has not yet lived up to expectations even though in the last couple of years the growth rate of mobile phones operating in countries like Germany has exceeded that of the fixed network (Bundesnetzagentur 2006).

Several surveys indicate that perceived usefulness and the relative advantage provided are of major relevance for customers to adopt mobile banking services (Brown et al. 2003; Lee et al. 2003; Luarn and Lin 2005). However, most of mobile banking research concentrates on behavioral and technical issues related to applications and services currently available. These are mainly reproductions of the traditional banking services such as payment services, basic information services such as bank statements or banking account management (e.g. Barnes and Corbitt 2003; Herzberg 2003; Lanedri 2002; Mallat et al. 2004).

Utilizing the reduction of temporal and spatial constraints provided by mobile communication infrastructures, this work aims to identify and explore a new, promising mobile banking scenario. Focusing on the highly time-critical mobile brokerage domain, a novel event-driven mobile financial decision support system is introduced and its relative advantages are illustrated. Compared to existing mobile banking concepts, the explored scenario benefits from increased ubiquity due to a limited period of reaction time available and explicitly addresses the relative advantage demanded by customers.

Section 1.1 further illustrates the gap between current mobile financial service concepts and the user acceptance serving as research motivation. Then, Section 1.2 explicates the addressed research objective and the derived research questions. The general structure is then presented in Section 1.3 providing an overview of scientific foundations as well as major contributions for each of the chapters. Finally, Section 1.4 summarizes relevant methodical issues, with special focus on a design science research framework providing a methodical basis for the entire work presented in the following.

1.1 Mobile Financial Services

When planning novel mobile financial services, companies face the problem of identifying suitable service concepts that will be taken up by customers searching for the most promising investment strategies. In recent years, online brokers and banks have invested significantly in their online services with the aim of attracting more customers. In the online and mobile brokerage domain companies intend to increase the number of transactions performed in order to realize higher profits from transaction fees. Furthermore, the corresponding product and service development strategies in this industry are of major relevance since they empower firms to control switching costs of their customers (Chen and Hitt 2002).

Most of the existing mobile financial services are pull-based, and typically modified versions of standard online banking services, i.e. they address similar application scenarios such as providing access to stock quotes, calculating currency conversion, trading of stocks or conducting payments (Mallat et al. 2004). Online brokers have developed specific business models for mobile brokerage services in order to manage customer segments, pricing models and products (Looney et al. 2004). Looney and Chatterjee (2002) show that appropriate mobile financial information services can enhance customer satisfaction in order to retain the most profitable customers, which will improve long-term profitability. The authors conclude that the value provided to customers is a central success factor for mobile financial services and therefore technological opportunities need to be recognized and evaluated.

While around 40% of today's mobile device users believe that banking and stock trading can be supported adequately by mobile services, only 2% of mobile Internet users utilize corresponding financial services (van Veen et al. 2006). In consequence, the diffusion of mobile banking services has not met expectations (Shen et al. 2006).

Thus, the design and evaluation of novel mobile financial services that provide additional value to customers is an ongoing challenge. Lanedri (2002) points out that mobile brokerage services enable private investors to react promptly to changing market conditions since they can be reached in an unrestricted environment. Mattila (2003) analyzes factors affecting the adoption of mobile financial services and shows that customers demand user-friendly services that provide additional value compared to the existing offerings. In a survey analyzing requirements of mobile brokerage services, Laukkanen and Lauronen (2005) identify the most relevant service characteristics demanded by customers. Their results indicate that location-independent service access to real-time information and transaction services is highly relevant, when prompt reaction is required (Laukkanen and Lauronen 2005).

This raises the question how private investors should recognize the need for reaction since corresponding personalized mobile notification services are currently still rare and, at any rate, do not reach very far. Keeping in mind customers' value as a dominant service characteristic, this question will be addressed in the following.

1.2 Research Objective and Questions

Many researchers have emphasized the potentials of mobile banking services (e.g. Barnes and Corbitt 2003; Herzberg 2003; Mallat et al. 2004). There is wide evidence that the usefulness and relative advantage provided by mobile banking services is of major relevance for the users' willingness to adopt mobile banking services (Mattila 2003; Lee et al. 2003; Luarn and Lin 2005).

Being based on the behavioral science paradigm, these analyses provide valuable insights into the success factors of mobile banking services. However, little research addresses the question how this relative advantage can be achieved. In contrast, there is a focus on traditional banking services, such payment, bank account management or the provision of financial information, being shifted to the mobile infrastructures (e.g. Barnes and Corbitt 2003; Mang and Georgi 2006, Pousttchi and Schurig 2004).

Consequently, the lack of novel concepts for mobile banking services providing the postulated relative advantage has resulted in little adoption rates in the banking industry (Shen et al. 2006). Kock et al. (2002) point out that the information systems (IS) research community faces the opportunity to broaden its scope and learn from science and engineering. Creating something new such as novel IT artifacts can contribute to IS research as much as studying an already existing item or issue (Kock et al. 2002). With respect to the existing research in mobile banking services, few contributions exist that explore new promising service concept or address novel system designs including sound evaluations of the business value provided.

Focusing on the particular characteristics of mobile communication infrastructures, this thesis aims to bridge this gap by exploring a novel and promising mobile banking application domain. Being based on the design science research paradigm, which is further introduced in Section 1.4, the research objective addresses the design and evaluation of a novel IT artifact that provides event-driven notification and decision support to private investors. Therefore, a combination of hard and software system (the IT artifact) is explored, prototypically implemented and evaluated. This artifact notifies private investors about critical market events that can affect the prices of stocks held by the investors. When stock prices react quickly to these events, traditional online banking services do not enable users to react in time due to limited service access, whereas ubiquitous service access is one of the major value propositions for mobile commerce in general (Sun et al. 2005). Using mobile push services, a notification is sent automatically to the mobile device of the investor, when a critical market event has occurred. Furthermore, the artifact provides decision support by estimating the stock price effect following the event. The research objective will be addressed in a way to provide valuable contributions to IS research that should also be practically applicable.

From this research objective, the following research questions are derived:

- What are relevant market events that affect stock prices in a way so that they provide trading opportunities for private investors (Chapter 2)?

- What are the characteristics and components of a suitable decision support system that supports the investors making their time-critical investment decisions (Chapter 3)?

- How can a corresponding IT artifact be designed that provides intraday decision support to investors and utilizes mobile communication infrastructures (Chapter 4)?

- How can such a kind of mobile service be evaluated in order to prove the benefits, and the relative advantage, it provides (Chapter 5)?

1.3 Structure of the Thesis

The previous sections of this introduction have illustrated the status quo of mobile commerce research with special focus on mobile banking research from which the problem definitions and research questions were derived. In this thesis, these research questions are mainly addressed with the help of the design science research paradigm and further research methodologies that are summarized in the following section.

Apart from this introduction, the thesis consists of five chapters as shown in the following Figure 1.1.

The introducing motivation has shown that research into mobile financial information and decision support systems within the mobile brokerage application domain can provide economically relevant contributions, so there is relevance to the problem field addressed. The relevance of IS research to practice has been emphasized in many publications in the past (e.g. Kock et al. 2002; Lee 1999). This relevance also needs to be assured for rigorous design science research (Hevner et al. 2004). Problem relevance is further substantiated in Chapter 2, which provides evidence of the existence, and an analysis of the duration, of intraday stock price effects on the German capital market that could be exploited by investors when being supported with appropriate mobile services. The chapter starts with an introduction to the theory of efficient capital markets laying a theoretical foundation for the subsequent analysis. The stock price analysis is based on the event study methodology which originates from research in financial market analysis (Dolley 1933) and which has been adopted in the field of information system research in the past (e.g. Chatterjee et al. 2001). Furthermore, methods required for statistical hypothesis testing are introduced and applied. The empirical results presented in the following substantiate the relevance to practice since significant intraday price effects are observed for a relatively short period of time necessitating a prompt notification of, and a reaction by, the investor. Supporting investors during investment decisions is of

major relevance to business and is an ongoing challenge that has been addressed by both practitioners and researchers for several decades.

Figure 1.1: Structure of the Thesis

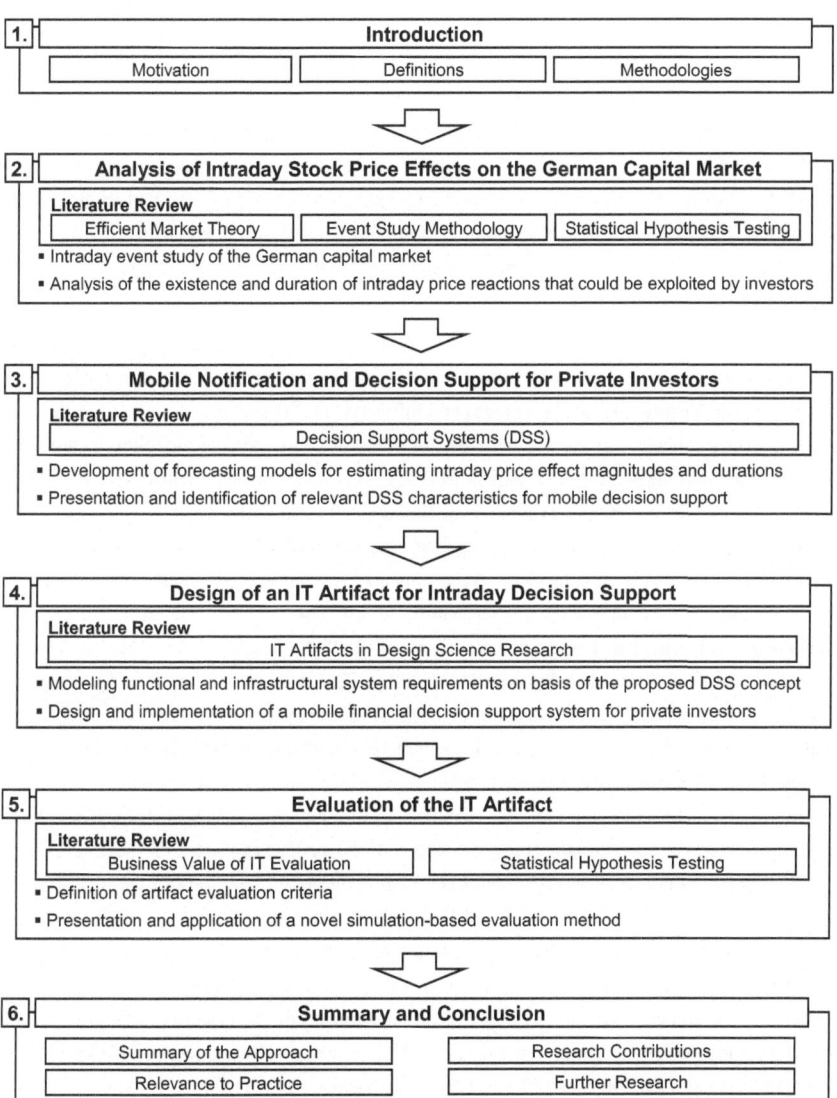

Then, Chapter 3 addresses this research field and therefore starts with a literature review summarizing the status quo of decision support system (DSS) research. The presentation of recent DSS approaches and characteristics serves as a foundation for analyzing the characteristics of a corresponding mobile financial DSS concept supporting investors being pressed for time. Therefore, two forecasting models are developed using ordinary-least-squares (OLS) regression analysis, which enable the DSS and the investors to assess the relevance of an event observed. This is measured by the stock price effect magnitude and its duration as estimated by the forecasting models. These forecasting models represent the dominant components of the DSS to be designed. An empirical evaluation attests superior out-of-sample model forecasting quality compared to previous approaches working with text mining techniques (e.g. Mittermayer 2004; Spiliopoulou et al. 2003). In order to demonstrate the feasibility of these models, they are incorporated into a prototypical application design in the following chapter.

After providing an overview of the role of IT artifacts in design science research, Chapter 4 presents an IT artifact, which considers relevant identified system characteristics and uses the developed forecasting models. Functional and infrastructural system requirements are derived from the DSS concept and are documented, for example, with suitable modeling techniques. The designed and implemented IT artifact *MoFin DSS* demonstrates the feasibility of the DSS concept. It enables a concrete evaluation of the artifact's suitability to its intended purpose, i.e. supporting private investors in making time-critical intraday investment decision by using appropriate mobile financial services. According to Srinivasan et al. (2005), the IT artifact designed comprises combination of hardware and software systems. The software components were implemented using, first, Visual Basic 2005 for implementing the *MoFin DSS* prototype server application software and, secondly, FTL, a scripting language for programming server-side interfaces used by *MoFin DSS*. These interfaces provide access to dynamically generated XML documents, which contain required input data such as news or stock prices. The *MoFin DSS* software provides the functionality to observe continuously company announcements (so-called ad hoc disclosures) that are published during stock exchange trading hours. When a new announcement is observed, the system evaluates the potential effect on the corresponding stock price (price effect magnitude) and the period of time in which the stock price (price effect duration) not yet fully reflects the new information available. When the price effect is identified to be significant, a mobile message is sent to a mobile device of the investor with further information such as details of the company announcement, estimated effects, or a graphical illustration of the adjustment process of the affected stock price, all of which provide decision support to the investor. This prototypically implemented DSS concept demands management of a complex server infrastructure that needs to be realized by the *MoFin DSS* software.

The evaluation of the proposed and implemented IT artifact is addressed in the following Chapter 5. A literature review of business value of IT evaluations provides an introduction to current approaches and relevant theoretical foundations. Statistical test procedures for addressing statistical hypothesis testing for two samples are presented in the following. These provide a methodic basis for comparing different evaluation results.

In the following, new artifact evaluation criteria and a novel simulation-based evaluation methodology are introduced that provide a basis for evaluating customers' benefits of the IT artifact presented. The simulation results then illustrate that investors being supported by *MoFin DSS* can realize statistically higher trading profits. Furthermore, it is explicated how to assess the total value provided to customers for different scenarios determined by investors' behavior, transaction costs, and other variables.

Finally, Chapter 6 summarizes the research approach of this thesis and presents its major research contributions. This, for example, comprises empirical results of an intraday event study, a decision support system concept comprising econometrically estimated forecasting models, an IT artifact that prototypically deploys this concept, and an evaluation methodology developed for assessing the IT business value provided. Next, practical implications are presented and their relevance is discussed. Finally, areas of further research are identified and discussed. These include possible extensions of the chosen design science approach, as well as behavioral science issues, which could be based on the contributions of this work.

1.4   Definitions and Research Methodology

1.4.1   Empirical Datasets and Data Analysis

There are several empirical sections in this thesis, especially in Chapter 2, 3, and 5 that rely on extensive empirical data. All this data has been collected within the period of 2003-08-01 and 2005-07-31, stems from primary data sources, and was collected automatically by server-scripts that were programmed in preparation.

The kind of event which has been selected as event of interest are ad hoc disclosures according to article 15 of the German Securities Trading Act (WpHG) published by the Deutsche Gesellschaft für Ad-hoc-Publizität (DGAP). The ad hoc disclosures were accessed via a news feed provided by DPA-AFX including publication date exact to the second. In total 4,998 ad hoc disclosures were collected of which 425 were used for further analyses. Most of the ad hoc disclosures were removed form the sample analyzed due to different filter rules, for example because they were not published during stock exchange trading hours.

The analysis of the price effect following these events is based on intraday stock price series of those companies that have published the disclosures. These price series and CDAX index prices were collected from the Frankfurt Stock Exchange (Xetra and floor trading). Furthermore, trading volumes were collected for the transaction prices observed. Both intraday stock prices and trading volumes were collected exact to the minute. If there has been more than one transaction price within the period of one minute, the last price has been taken. The trading volumes have been summed up for the one-minute interval.

Further data stems from *FactSet / JCF Group* providing the number of analysts covering the companies at the publication date of the all ad hoc disclosures observed.

All the data was analyzed using different software packages. Data formatting and preparation was done using Microsoft Excel 2003. The statistical hypothesis tests were performed with the econometric software package EViews 4.1 and the linear OLS regressions were calculated using SPPS 11.5. Graphical illustrations were plotted with Maple V and Microsoft Excel 2003.

1.4.2   IT Artifact Definition

In this thesis, the term *IT artifact* is used according to Srinivasan et al. (2005) who define IT artifacts "as a combined hardware and software system that is designed and implemented within an organizational context and whose purpose is to collect, organize, and store data, and transform it into information needed for operating and managing the organization".

IT artifacts are generally designed and deployed for a specific purpose and need to be evaluated for appropriateness and effectiveness within a particular organizational context. Other relevant definitions of the term can be found in Section 4.1 providing a brief overview of the role of IT artifacts in IS research.

1.4.3   Design Science Research Framework

Simon (1969 and 1996) originally described design science as a science of the artificial, having its roots in both computer and management sciences. Today, the design, deployment, and evaluation of prototypical concepts and applications are applied in both computer science (CS) (Olivier 2004) and information systems (IS) research (Srinivasan et al. 2005). Providing a basis for prescriptive research, the design science paradigm seeks to address relevant unsolved problem domains with the design, development, and evaluation of innovative IT artifacts such as hard- and software prototypes.

March and Smith (1995) emphasize the dual nature of IT research with artificial phenomena being designed and created as well as being observed and studied. This distinction between design and behavioral science, and its implications for IS and CS research has been a feature of an ongoing discussion in recent years (e.g. March and Smith 1995; Simon 1996; Hevner et al. 2004; Vahidov 2006).

Having its roots in natural science, the behavioral science paradigm focuses on developing and testing theories, with the aim of understanding and explaining observations made (March and Smith 1995). In contrast to this, design science research focuses on the creation and evaluation of artifacts that provide value for users or organizations (Banker and Kauffman 2004). However, the role of theories in design science is currently being discussed (e.g.

Venable 2006). Within this work, theoretical foundations play an important role in addition to the design science paradigm, especially with regard to the addressed problem field and the artifact evaluation since the corresponding chapters are theoretically founded, e.g. by deriving research hypotheses from relevant theories.

Within CS and IS literature, the prominent role of design science has been well recognized because the design of useful and innovative IT artifacts can provide new knowledge which in turn can push back the boundaries of existing theories in behavioral science research (Hevner et al. 2004; Olivier 2004).

Hevner et al. (2004) present a widely cited framework for conducting design science research in the IS field that lays a methodological basis for this thesis. Their framework has attracted attention in the call for papers for the *MISQ Special Issue on Design Science Research*, which prompts authors to conform to the corresponding design science research guidelines (March and Storey 2006).

The framework is based on the definition of guidelines that should assist researchers in conducting rigorous design science research. These seven guidelines should help to understand, execute, and evaluate design science research. This framework and the proposed guidelines are used in this work as methodological background. They are presented and summarized in the following, including an illustration of how they are incorporated into this work.

- Problem relevance

  Design science research aims at designing technology-based solutions to address unsolved problems with business or economic relevance. The identification and analysis of a relevant problem field is generally a starting point since the goal of the designed artifact is to address and solve these problems to some extend. The identification and analysis of relevant problem fields including relevant research questions raised are usually based on behavioral science approaches or statistical analyses.

  The following Chapter 2 explores the addressed problem field by presenting an intraday event study analysis that proves the existence of significant intraday stock price effects that could be exploited by investors. By analyzing the temporal persistence of these price effects, the analysis provides evidence that a suitable mobile financial service could provide benefits for some investors.

- Design of an artifact

  The design of an IT artifact that is useful within an organizational context is the main result of design science research. Therefore, researchers need to produce IT artifacts that demonstrate the feasibility of a concept.

  These artifacts are usually not fully working information systems that are already used within an organizational context. They are rather designed in several ways (e.g. in iterative loops) and tested in order to find the most appropriate concepts, designs, or prototypical implementations in order to solve the identified problems (Denning 1997). These innovations can therefore play a major role for finding suitable approaches for appropriate information systems.

This work presents the design and implementation of an IT artifact called *MoFin DSS*, which is a combination of both software and hardware infrastructure and is presented in Chapter 4. It empowers and supports private investors to react promptly to critical market events affecting stock prices. Following the IT artifact definition of Srinivasan et al. (2005), the stock price effect forecasting models that are presented in Chapter 3 are no IT artifacts in this sense. Here, these models are presented as DSS components becoming part of the *MoFin DSS* IT artifact.

- Design evaluation

An IT artifact is not built as an end in itself and therefore should provide substantial benefits to company employees, authorities and customers, i.e. within an organizational context (Hevner et al. 2004). These benefits can be evaluated directly by assessing the utility provided to users of the system, or indirectly with business profitability or productivity assessments (Hitt and Brynjolfsson 1996).

Furthermore, prototypes are used as a proof of concept for innovations, or for experimentations that illustrate the innovative character (Olivier 2004).

Hevner et al. (2004) present a set of evaluation methods that can be applied for assessing the utility, quality, and efficacy of designed artifacts such as field studies, architecture analyses, or simulations that demonstrate potential benefits of the artifact with artificial data.

In this work, Chapter 5 addresses the evaluation of the IT artifact designed. Appropriate evaluations metrics are defined and a novel simulation-based methodology for evaluating the business value of IT is developed and applied.

- Research rigor

Rigor can be achieved by using appropriate research methods and theoretical foundations (Lee 1999). The design science research paradigm and the corresponding research guidelines presented here constitute a concise conceptual research framework used in this thesis.

Furthermore, each of the Chapters 2 to 5 starts with a section that introduces theoretical foundations, methodologies and research frameworks used or applied. For example, Chapter 2 starts with an introduction to the efficient market hypothesis which constitutes the theoretical basis of the chapter. Furthermore, principles of the event study methodology and statistical hypotheses testing are presented. At the beginning of Chapter 3 a DSS research framework is introduced, which is used to present and explain the proposed DSS concept. Furthermore, the model creation is based on statistical analysis (regression) of primary data sources. A review of the role of IT artifacts in information systems is presented in Chapter 4. The following chapter, which addresses the evaluation of the proposed IT artifact, starts with an introduction to theoretical foundations of measurement concepts for business value of IT measurement concepts. All these theoretical foundations and methods applied are essential for rigorous research.

- Research contributions

Design science research results can provide new knowledge to the environment of the problem space addressed such as people and organizations involved, or the technologies used or affected. Furthermore, design science research calls for clear research contributions to the knowledge base such as contributions to the design science research framework or new methodologies (Hevner et al. 2004). This work provides research contributions in both dimensions, i.e. to the knowledge base and the environment of the problem space addressed.

The empirical stock price analysis and the DSS concept, which are presented in Chapter 2 and 3, illustrate the problem relevance and a basis for an appropriate information system approach. This provides evidence to the financial community that and how the observed event type causes significant price effects that could be exploited by investors.

The IT artifact designed and prototyped in Chapter 4 addresses an important unsolved problem in a novel way that provides several advantages compared to previous approaches and therefore contributes to the foundations.

Finally, a new evaluation methodology is introduced and applied in Chapter 5, which provides a basis for evaluating customers' benefits of new financial information services. Addressing both the application in the environment and contributions to the knowledge base, the presented research approach in this work claims to be both relevant and rigorous (Benbasat and Zmud 1999; Hevner et al. 2004).

A detailed presentation of these and other research contributions is provided in the last chapter.

- Design as a search process

Conducting design science is an iterative process that aims at improving the artifact's capability of solving the addressed problem field (Hevner et al. 2004). Thus, researchers should perform a heuristic search for better alternatives that could involve the artifact itself, the problem analysis, or the evaluation methodologies (Simon 1996).

The proposed artifact is the result of an iterative research process of three years in which more than ten research papers were published in journals and conference proceedings being subject to a double-blind review process in order to assess and increase the quality of theoretical foundations and research contributions (e.g. Muntermann 2004; Muntermann and Güttler 2007). Consequently, the comments of reviewers and conference participants are incorporated into this work.

- Communication of research

  Finally, research results should be presented appropriately for the technology and management oriented community. This is essential to broaden the knowledge base by all relevant aspects, which enables researchers to present, evaluate, and refine the different dimensions of design science research, such as problem definition, artifact proposal, and approach evaluation.

  Therefore, relevant previous work was submitted to and published in international journals and conference proceedings[1]. Different research communities and research fields were addressed, such as information systems, computer science, and finance. Moreover, the problem field and the proposed system design were presented to several practitioner audiences. The reviewer's comments and the discussions with conferees and practitioners were fruitful to enhance the manuscript in several aspects, such as the effectiveness of the solution approach of the proposed and evaluated IT artifact, or the theoretical foundations including relevant theories and methodologies applied.

The previous paragraphs have illustrated how the presented design science research guidelines are addressed by this thesis. Starting with the problem relevance of the domain addressed in this work, the subsequent Chapter 2 explicates an analysis of the addressed financial problem field and illustrates how the observed and analyzed intraday stock price effects can provide an opportunity for investors.

---

[1] Further information can be found on the author's website: www.muntermann.com

2 Analysis of Intraday Stock Price Effects on the German Capital Market

Analyzing the adjustment process of stock prices reacting to new information available has a long tradition in empirical financial research and plays a major role in understanding the dynamics of financial markets. In this chapter, the analysis of the intraday stock price adjustments on the German capital market lays an empirical basis and motivation for the design and development of a novel IT concept that supports investors to react quickly to new information available before stock prices fully reflects this information.

In the following, Section 2.1 details the theoretical foundation and research methodology being relevant for the analysis of the stock price developments observed. This comprises the efficient market hypothesis (Section 2.1.1) as theoretical foundation, event study analysis (Section 2.1.2) as methodological framework and an introduction to statistical hypothesis testing (Section 2.1.3) used for testing the statistical significance of intraday stock price reactions on the German capital market.

The analysis procedure and empirical results are then presented in Section 2.2, which illustrates the significance of intraday stock price adjustments on the German capital market following so-called ad hoc disclosures observed in the years 2003, 2004 and 2005.

The chapter concludes with a summary of the results (Section 2.3) with special focus on implications for information systems in this field. Furthermore, the results are used in the following as an empirically proved motivation since they indicate both practical relevance and academic challenge.

2.1 Theoretical Foundation and Research Methodology

2.1.1 Efficient Market Hypothesis

The efficient market hypothesis is based on the theory of efficient markets after which market prices fully reflect all information available (Fama 1970). The corresponding efficient market hypothesis addresses this information efficiency and states that it is not possible to outperform consistently the market taking both risk and returns into account. There are three different forms of testing the efficient market hypothesis (Fama 1991).

First, the strong form test assumes that stock prices reflect all information available and addresses the question whether any investors possess private information that is not yet reflected by these prices. Second, the semi-strong form implies that security prices adjust efficiently to new information available within a short period of time. The test addresses the question how quickly security prices react to new information available. Finally, and third, the weak form implies that historic prices and returns do not provide any information about future prices and can be used for according tests, e.g. when developing time series models (Diebold 2001).

The different forms of market efficiency are the basis for many empirical analyses performed in the past (Smith 1978). In this chapter, the efficient market theory is a theoretical basis for the analysis of intraday stock price adjustments on the German capital market and corresponding research hypotheses are formulated. Event study analysis, which is presented in the following section, represents a methodical framework for testing the efficient market hypothesis, especially for testing the semi-strong form by analyzing stock price adjustments following market events observed such as company announcements or stock splits (Fama et al. 1969).

2.1.2   Introduction to Event Study Analysis

Event study methodology was developed in order to assess stock price effects caused by unanticipated market events (McWilliams and Siegel 1997). The analysis of market events and their economic impact on asset prices has a long tradition in finance and applied economics. Dolley (1933), for example, analyses the impact of stock splits on the market prices observed at the New York Stock Exchange between 1921 and 1930[2]. The results indicate that stock splits appear with increased frequency during boom years (more than 35% of all stock splits were observed during the years 1928 and 1929) and most of the stock splits led to increased stock prices in the short run.

Among the first to make use of the event study methodology are Ashley (1962), Ball and Brown (1968) and Fama et al. (1969). Ashley (1962) analyzes stock price reactions following earnings and dividend announcements. He detects significant price reactions within the first four days following the announcement date whereby the capital market reacts more quickly to bad news and slower to good news. Ball and Brown (1968) evaluate price movements before and following the publication of annual report announcements. They observe that most of the price reaction is completed prior to the announcement date, i.e. market participants anticipate most of the information provided. Fama et al. (1969) examine the speed of stock price adjustments to new information. They observe stock splits and monthly returns before and after the split between 1927 and 1957 and conclude efficiency of the capital market since the observed stock prices reflect quickly new information.

The procedure of the event study methodology is usually summarized in the literature as a set of several steps (e.g. Bowman 1983; Campbell et al. 1997; Peterson 1989; MacKinlay 1997), which are described in the following:

1. Event identification and definition of analysis windows

    At first, the events of interest, which should be observed, have to be determined. Relevant events can be single events, which occur at a certain date or event types, such as company announcements being published by different companies at different dates. Therefore, it is essential to identify the exact event date (and time) as imprecise event dates may bias the

---

[2] Dolley (1933) defines stock split-up as "a multiplication of the number of shares into which the existing common-stock capital account is divided".

empirical results of the event study (Brown and Warner 1985). For a detailed analysis, it is required to define two analysis windows, relative to the event date, as illustrated in Figure 2.1.

First, an *estimation window* with a start date t_{-S} and end date t_{-E} has to be defined prior to the event window. This period is determined to capture common movements of the stock or benchmark price when no relevant event occurs. The definition of the length of the estimation window involves a tradeoff between advantages and disadvantages. On the one hand, a longer estimation window covers more input data while on the other hand, it may result in model parameter instability e.g. because of data with lower explanatory power and a higher probability of confounding events (Brown et al. 1985)[3]. Typically, the selection of the length of the estimation window depends on the focus of the analyzed price effects and is shorter for studies with a shorter focus, e.g. the estimation window of daily studies is usually shorter than for monthly studies (Peterson 1989).

Figure 2.1: Analysis Windows of the Event Study

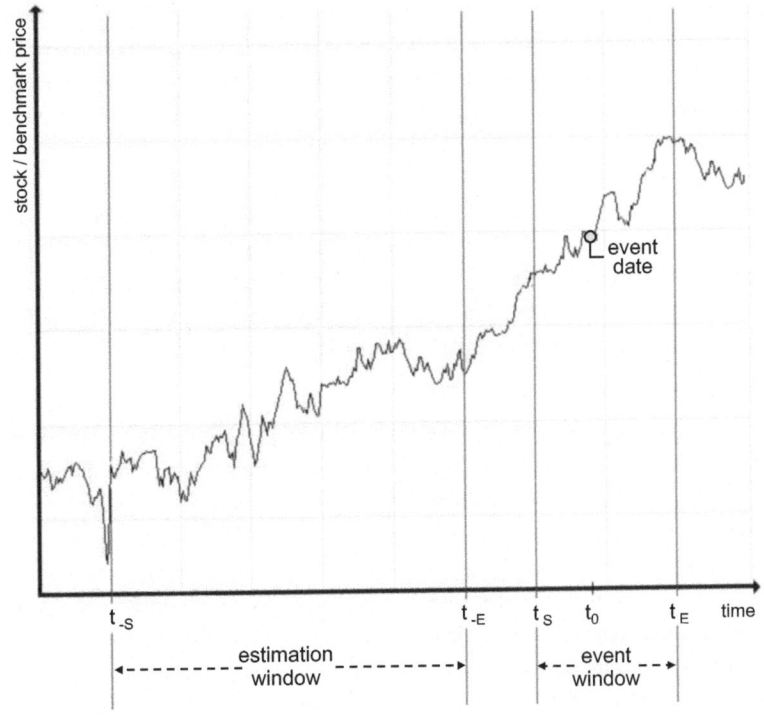

---

[3] Confounding events and their treatment are discussed in the next step.

The *event window* is the period of time in which the stock price reaction caused by the event is analyzed. It is defined with a start date t_S and end date t_E. For example, the event window might cover the trading hours following the event date or several more days (e.g. in order to assess the speed of stock price adjustments). If the study addresses price effects prior to the announcement date (e.g. for analyzing insider trading or anticipation effects) the event window also covers a period before the event date. Generally, there is no overlap between the estimation and event window, as the methodology works with a comparison of stock price movements between these two periods. Moreover, it can be reasonable to work with a gap between the end of the estimation window and the start of the event window. Doing so, should ensure that the estimation window does not include prices already affected by anticipation or insider effects.

2. Criteria for sample selection and filter rules

   Within the estimation window and the event window, events might occur which affect the observed stock prices (so-called *confounding events*). It is essential to reduce this impact as much as possible, e.g. by applying several filter rules. Patel and Wolfson (1982) observe earnings and dividend announcements published during stock exchange business hours. They propose to discard an event from the sample if a second event was observed during the estimation window, which might confound the stock price behavior analyzed. Furthermore, the analysis can focus on specific companies having particular characteristics (e.g. within a defined industry segment) or periods (e.g. event dates during trading hours vs. non-trading hours). Moreover, the analysis heavily depends on the availability of data sources. Events and stock price effects can only be analyzed if the used data sources comprise event details (e.g. the exact publication date) and the price series of the affected stocks are provided by the stock exchanges. In order to illustrate dataset qualities, Campbell et al. (1997) propose to provide further sample characteristics, such as market capitalization of the firms, or the temporal distribution of the observed events.

3. Modeling normal and abnormal stock returns

   In order to evaluate the impact of the observed events on stock prices, it is required to model normal and abnormal stock returns. The normal return is the expected price movement, which would have occurred when the event did not have happen and is determined using the available stock prices observed during of the estimation window. Normal returns are usually calculated using a constant-mean-return model assuming constant stock returns over time or with a market model where the stock returns depend on the development of market returns. After estimating normal returns, abnormal returns can be calculated by adjusting the observed returns during the event window by the normal returns estimated from the estimation window. These abnormal returns can directly be used for testing formulated hypotheses. Moreover, the abnormal returns can also be cumulated as a group of abnormal returns first (e.g. over time) and then be used for conducting statistical tests. For example when working with daily returns, it is possible to use the abnormal returns on a daily basis (Carter and Soo 1999) or to cumulate the abnormal returns over several trading days (Aharony and Swary 1980; Salinger 1992) during the event window. Besides aggregating abnormal returns through time, it is possible to aggregate stocks, for example to analyze specific characteristics of company segments or branches (Campbell et al. 1997).

4. Testing setup

Besides calculating abnormal stock returns for all observed events and different dates during the event window, it is required to formulate a set of hypotheses, which should be tested. These hypotheses depend on the focus of the event study and the determined abnormal return series. The latter provide the basis for the statistical tests performed since they are interpreted as distribution of price effects. The first event studies were initially conducted for testing the semi-strong form of capital market efficiency and hypothesize if prices efficiently adjust to new information available (Fama et al. 1969; Fama 1970). Later on, event studies addressed the price effects following specific event types or price effects that have been observed in specific market segments (Dolley 1933; Jennings and Starks 1986; Kalay and Lowenstein 1986). The outcome of the testing setup is one or more null hypotheses to be tested. These hypotheses are tested using different kinds of statistical test procedures featuring considerable advantages and disadvantages. The selection of suitable test statistics depends on different circumstances, e.g. the sample size or the characteristics of the abnormal return distribution. Usually, parametric (e.g. Student t-test), nonparametric test statistics (e.g. Wilcoxon signed rank test), or a combination of both are applied, each featuring specific advantages and disadvantages (Campbell and Wasley 1993). Brown and Warner (1980) analyze the impact of chosen tests procedures on test results. They show that parametric test procedures are well suited since the mean of excess returns converges to normality. However, Campbell et al. (1997) suggest to apply both parametric and nonparametric test procedures in order to cross-check potential methodical impacts.

5. Analysis of empirical results

As a last step, analysis and interpretation of the empirical results is required. Therefore, the results of the statistical test are presented in tables and figures in order to corroborate or abandon the hypotheses formulated within the testing setup. These statistics should shed light on the question how and within which period of time the observed events impact upon the analyzed stock prices. Furthermore, the presentation of descriptive statistics can help to analyze and classify the results. A comparison with prior research helps to evaluate and interpret the findings.

One essential difference between event studies is the temporal focus of the analyzed security prices and the used stock price intervals. Whereas most of the existing event studies use daily, weekly, or monthly return series (e.g. Aharony and Swary 1980; Kalay and Lowenstein 1986; Nowak 2001; Röder 1999), there are some studies working with intraday returns addressing the intraday speed of stock price adjustments.

For research, the use of intraday data has the advantage of enabling short-term analysis of price reactions before and following the observed events. However, the availability and management of such stock price series, which can be quite voluminous, is a big challenge. Since the data volume quickly increases over time it makes high demands on the data processing (e.g. when working with a one-minute interval and 8.5 business hours, up to 510 quotes need to be managed for each stock per day).

So far, there exist three widely cited empirical studies analyzing the German capital market between 1995 and 1997, all of which concentrate on daily price effects (Nowak 2001; Oerke 1999 and Röder 1999). All studies examine the existence of significant abnormal returns before, during, and after the event date. Their research goal is to prove the existence of insider trading prior to the announcement date, efficient market reaction at the announcement date and phenomena like herding after the announcement.

An overview of these studies is provided by Nowak (2001). According to Kaserer and Nowak (2001), the studies by Oerke (1999) and Röder (1999) show methodological problems regarding the calculation of abnormal returns as their method of calculating abnormal returns leads in most cases to significant results (Kaserer and Nowak 2001). All these studies focus on long-term price effects, which can be observed over several trading days.

When analyzing the market and information efficiency level of capital markets with daily data, the intraday speed at which the information is processed into stock prices is not discernable. Since the question of market efficiency and prompt price reactions is concerned with the speed at which stock prices reflect new relevant information, the question of degree of efficiency in a certain market can be further refined by using intraday data. As mobile financial information systems should reduce reaction time of investors during their daily activities, only the analysis of intraday data provides insights into their capabilities and requirements.

There exist a few event studies addressing intraday price behavior and most address the US capital market. Patell and Wolfson (1984) analyze the intraday speed of stock price reactions after earnings and dividend announcements. They can show that most of the detected price reactions occur within the first fifteen minutes after the announcement has been published. Besides, they observe moderate abnormal price reactions during the 90 to 30 minutes interval prior to the announcement date.

Woodruff and Senchak (1988) observe intraday price reactions caused by unexpected earnings results and find prompt price reactions following the announcements up to one hour.

Barclay and Litzenberger (1988) analyze intraday price reactions caused by announcements of new equity issues. They detect an abnormally high trading volume and a negative average return for a period of 15 minutes after the announcement has been published. They also find abnormal price reactions during 75 to 50 minutes and during the last four price fixings prior to these announcements. Jennings and Starks (1985) divide their sample into earnings announcements with high and low informational content. They observe abnormal price reactions in the first twenty price fixings following the announcement of earnings forecasts. The price adjustment process for announcements with high informational content takes longer than for those with low information context. Abnormal price reactions are found in the first eight hours following the announcement[4]. Smith et al. (1997) analyze abnormal trading volume following announcements of takeovers. They find significant abnormal returns in the first three hours following the announcement date and to some extent in the fourth and fifth hour. Lee at al. (1994) examine the development of the trading volume during the first business hours. They observe that the price adjustment process needs approximately four hours after which stock prices fully reflect the new information available.

There exist only few intraday event studies addressing the intraday speed of stock price adjustments on the German capital market resulting from published ad hoc disclosures.

Oerke (1999) analyzes intraday price series between January 1995 and June 1997 and considers intraday price effects following ad hoc disclosures. The analysis is based on intraday stock prices taken from IBIS and covers 131 observed ad hoc disclosures of which 29 were published during stock exchange business hours[5]. The results indicate that positive disclosures (19) cause prompt price adjustments whereas negative disclosures (10) are reflected in stock prices with a delay of more than thirty price fixings. However, the small sample size of 29 observed events limits the statistical significance of these results. Furthermore, the author notes that institutional investors dominate trading on IBIS, as there is a minimum order size of one hundred shares (Oerke 1999).

Röder (2000) observes intraday stock prices and trading volumes taken from the Frankfurt Stock Exchange (floor trading) and Xetra between January 1998 and December 1998 and analyses abnormal behavior in the course of the day of publication. The price effect analysis following the event date is limited to five periods of analysis (four within the first hour and covering the period until the close of trading) and is performed separately for floor trading and Xetra transaction prices. A classification into good and bad disclosure content is done by the positive or negative sign of the calculated price effect. The results for floor trading and disclosures with positive announcement content show significant price effects following the event date until the close of market. Due to the small sample sizes, no statistical analyses are

---

[4] Jennings and Starks (1985) use data of the trading day following the event day.

[5] The electronic trading system IBIS (Integriertes Börsenhandels- und Informationssystem) has been replaced with Xetra on 1997-11-28.

made for floor trading (bad announcement content) and Xetra (good and bad announcements) (Röder 2000).

In a second intraday analysis, Röder (2000b) analyses price adjustments following ad hoc disclosures between July 1996 and June 1997. The stock price series used for the statistical analysis are limited to one opening, spot, and close stock price per day and consequently do not provide insights into the intraday speed of stock price adjustments.

Since 2002-08-01 the minimum lot size has been reduced to one stock per Xetra order with the aim of increasing market liquidity, to decrease implicit transaction costs and to attract more private investors (Deutsche Börse Group 2002). Furthermore, online banks and brokers have invested significant amounts of money in modern information and transaction services and related IT infrastructure in recent years, which contributes to improved information supply for private investors. Since the existing analyses presented above are based on earlier datasets, they do not regard corresponding changes in trading behavior and the level of information of private investors. Consequently, these analyses provide little information regarding the intraday speed of stock price adjustments on the German capital market today.

2.1.3   Statistical Hypothesis Testing for One Sample Parameters

The question whether or not an observed stock price movement is exceptional can be addressed with statistical hypothesis testing. In general, it is applied to an abnormal stock return sample that has been calculated using datasets observed. Therefore, a test methodology computes estimators for the true population parameters derived from the sample (Studenmund 2006).

After formulating a null hypothesis H_0 (e.g. that the mean of a sample is zero) and the alternative hypothesis H_A (that the mean is not zero), the statistical test provides insights if the hypothesis can be rejected at a given significance level such as 1%, 5%, and 10%. Depending on this level of significance and given the observed sample data, it is very unlikely that the null hypothesis is correct when it has been rejected. Correspondingly, the rejection would then rather indicate that the mean is not zero with a small level of uncertainty.

There exist many different statistical hypothesis test procedures and selecting a suitable one depends on several factors. First, one has to decide whether the test should work with one or more populations. One-sample tests are used for estimating population parameters such as the mean or median and two (or more) sample tests compare these parameters of several samples. As the research hypotheses formulated in the following Section 2.2.3 addresses the existence and persistence of abnormal price behavior, one-sample tests are appropriate in this situation and can be applied separately for the different time frames.

Hypothesis tests work with or without assumptions about the shape of the population, e.g. that the population is normally distributed. All statistical tests that assume a certain kind of sample shape are summarized as parametric hypothesis testing and tests without any assumptions are called nonparametric testing (Weiers 2005). Selecting the most suitable test statistic is of major relevance for event studies, as this choice can have significantly impact upon the results. This choice is influenced by the characteristics of the empirical distributions which will be illustrated in Section 2.2.4.

Prior research has shown that daily and monthly excess return series are generally not normal (e.g. Berry et al. 1990). However, several authors suggest the application of the parametric t-test statistic and report lower error rates compared to nonparametric test statistics (e.g. Berry et al. 1990; Brown and Warner 1985). According to the Central Limit Theorem, the t-test statistic can also be used for populations that are not normal when the sample size is larger than 30. Here, the sampling distribution of the mean is approximately normal (Groebner et al. 2001).

However, Corrado (1989) reports that nonparametric test statistics have more power to detect excess returns than their parametric counterparts (Corrado 1989). His empirical results confirm the theoretical advantage of nonparametric tests over parametric tests regarding the resistance to outliers. Therefore, several authors propose that event-study test statistics should be conducted with parametric tests and the statistical results should be cross-checked with a nonparametric test statistic to ensure that the results are not influenced from outliers (Sanger and Peterson 1990; McWilliams 1990; Campbell et al. 1997).

The following sections 2.1.3.1 and 2.1.3.2 introduce two such procedures for testing parameters of one sample populations that have been applied in several event studies before (e.g. Patell 1976; Dodd and Warner 1983; Brown and Warner 1985; Barclay and Litzenberger 1988; Patell and Wolfson 1984). These statistical tests will then be used for the statistical test procedures of the event study performed.

To address potential problems arising from high non-normal excess returns and from outliers, one parametric (Student t-test) and one nonparametric test (Wilcoxon signed rank test) are presented and applied in the following.

2.1.3.1 Parametric Test Procedure: Student t-Test

The Student t-test is the most common parametric statistical test procedure for testing a sample mean given a sample with unknown standard deviation (Weiers 2005)[6]. The test can be applied when the sample is truly or approximately normal distributed or the sample size is larger than 30. The t-test statistic is given as (Groebner et al. 2001):

---

[6] When the standard deviation is known, the z-test is used.

$$t = \frac{\bar{x} - \mu_0}{\frac{s}{\sqrt{I}}}$$

where

$\bar{x}$ =   sample mean

μ_0 =   hypothesized population mean

s =   sample standard deviation

I =   sample size

Equation 2.1: *t*-Test Statistic

The calculated *t*-value, the level of significance α, and the number of degrees of freedom (*df* = *I*-1) are then used for identifying the critical values of the test statistic given the *t*-distribution for this *df*, which is illustrated in the following figure for *df* = 30 and α = 0.05. When the number of degrees of freedom exceeds 100, the Student *t*-distribution converges to the normal distribution (Groebner et al. 2001).

Figure 2.2: Critical Values for the *t*-Distribution

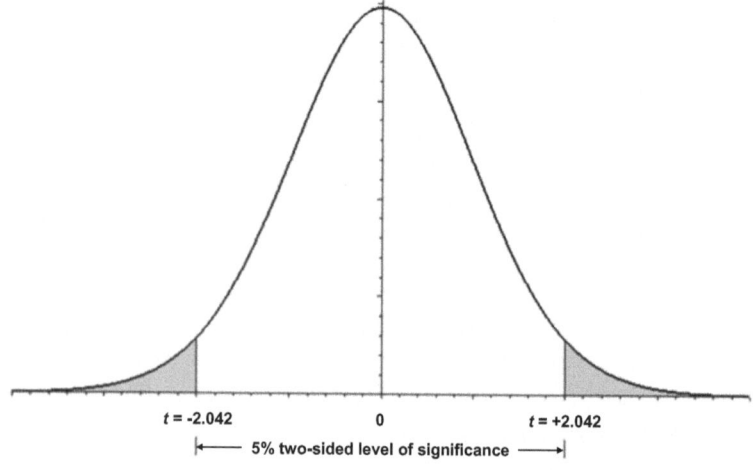

The resulting critical *t*-values -2.042 and +2.042 imply that 95% of the area beneath the curve is between these values. If the calculated *t*-test value lies outside these limits (the gray areas under the curve), i.e. its absolute value is greater than the absolute critical *t*-value, the null hypothesis can be rejected.

2.1.3.2   Nonparametric Test Procedures: Wilcoxon Signed Rank Test

The two most commonly used nonparametric test procedures for using data from a single sample are the *sign test* and the *Wilcoxon signed rank test*; the latter one uses more information from the sample and is therefore often a more powerful test than the sign test (Daniel 1978). Therefore, it has been chosen as the nonparametric test procedure to be applied in the following.

The Wilcoxon signed rank test is the nonparametric counterpart of the parametric Student *t*-test featuring several advantaged and disadvantages (Weiers 2005). Compared to the parametric Student *t*-test introduced in the preceding section it does not require any assumptions regarding the sample distribution and can also be used when working with small sample sizes (Wilcoxon 1945).

However, the information provided by the sample data is used less efficiently because the sample data is converted into ranks, which decreases the power of the test. Calculating the Wilcoxon signed rank test statistic W^+ is a 3-step procedure (Sheskin 2004):

1. Calculation of median differences d_i :

$$|d_i| = |x_i - m_0| \quad \forall \ i = 1...I$$

   where

   d_i =   median difference

   x_i =   sample value

   m_0 =   hypothesized population median

   I =   sample size

Equation 2.2: Wilcoxon Sign Rank Test Median Difference

2. Ranking of the $|d_i|$ values so the smallest $|d_i|$ has the rank of 1, while ignoring all $|d_i|$ with a value of 0 (i.e. the sample value is equivalent to the sample median). The result is a ranking list for the whole sample except those with $|d_i| = 0$.

3. Calculate the W^+-test statistic with:

$$W^+ = \sum_{i=1}^{I} rank_i \cdot b_i \quad with \quad b_i = \begin{cases} 1 & if\ d_i > 0 \\ 0 & else \end{cases}$$

where

$rank_i$ =   rank of $|d_i|$

b_i =   binary variable

d_i =   median difference

I =   sample size

Equation 2.3: Wilcoxon Sign Rank Test Statistic

According to Equation 2.3 the Wilcoxon signed rank W^+-test statistic is the sum of sample ranks with a median difference larger than 0. The test is based on the idea that the sum of the sample ranks should be similar above and below the median. The critical W^+-values for this test statistic can be obtained for different levels of significance and sample sizes from corresponding tables (Sheskin 2004). The EViews software used for this analysis reports an approximated Wilcoxon t-statistic and the corresponding p-values that can be interpreted easily.

2.2 An Event Study Analysis of the German Capital Market

In this section, the results of an intraday event study are presented, which provide insights into the intraday behavior of the German capital market. The event study is based on earlier studies that have been presented by Muntermann and Güttler (2005 and 2007). These studies use intraday price and trading volume series taken from the Frankfurt Stock Exchange (Xetra and floor trading) and address abnormal stock price and trading volume effects observed before and after the publication of ad hoc disclosures. The empirical analysis covers the period between 2003-08-01 and 2004-07-31 with a sample size of 160 observed events. The price effect analysis comprises five price fixings (and 30 minutes) prior to and fifteen price fixings (and two hours) following the event date. The authors find little evidence for significant abnormal price reactions and trading activity prior to the event date but a price adjustment process of, on average, thirty minutes following the event date. The trading volume effect holds for the whole analysis period of two hours and accordingly for the fifteen price fixings following the announcement and is not completed within this time interval.

Based on the methodological approach presented by Muntermann and Güttler (2007), an intraday event study analysis is presented in the following, with special focus on practical implications for financial information systems that could assist investors to exploit potential price effects.

After describing the dataset used (Section 2.2.1), Section 2.2.2 introduces a return-generating model for calculating abnormal stock returns. These returns form the basis for two research hypotheses formulated in the following Section 2.2.3. Then, Section 2.2.4 presents descriptive statistics for the samples analyzed. Finally, Section 2.2.5 reports the empirical results of the intraday event study.

2.2.1 Dataset

The following sections introduce the dataset used, which comprises the observed market events (Section 2.2.1.1) and intraday stock price series (Section 2.2.1.2). Due to voluminous data quantities and the necessity of daily data processing, much of this data processing was automated, as presented in Section 2.2.1.3.

2.2.1.1 Market Event Definition

Immediate publication of new information potentially effecting stock price developments is a helpful communication instrument between the management and the investors. Furthermore, this instrument prevents insider trading resulting from asymmetric information supply. On the other hand, the management might use the publication of company announcements for its own purposes, e.g. because (1) the management has a higher level of information regarding the business strategy and the operational business; (2) the incentives of the management differ from those of the shareholders; (3) accounting rules and supervision are imperfect (Healy and Palepu 1993).

The performed event study focuses on ad hoc disclosures according to article 15 of the German Securities Trading Act (WpHG) published by the Deutsche Gesellschaft für Ad-hoc-Publizität (DGAP). Article 15 demands immediate publication of insider information and regulates in which situation companies, whose shares are admitted to trading on an organized market within Germany, have to publish ad hoc disclosures (Bundesaufsichtsamt für den Wertpapierhandel 1998). This type of event is chosen since the legal regulation permits a clear definition and delimitation. Furthermore, previous research provides evidence for significant effects on the capital market (e.g. Leis and Nowak 2001; Nowak 2001; Oerke 1999; Röder 2002). A typical disclosure is depicted in the following Figure 2.3 in which the reelection of the Chairman of the Supervisory Board of *AdPhos AG* is disclosed.

The publication and distribution itself is done in most cases (98% in 2001) by the Deutsche Gesellschaft für Ad hoc Publizität (DGAP) on behalf of the companies. As a first step, DGAP sends new company announcements to the stock exchanges and the regulatory authorities to fulfill legal requirements (Deutsche Gesellschaft für Ad-hoc-Publizität 2002). Then the ad hoc disclosures are sent to and published by several news services and agencies. In this study, a digital news feed provided by DPA-AFX is used, which contains all ad hoc disclosures published by the DGAP. Each announcement can be identified by a unique timestamp exact to the second.

Figure 2.3: Example Ad Hoc Disclosure by Adphos AG[7]

DGAP-News: AdPhos AG :Reelection of the Chairman of the Supervisory Board of AdPhos AG

```
Corporate-news announcement sent by DGAP.
The sender is solely responsible for the contents of this announcement.
-------------------------------------------------------------------
Reelection of the Chairman of the Supervisory Board of AdPhos AG -
Prolongation of contracts of the board of directors until the middle of the
year 2008

Bruckmühl, 18th January 2005 - The Supervisory Board of Advanced Photonics
Technologies AG has appointed a new chairman, Mr. Dieter R. Kirchmair, and a
new deputy of the chairman, Mr. Robert E. Weidinger. The previous chairman of
the supervisory board of Advanced Photonics Technologies AG, Dr. Kai K. O. Bär
has resigned from the board in order to take over the management board of the
company subsidiary AdPhos Steel GmbH. As a new member of the supervisory
board, Dr. Wolf Rüdiger Willig has been appointed.
Mr. Kirchmair, who was deputy of the chairman at last, has been a member of
the supervisory board since 2001. Mr. Weidinger already belongs to the
supervisory board since 2003.

Dr. Rainer Gaus and Mr. Andreas Geitner, both members of the Managing Board of
AdPhos AG, were confirmed in their offices until the middle of the year 2008.
Due to this decision, the continuity in the leadership of the company is
warranted.

end of message, (c)DGAP 18.01.2005
-------------------------------------------------------------------
WKN: 828820; ISIN: DE0008288200; Index:
Listed: Geregelter Markt in Frankfurt (Prime Standard); Freiverkehr in Berlin-
Bremen, Düsseldorf, Hamburg, Hannover und Stuttgart

181358 Jän 05
```

The empirical analysis covers the period between 2003-08-01 and 2005-07-31, i.e. covers double the period of a study performed by Muntermann and Güttler (2007) and the announcement sample consists of 4,998 ad hoc disclosures. Figure 2.4 shows a bar chart of the temporal distribution of this dataset[8].

---

[7] Source: Deutsche Gesellschaft für Ad-hoc-Publizität (www.dgap.de), accessed 2005-01-20.

[8] Identical announcements published in different languages were treated as one disclosure.

Figure 2.4: Temporal Frequency Distribution of the Ad Hoc Disclosure Sample

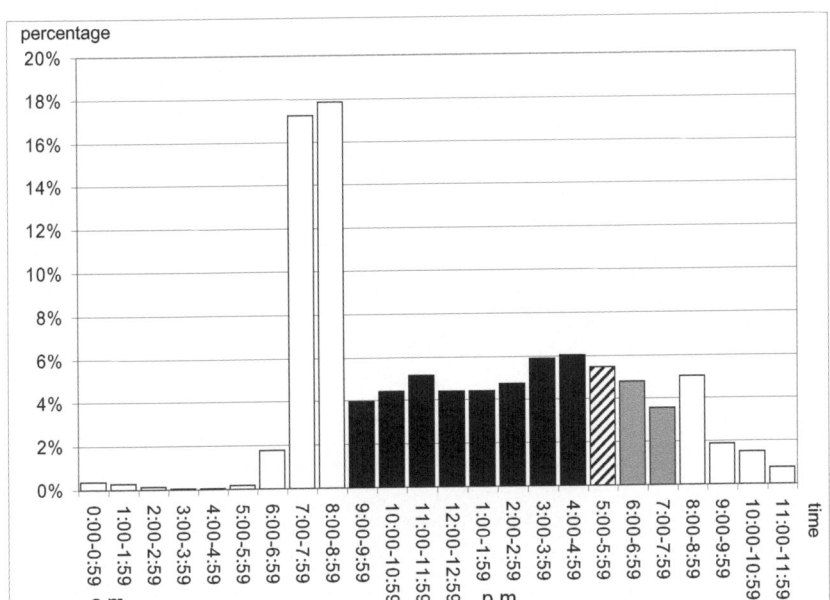

White bars indicate a publication off trading hours, black bars a publication during trading hours for the entire sample and grey bars indicate a publication during trading hours when the disclosure has been published before 2003-11-03. The striped bar illustrates the overlap of trading and non trading hours as trading as Xetra trading hours halt at 5:30 p.m. after 2003-11-02. Most of the ad hoc disclosures were published during the two hours before trading starts at Xetra and they are therefore not relevant for the intraday analysis. Companies publishing announcements after their actual time of occurrence might wish to prevent possible suspended trading, an issue that has already been criticized by the German Federal Financial Supervisory Authority (BaFin) in 2002 (BaFin 2002).

Figure 2.5 summarizes the data filter rules and the effect on the sample selection. The original dataset consists of 4,998 ad hoc disclosures, which were published by DGAP in the period of two years between 2003-08-01 and 2005-07-31 on behalf of the companies. Ad hoc disclosures published by companies with non-domestic shares were discarded from the sample since these companies are also subject to other disclosure regulations. If the foreign regulation is stricter than the German one, a different informational content can be expected from these ad hoc disclosures. Confounding events have a significant impact on the calculation of abnormal returns (Bowman 1983), so these were eliminated by identifying companies that had published other ad hoc disclosures during the ten days prior to the ad hoc disclosure of interest. Because the focus of the analysis lies on intraday short-term price adjustments, only ad hoc disclosures published during trading hours were taken into account. To ensure sufficient liquidity, ad hoc disclosures with less than twenty price fixings between the announcement date and the close of the market were also excluded from the sample.

Figure 2.5: Filter Rules and Dataset Creation

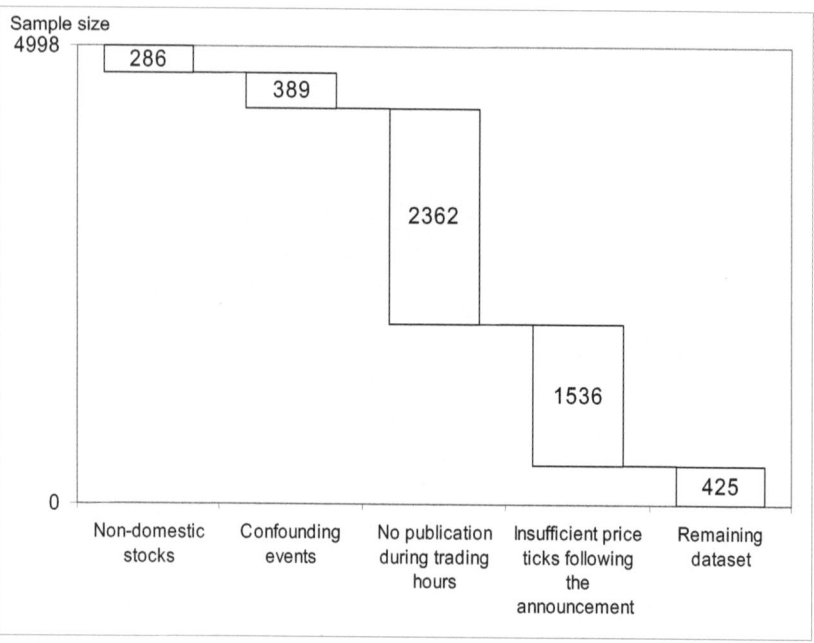

Figure 2.5 illustrates the effect of these filter rules on the master data of 4,998 ad hoc disclosures and the reduction to a sample size of 425 disclosures. The first two filter rules reduce the sample size by 286 (5.7%) and 389 (7.8%). Most (2362) of the disclosures are discarded (47.3%) because they were not published during stock exchange trading hours and are therefore unsuitable for an intraday analysis. Sufficient price fixings and corresponding intraday stock prices are not available for 1,536 (30.7%) disclosures and hence their price adjustment cannot be evaluated. After applying all filter rules there remain 425 (8.5%) ad hoc disclosures that can be used for the event study.

For this remaining sample descriptive statistics are presented in Table 2.1 for the companies which have published the announcements. All measures are given for the trading day's close prior to the event date.

Table 2.1: Descriptive Dataset Analysis

	Panel I: Market capitalization in billion EUR					
	> 0 ≤ 0.025	$> 0.025,$ ≤ 0.05	$> 0.05,$ ≤ 0.1	$> 0.1,$ ≤ 1	$> 1,$ ≤ 5	> 5
Number of ad hoc disclosures	111	61	48	107	46	52
Frequency	26.1%	14.4%	11.3%	25.2%	10.8%	12.2%
Cumulative frequency	26.1%	40.5%	51.8%	76.9%	87.8%	100.0%
	Panel II: Number of analysts					
	0	$> 0,$ ≤ 2	$> 2,$ ≤ 5	$> 5,$ ≤ 15	$> 15,$ ≤ 25	> 25
Number of ad hoc disclosures	122	103	59	55	43	43
Frequency	28.7%	24.2%	13.9%	12.9%	10.1%	10.1%
Cumulative frequency	28.7%	52.9%	66.8%	79.8%	89.9%	100.0%
	Panel III: Volume of traded stocks in 1,000					
	$> 0,$ ≤ 10	$> 10,$ ≤ 50	$> 50,$ ≤ 100	$> 100,$ $\leq 1,000$	$> 1,000,$ $\leq 5,000$	$> 5,000$
Number of ad hoc disclosures	43	91	77	144	48	22
Frequency	10.1%	21.4%	18.1%	33.9%	11.3%	5.2%
Cumulative frequency	10.1%	31.5%	49.6%	83.5%	94.8%	100.0%
	Panel IV: Index membership					
	DAX	MDAX	TecDax	No HDAX member		
Number of ad hoc disclosures	44	68	27	286		
Frequency	10.4%	16.0%	6.4%	67.3%		
Cumulative frequency	10.4%	26.4%	32.7%	100.0%		

Panel I shows the market capitalization in billion EUR of the companies, which published the respective ad hoc disclosure. More than 50% of these companies had a market capitalization of less than 100 million EUR at this time. Only 12.2% stem from large caps with a market capitalization of more than five billion EUR. Therefore, small caps dominate the data sample.

Panel II presents the number of analysts covering the respective company, which has published the ad hoc disclosure[9]. The number of analysts covering the companies draws a similar picture with 28.7% of the ad hoc disclosures having been announced by companies, which are not covered by any analyst. 38.1% are covered by one to five analysts only and 20.2% are covered by more than fifteen analysts.

---

[9] The number of analysts covering a company has been provided by FactSet / JCF Group.

The third Panel gives the trading volume in 1,000 stocks of the respective company. The companies in the sample are traded quite frequently. Less than one third of the ad hoc disclosures, and the respectively stocks of the disclosing company, feature a trading volume of less than 50,000 shares.

Panel IV shows whether the companies are members of the DAX, MDAX, or TecDAX that cover the shares of the largest companies listed in Prime Standard. More than two-thirds (67.3%) of the companies are not member of one of these three indices and the HDAX respectively as HDAX comprises all shares listed in the indices DAX, MDAX, and TecDAX (Deutsche Börse Group 2005). This corroborates the finding that small and medium caps dominate the data sample.

No statistics regarding the announcement categories were assigned to the ad hoc disclosures for the data samples for several reasons: First, there is no common category list for ad hoc disclosure. Consequently, there exist different kinds of ad hoc disclosures category definitions (e.g. Leis and Nowak 2001; Röder 1999; Muntermann and Güttler 2007). Second, the classification mapping is often not definitely, when an announcement can be assigned to more than one category. Third, the categorization has to be done subjectively according to the announcement category list used. However, as the first year of the data sample used is similar to the sample used by Muntermann and Güttler (2007) a similar frequency distribution of announcement categories can be expected. Within their sample more than one-third (35.5%) of the disclosures address financial statements and dividend statements. Less than one forth (23.7%) were expected to contain positive announcement content (takeovers by the company, substantial orders, cooperation, changes in strategy, stock repurchases, stock splits, and innovations) and 20.3% largely negative news (increases of the share capital, bankruptcies, litigations, capital reductions, and adverse value adjustments by the company). The remaining disclosures cover takeovers of other companies (7.9%), disposition of assets (7.9%), and changes in the management board (5.6%).

2.2.1.2 Intraday Stock Prices

The stock exchange symbols of the companies behind the ad hoc disclosures were determined automatically. Using this symbol and given the event dates, eleven day histories of intraday stock prices were requested per ad hoc disclosure starting at the event dates. This period covers both the estimation and event window. Given these price series, all price information observed during a period of one minute was aggregated using the closing price of this period. This aggregation is done for two reasons. First, data volumes had to be reduced to a manageable complexity. Second, the intraday returns should be adjusted by general market trends with a common market index. Since the price information of indices was not calculated for each second, it was necessary to have consistent timestamps. Therefore, the study is based on stock and index price information exact to the minute, as a compromise between manageability and accuracy[10].

All stock prices and trading volumes are taken from the Frankfurt Stock Exchange (Xetra and floor trading). Xetra is an electronic trading platform, aggregating orders of licensed traders and is operated by the Deutsche Börse Group. Xetra covers more than 90% of the entire share trading in Germany (Deutsche Börse Group 2003).

In order to analyze the price effects following the ad hoc disclosures, intraday price series (of stocks and the benchmark index) need to be observed for a period of two years and ten days (two years covering the observation period plus ten days estimation period for the first ad hoc disclosures observed). For technical reasons the estimation period of the intraday stock and index price data is limited to ten days prior to the event dates and therefore, the analysis is restricted to this period[11].

In detail, intraday price series were collected and analyzed from 2003-07-22 to 2003-11-02 between 9 a.m. and 8 p.m. and from 2003-11-03 to 2005-07-31 between 9 a.m. and 5:30 p.m. The shorter daily observation periods resulted from a change in Xetra trading hours during the study.

2.2.1.3 Data Processing Automation

The data collection process for collecting market events and intraday price series has been automated by a developed batch script running on a specific application server. This server is hosted by *Interactive Data Managed Solutions AG* and provides access to the different data sources used. The batch script started every day at 2 a.m. and compiled data from different data sources for further processing. This automation has been done for practical and technical reasons: (1) to eliminate potential sources of error from manual processing, (2) to be able to process big data volumes collected daily over a period of two years and (3) to be able to dynamically generate a single spreadsheet compiled from different data sources. Figure 2.6 illustrates the data processing automation executed by the developed batch script.

---

[10] Previous intraday event studies for the German capital market work with higher aggregation levels such as several minutes (e.g. Röder 2002) or hours (e.g. Röder 2000).

[11] The data sources used provided historical intraday stock price series for a period of the past ten days plus the event date.

Figure 2.6: Event Study Process Automation

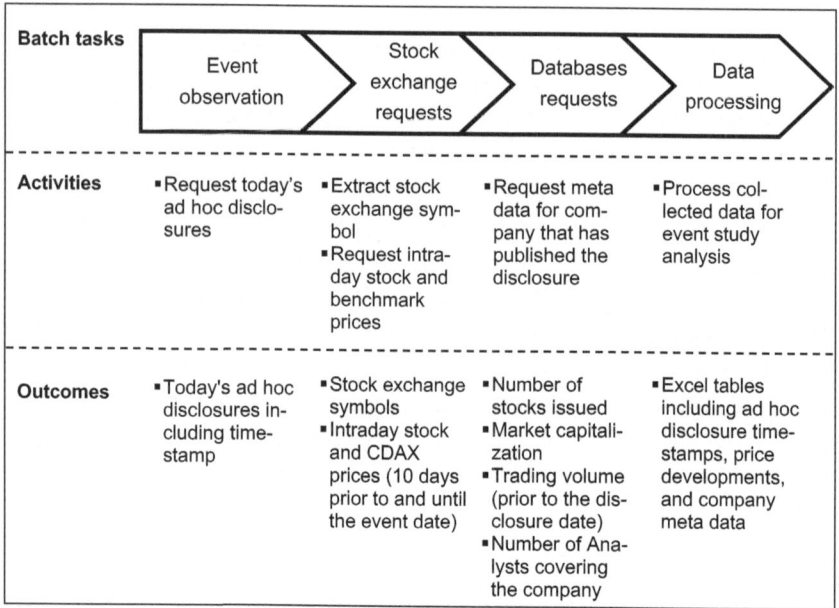

Each batch task uses the output generated by the previous task and the final output is generated as Excel spreadsheets, which were used for the event study analysis. Over the course of two years the batch script processed 4,998 ad doc disclosures and the corresponding intraday price series. Furthermore, five additional company figures were processed for each of the 4,998 ad doc disclosures.

2.2.2 Measuring Normal and Abnormal Stock Returns

To isolate price effects caused by the ad hoc disclosure, a single-index model is applied by using intraday price series of the CDAX Performance Index (ISIN: DE0008469602) taken from Xetra for the same period. The CDAX encompasses the shares of all domestic companies listed in Prime Standard and General Standard and therefore represents the entire German equity market (Deutsche Börse Group 2005).

The calculation of normal and abnormal returns is based on the calculation of (logarithmic) transaction returns according to Barclay and Litzenberger (1988). The calculation is done for each stock of the company that has published an ad hoc disclosure (event i) at time t using intraday prices P. These returns are calculated for all existing prices (and companies) starting ten days prior to the publication date. The returns of the CDAX returns are calculated accordingly.

$$R_{i,t} = \ln\left(\frac{P_{i,t}}{P_{i,t-1}}\right) \qquad\qquad R_{CDAX,t} = \ln\left(\frac{P_{CDAX,t}}{P_{CDAX,t-1}}\right)$$

where

i = event index

$P_{i,t}$ = stock price with indices i and t

$R_{i,t}$ = logarithmic return with indices i and t

$R_{CDAX,t}$ = logarithmic CDAX return with index t

t = price fixing index

Equations 2.4: Logarithmic Returns

Hence, abnormal returns $AR_{i,t}$ are calculated by subtracting CDAX returns $R_{CDAX,t}$ from the stock returns $R_{i,t}$.

$$AR_{i,t} = R_{i,t} - R_{CDAX,t}$$

Equation 2.5: Abnormal Returns

Klein and Rosenfeld (1987) examine the quality of different return-generating models for calculating abnormal returns. They show that results of the single-index model lead to the same conclusions as those of the market-adjusted return model.

Unlike event studies of a single item such as short sales (Aitken et al. 1998), where only negative stock market reactions can be expected, ad hoc disclosures are published because of different types of events, such as earnings surprises, new equity issues, changes in the management board or takeovers. For some of them one should expect negative market reactions and for others positive market reactions. Therefore, a common direction of market reactions cannot be expected for all ad hoc disclosures.

As no ex ante classification into ad hoc disclosures with probably good or bad new information was made, positive and negative stock reactions might neutralize. Hence, the analysis is based on absolute values of the abnormal returns $AR_{i,t}$ to avoid a possible neutralization of positive and negative returns. However, these returns cannot be used for statistical tests without any further adjustment because it would be possible with the utmost probability to reject the null hypothesis that 'a sum of absolute values is zero'.

For this reason, an adjustment according to Carter and Soo (1999) is needed. Given that the data sources used provide intraday stock price series for ten days prior to the publication date only, the estimation window is limited to this period. Since the intraday event study performed by Muntermann and Güttler (2007) presents no evidence for abnormal stock price reactions prior to the publication of ad hoc disclosures, the day prior to the event date has been excluded for the calculation of $MAAR_i$ only. Therefore, the mean of the absolute abnormal returns $MAAR_i$ are calculated for the estimation window of nine days, which starts ten days prior to the publication date (this means up to 11 hours · 60 min · 9 days = 5,940 prices per stock and ad hoc disclosure depending on the price ticks received from the stock exchanges).

$$MAAR_i = 1/T \sum_{t=1}^{T} |AR_{i,t}|$$

where

$|AR_{i,t}|$ =   absolute abnormal return

T =   number of price fixings exact to the minute observed between t_S and t_E

t_E =   end date of the estimation window

t_S =   start date of the estimation window

Equation 2.6: Mean Absolute Abnormal Returns

The time interval of each $MAAR_i$ calculation (i.e. the estimation window) covers the period from ten to two days prior to the event date. The absolute abnormal returns $|AR_{i,t}|$ of the event day are adjusted by these averages. The result is the corrected absolute abnormal return $CAAR_{i,t}$:

$$CAAR_{i,t} = |AR_{i,t}| - MAAR_i$$

where

$|AR_{i,t}|$ =   absolute abnormal return with indices i and t

$MAAR_i$=   mean absolute abnormal return

Equation 2.7: Corrected Absolute Abnormal Returns

Compared to Carter and Soo (1999) this $CAAR$ can be interpreted more easily because Equation 2.7 is not standardized with the standard deviation of $|AR_{i,t}|$. The calculated $CAAR$ is therefore adjusted by a combination of an index model and an average return model (Armitage 1995). Positive (negative) $CAAR$ values can be interpreted as the part of the absolute abnormal returns lying above (below) the level that can be observed on an average day when no ad hoc disclosure is published. An example analysis of a stock price adjustment process is presented in Figure 2.7.

Figure 2.7: Example Analysis of a Stock Price Reaction Following an Ad Hoc Disclosure

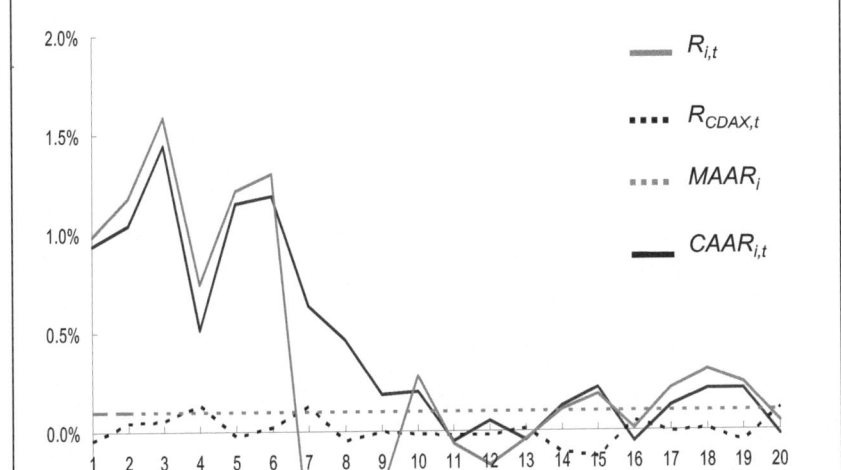

This explanatory analysis figure illustrates the relation of the calculated figures for the price reaction following an ad hoc disclosure i published by *SAP AG* on 2003-10-08. It shows the changes of R_i, R_{CDAX}, $CAAR_{i,t}$ and the value of $MAAR_i$. These are calculated for the affected stock of *SAP AG* and the CDAX index (both taken from Xetra) for the first twenty intraday prices following the event date. The return values were connected by lines for illustration only, since there is no real (here linear) adjustment between the price fixings.

For testing the existence of significant abnormal returns caused by the published ad hoc disclosures, mean and median corrected absolute abnormal returns ($\mu(CAAR_{i,t})$ and *median($CAAR_{i,t}$)*) are calculated over the I ad hoc disclosures and the corresponding stock prices for twenty price fixings following the event date.

$$\mu(CAAR_t) = 1/I \sum_{i=1}^{I} CAAR_{i,t}$$

Equation 2.8: Mean Corrected Absolute Abnormal Returns

$$median(CAAR_t) = \begin{cases} CAAR_{(I+1)/2,t} & \text{if } I = uneven \\ 1/2(CAAR_{(I/2),t} + CAAR_{(I/2+1),t}) & \text{if } I = even \end{cases}$$

Equation 2.9: Median Corrected Absolute Abnormal Returns

where

$CAAR_{i,t}$ =   corrected absolute abnormal return with indices i and t

I =   sample size

Cumulating abnormal returns to a group of abnormal returns is a standard event study procedure when analyzing abnormal price behavior (Barclay and Litzenberger 1988; Bowman 1983; Mandelker 1974). Cumulated corrected absolute abnormal returns $CCAAR_{i,t1,t2}$ are calculated over different periods between $t1$ and $t2$ for all I events and the corresponding stock prices (Equation 2.10):

$$CCAAR_{i,t1,t2} = \sum_{t=t1}^{t2} CAAR_{i,t}$$

where

$CAAR_{i,t}$ =   corrected absolute abnormal return with indices i and t

Equation 2.10: Cumulated Corrected Absolute Abnormal Returns

This accumulation is done for two different dimensions. First, the accumulation covers a given number of price fixings (price fixing timeframes $(t1,t2) = (1,2), (3,5), (6,10), (11,15), (16,20)$) and, secondly, different timeframes on a minute basis (minute-by-minute timeframes $(t1,t2) = (0,15), (16,30), (31,45), (46,60), (61,75), (76,90), (91,120)$). Compared to Muntermann and Güttler (2007), this analysis covers ex post analyses following the event date only. In contrast to this reduction, the analyses covers a longer ex post analysis period including five more price fixings and more detailed timeframes on a minute basis respectively.

The accumulation of corrected absolute abnormal returns is illustrated in Figure 2.8 showing the development of $CCAAR_{i,t1,t2}$ also for the stock price adjustment process following the ad hoc disclosure published by *SAP AG* on 2003-10-08.

Figure 2.8: Example Accumulation of Abnormal Stock Price Reactions Following an Ad Hoc Disclosure

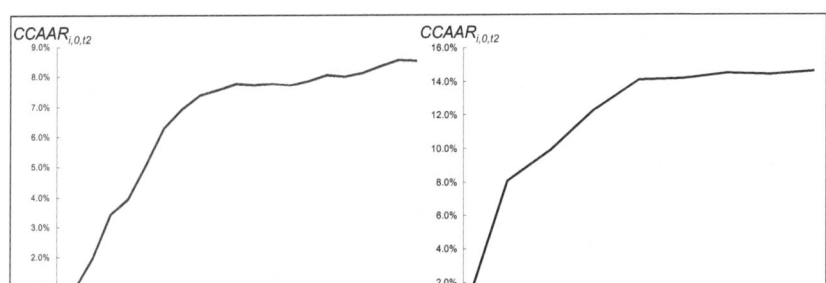

In addition, mean and median cumulated corrected absolute abnormal returns ($\mu(CAAR_{i,t})$ and $median(CAAR_{i,t})$) are calculated over the I number of ad hoc disclosures for the different time-frames, which can be used for hypotheses tests.

$$\mu\left(CCAAR_{t1,t2}\right) = 1/I \sum_{i=1}^{I} CCAAR_{i,t1,t2}$$

Equation 2.11: Mean Cumulated Corrected Absolute Abnormal Returns

$$median\left(CCAAR_{t1,t2}\right) = \begin{cases} CCAAR_{(I+1)/2,t1,t2} & \text{if } I = uneven \\ 1/2\left(CCAAR_{(I/2),t1,t2} + CCAAR_{(I/2+1),t1,t2}\right) & \text{if } I = even \end{cases}$$

Equation 2.12: Median Cumulated Corrected Absolute Abnormal Returns

> where
>
> $CCAAR_{i,t1,t2}$ =   cumulated corrected absolute abnormal
>
>   return with indices i and $t1$ and $t2$

The resulting values are used for addressing a set of research hypotheses formulated in the following.

2.2.3 Research Hypotheses

Following the findings of Nowak (2001), Oerke (1999), and Röder (1999), different research hypotheses are formulated regarding the efficiency with which the German capital market reacts to the information content provided by ad hoc disclosures.

As the analysis addresses the potential of suitable mobile notification systems, it covers ex post reactions of stock prices to ad hoc disclosures only. Muntermann and Güttler (2007) conducted an event study analysis covering ex ante intraday stock price reactions to ad hoc disclosures. They do not observe any significant abnormal trading volumes or price effects five price fixings prior to this event type. Consequently, they do not provide evidence for intraday insider trading or anticipation effects.

In order to prove the relevance of the selected event type a research hypothesis regarding observable price effects is formulated. This hypothesis addresses the presence of nonzero abnormal market returns.

Research hypothesis Ia: Stock prices react after the publication of ad hoc disclosures.

Furthermore, it is of utmost importance to ascertain after which time span the observed price effects are completed, as investors would have to react within this period. The hypothesis is theoretically derived from the semi-strong form of the efficient market hypothesis after which stock prices should adjust efficiently to new information available. Therefore, an analysis of the period following the event date provides evidence regarding the window of opportunity, which opens for a limited time span only. Consequently, a second research hypothesis is formulated.

Research hypothesis Ib: The observed price effects persist for a short period of time only (several minutes, up to a few hours).

Given the mean (median) corrected absolute abnormal returns $\mu(CAAR_{i,t})$ $(median(CAAR_{i,t}))$ and the mean (median) cumulated corrected absolute abnormal returns $\mu(CCAAR_{i,t1,t2})$ $(median(CCAAR_{i,t1,t2}))$, the *research hypotheses Ia* and *Ib* are tested with statistical test procedures that were introduced in Section 2.1.3.

If the statistical null hypotheses can be rejected at a given significance level (i.e. *research hypothesis Ia* and *Ib* can be corroborated), suitable information systems could support investors to exploit the observed price movements. Furthermore, the selected event type (ad hoc disclosures pursuant to article 15 of the German Securities Trading Law) could be identified as interesting market events, for which timely information supply would open a window of opportunity for investors. As the null hypotheses are tested for different time intervals, the test statistics provide evidence regarding possible reaction delays and the persistence of abnormal price behavior. These different analysis periods are used to corroborate or reject *research hypothesis Ib*. If the statistical analyses provide evidence for only a limited period of time within which abnormal market behavior can be observed, this can constitute a motivation for the introduction of mobile financial services providing timely information supply.

2.2.4 Sample Analysis and Descriptive Statistics

Each of these samples represents the calculated $CCAAR_{t1,t2}$ for a time interval covering a set of price fixings or minutes. The analysis covers the first 20 price fixings, and the first 120 minutes following the event date respectively. For the analyses of the first 20 price fixings, the total sample of 425 disclosures can be used. Since there is not necessarily at least one price fixing observable in every interval of fifteen minutes, not every $CCAAR_{t1,t2}$ can be calculated and the sample has to be adjusted accordingly. Table 2.2 shows the results of these adjustments with panel I summarizing the sample sizes for intervals determined by price fixings and panel II showing the number of samples drawn from (15-minutes) time intervals.

Table 2.2: Sample Adjustments for Different Time Intervals

	Sample size I		
	All disclosures	Disclosures of index members	Disclosures of non-index members
Panel I: Interval by price fixings			
All intervals	425	140	285
Panel II: Interval by minutes			
(1,15)	377	132	245
(16,0)	368	128	240
(31,45)	355	124	231
(46,60)	348	124	224
(61,75)	349	127	222
(76,90)	356	127	229
(91,105)	349	123	226
(106,120)	326	116	210

The descriptive statistics presented in this section provide detailed information regarding the distributions of the evaluated price reactions. All reported statistics are produced with the econometric software package EViews 4.1.

The descriptive statistics (Table 2.3, Table 2.4, and Table 2.5) comprise information regarding the maximum and minimum value, the 90th, 75th, 25th, and 10th percentile, and the population mean. Furthermore, the $CCAAR_{t1,t2}$ populations' skewness and kurtosis are presented in the two right-hand columns. Whereas skewness measures distribution's asymmetry around its mean, the kurtosis is a measure for the peakedness or flatness of the distribution (Poddig et al. 2003). For symmetric distributions, such as the normal distribution, the skewness is zero. Positive skewness implies that the distribution has a long right tail and negative skewness a long left tail. The kurtosis of distributions is usually compared with the kurtosis of the normal distribution, which has a kurtosis of three (Poddig et al. 2003). A computed kurtosis exceeding this value indicates that the distribution is peaked (leptokurtic) relative to the normal, whereas a value of less than three implies a flat (platykurtic) distribution.

Table 2.3 provides information regarding the entire sample and Table 2.4 presents results for 140 ad hoc disclosures of companies, which were included in the DAX, MDAX, or TecDAX.

Each row provides information regarding the $CCAAR_{t1,t2}$ population of the (t1,t2) time interval.

In Panel I, the $CCAAR_{t1,t2}$ distribution details are reported for the time intervals between price fixing 1 and 2, 3 and 5, 6 and 10, 11 and 15 and 16 and 20 following the event date.

Panel II provides the same details for eight sequential time intervals of fifteen minutes each, covering 120 minutes from the event time onwards.

Table 2.3: Distributions of the Price Reaction of All Disclosures

$CCAAR_{t1,t2}$ Interval	Percentiles and central tendency							Statistics	
	Max	0.9	0.75	Mean	0.25	0.1	Min	Skew-ness	Kurtosis
Panel I: Intervals by price fixings									
(1,2)	1.089	0.093	0.035	0.037	0.001	-0.005	-0.039	6.495	55.269
(3,5)	0.398	0.048	0.020	0.014	-0.004	-0.017	-0.094	3.804	26.133
(6,10)	0.420	0.061	0.018	0.012	-0.009	-0.028	-0.172	2.978	19.343
(11,15)	0.310	0.031	0.011	0.003	-0.011	-0.030	-0.123	2.646	18.769
(16,20)	0.284	0.030	0.010	0.001	-0.013	-0.030	-0.099	2.332	19.758
Panel II: Intervals by minutes									
(1,15)	1.150	0.089	0.046	0.033	0.000	-0.012	-0.102	8.533	117.083
(16,30	0.356	0.035	0.013	0.008	-0.007	-0.023	-0.155	3.817	28.736
(31,45)	1.068	0.024	0.008	0.005	-0.009	-0.027	-0.144	11.195	166.249
(46,60)	0.330	0.026	0.007	0.004	-0.009	-0.024	-0.109	4.027	26.617
(61,75)	0.821	0.030	0.007	0.014	-0.009	-0.019	-0.134	5.933	47.269
(76,90)	0.405	0.032	0.007	0.005	-0.007	-0.018	-0.155	4.639	38.673
(91,105)	0.645	0.024	0.004	0.004	-0.007	-0.018	-0.133	8.374	106.060
(106,120)	0.343	0.020	0.005	0.001	-0.008	-0.019	-0.144	4.842	43.629

Table 2.4: Distribution of the Price Reaction of Index Members

$CCAAR_{t1,t2}$	Percentiles and central tendency							Statistics	
Interval	Max	0.9	0.75	Mean	0.25	0.1	Min	Skew-ness	Kurtosis
Panel I: Intervals by price fixings									
(1,2)	0.175	0.026	0.014	0.012	0.001	0.000	-0.005	4.680	29.828
(3,5)	0.079	0.022	0.013	0.009	0.001	-0.002	-0.013	2.197	9.656
(6,10)	0.051	0.017	0.010	0.006	-0.001	-0.003	-0.016	1.696	7.451
(11,15)	0.037	0.015	0.006	0.004	-0.001	-0.004	-0.017	1.501	6.477
(16,20)	0.036	0.011	0.004	0.003	-0.001	-0.005	-0.015	1.573	7.103
Panel II: Intervals by minutes									
(1,15)	0.125	0.055	0.036	0.024	0.003	-0.001	-0.009	1.430	5.175
(16,30	0.054	0.017	0.008	0.005	-0.001	-0.005	-0.017	1.764	8.002
(31,45)	0.055	0.013	0.005	0.003	-0.003	-0.008	-0.043	1.712	10.282
(46,60)	0.076	0.016	0.006	0.004	-0.002	-0.006	-0.026	2.594	13.823
(61,75)	0.291	0.011	0.003	0.007	-0.004	-0.009	-0.026	5.592	37.560
(76,90)	0.084	0.011	0.004	0.001	-0.003	-0.008	-0.025	2.961	20.829
(91,105)	0.061	0.010	0.004	0.001	-0.003	-0.007	-0.034	1.538	11.587
(106,120)	0.043	0.009	0.003	0.001	-0.003	-0.007	-0.026	1.260	8.081

Finally, Table 2.5 shows results for the 285 ad hoc disclosures of non-index members.

Table 2.5: Distribution of the Price Reaction of Non-Index Members

$CCAAR_{t1,t2}$	Percentiles and central tendency							Statistics	
Interval	Max	0.9	0.75	Mean	0.25	0.1	Min	Skew-ness	Kurtosis
Panel I: Intervals by price fixings									
(1,2)	1.089	0.123	0.045	0.050	0.001	-0.009	-0.039	5.385	38.250
(3,5)	0.398	0.061	0.028	0.016	-0.008	-0.023	-0.094	3.150	18.239
(6,10)	0.420	0.081	0.030	0.015	-0.018	-0.039	-0.172	2.372	12.989
(11,15)	0.310	0.046	0.017	0.003	-0.020	-0.036	-0.123	2.208	12.879
(16,20)	0.284	0.037	0.017	0.000	-0.020	-0.039	-0.099	2.053	14.108
Panel II: Intervals by minutes									
(1,15)	1.150	0.111	0.053	0.037	-0.001	-0.021	-0.102	7.256	82.587
(16,30	0.356	0.056	0.016	0.009	-0.014	-0.028	-0.155	3.099	19.254
(31,45)	1.068	0.039	0.010	0.007	-0.015	-0.034	-0.144	9.143	110.212
(46,60)	0.330	0.031	0.008	0.004	-0.017	-0.030	-0.109	3.378	18.294
(61,75)	0.821	0.036	0.010	0.017	-0.013	-0.024	-0.134	5.085	34.299
(76,90)	0.405	0.042	0.010	0.007	-0.010	-0.024	-0.155	3.767	25.852
(91,105)	0.645	0.031	0.007	0.005	-0.011	-0.023	-0.133	6.871	70.852
(106,120)	0.343	0.025	0.006	0.002	-0.011	-0.027	-0.144	3.990	29.260

The statistics show a high positive skewness for all analyzed samples indicating long right tails and a higher probability of positive extreme values. Furthermore, the kurtosis calculated for all samples exceed the value of 3, which provides evidence for platykurtic distributions, i.e. the probability of extreme values is higher compared to a normal distribution (Abramowitz 1972).

These characteristics can be visualized in a frequency distribution histogram, e.g. for the $CCAAR_{1,2}$ sample (Figure 2.9).

Figure 2.9: $CCAAR_{1,2}$ Frequency Distribution Histogram

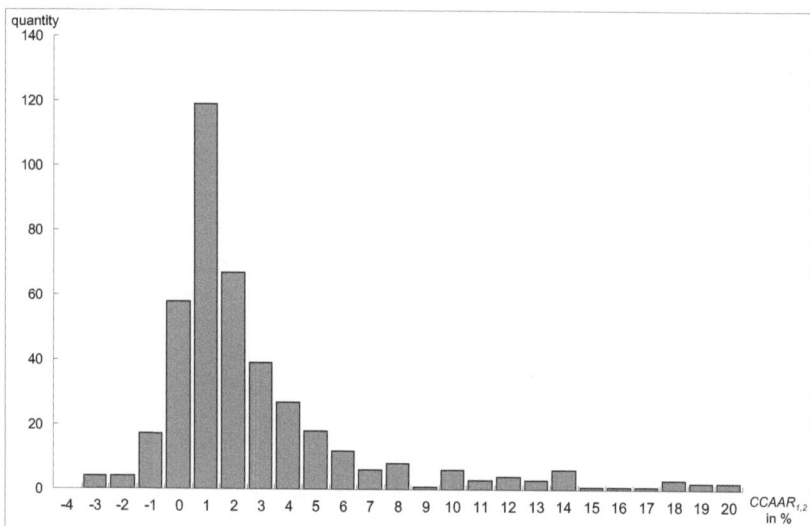

The observed fat-tail characteristic is typical for return distributions when working with high-frequency intraday data (Dacorogna et al. 2001). The $CCAAR_{1,2}$ sample depicted has a mean of 3.94% and more than 80% of the sample values are below this mean. On the other hand, the distribution histogram shows that there are much more extreme observations in the right-hand tail exceeding several times the sample mean, which illustrates that there exist more positive extreme values.

2.2.5   Empirical Results

The empirical results of the intraday stock price reactions following the publication of ad hoc disclosures are reported in the following sections 2.2.5.1 (parametric test results) and 2.2.5.2 (nonparametric test results).

Table 2.6 and Table 2.8 summarize the results for the first twenty price fixings and the price fixing intervals (1,2), (3,5) (6,10), (11,15) and (16,20). Table 2.7 and Table 2.9 respectively show the results for the eight sequential intervals (1,15), (16,30), (31,45), (46,60), (61,75), (76,90), (91,105) and (106,120), which are measured in minutes following the event date.

Compared to Muntermann and Güttler (2007) five additional price fixings were included to cover a longer period of analysis. Furthermore, the analyses of intervals in minutes cover two additional periods of analysis and all of these intervals have the same duration of 15 minutes in order achieve comparability between intervals.

The abnormal price reaction for each price fixing or interval is measured by the corrected absolute abnormal return $CAAR_t$ and the cumulated corrected absolute abnormal return $CCAAR_{t1,t2}$ as presented in Section 2.2.2.

2.2.5.1 Parametric Test Results

For the parametric test procedure, standard two-sided Student t-tests have been conducted. Since all sample sizes used are larger than 30, the sample means are assumed to be approximately normally distributed (Groebner et al. 2001).

$$H_0 : \mu(CAAR_t) = 0 \quad H_A : \mu(CAAR_t) \neq 0$$

and

$$H_0 : \mu(CCAAR_{t1,t2}) = 0 \quad H_A : \mu(CCAAR_{t1,t2}) \neq 0$$

Equations 2.13: Parametric Null Hypotheses

The t-statistics are reported (Table 2.6) for testing the null hypotheses that the sample mean of the $CAAR_t$ and the $CCAAR_{t1,t2}$ samples, respectively, is zero. Therefore, the test statistics cover the price fixings and several periods measured in price fixings or minutes following the event date.

The test statistics show abnormal high stock returns in the first thirteen price fixings following the publication of ad hoc disclosures for all 425 ad hoc disclosures except the twelfth price fixing. The event windows (1,2), (3,5), (6,10), (11,15) and (16,20) all show significant abnormal returns. After dividing the sample in index and non-index members, it can be shown that the adjustment process covers more price fixings for the index members.

For these 140 ad hoc disclosures, abnormal high price reactions were detected for all price fixings except the eighteenth one and for all intervals also.

For the 285 ad hoc disclosures of the non-index members, abnormal high price reactions were found only for the first thirteen price fixings (despite the eighth and twelfth) and the three intervals (1,2), (3,5) and (6,10) following the announcement.

Table 2.6: Intraday Price Reactions to Ad Hoc Disclosures According to Price Fixings (Parametric Test Statistics)

Price fixing (or interval)	All disclosures ($I = 425$)		Disclosures of index members ($I = 140$)		Disclosures of non-index members ($I = 285$)	
	Mean $CAAR_t$ or $CCAAR_{t1,t2}$ in %	Student t-statistic	Mean $CAAR_t$ or $CCAAR_{t1,t2}$ in %	Student t-statistic	Mean $CAAR_t$ or $CCAAR_{t1,t2}$ in %	Student t-statistic
1	2.6366	7.00***	0.8746	4.77***	3.5022	6.39***
2	1.1123	4.08***	0.3353	6.64***	1.4939	3.69***
3	0.5191	5.25***	0.3492	7.04***	0.6025	4.15***
4	0.5241	5.51***	0.2441	5.90***	0.6617	4.73***
5	0.2511	2.96***	0.1737	3.92***	0.2892	2.32**
6	0.1746	2.77***	0.1735	5.33***	0.1751	1.89*
7	0.3893	2.98**	0.1256	4.37***	0.5188	2.67**
8	0.1417	2.36**	0.1461	4.37***	0.1395	1.58
9	0.2017	3.18***	0.1210	4.31***	0.2414	2.58***
10	0.2485	2.96***	0.1350	4.15***	0.3042	2.45**
11	0.1617	2.28**	0.0544	2.24**	0.2145	2.04**
12	0.1276	1.57	0.0592	2.71***	0.1612	1.33
13	0.1418	2.19**	0.1013	4.16***	0.1617	1.69*
14	0.0895	1.52	0.0494	1.93*	0.1092	1.26
15	-0.0072	-0.12	0.0558	2.28**	-0.0381	-0.42
16	-0.0467	-0.96	0.0871	2.99***	-0.1124	-1.58
17	0.0715	1.15	0.0733	2.57**	0.0705	0.77
18	-0.0782	-1.55	0.0295	1.26	-0.1311	-1.76*
19	-0.0424	-0.89	0.0417	1.94*	-0.0837	-1.19
20	0.0887	1.48	0.0582	3.05***	0.1037	1.16
(1,2)	3.7489	7.51***	0.0121	6.45***	5.0049	6.85***
(3,5)	1.3766	6.23***	0.0088	7.74***	1.6083	4.95***
(6,10)	1.2094	4.59***	0.0061	6.81***	1.4988	3.83***
(11,15)	0.3493	1.68*	0.0035	5.15***	0.3389	1.10
(16,20)	0.0583	0.36	0.0026	3.93***	-0.0599	-0.25

***, ** and * indicate significance at the 1%, 5% and 10% level respectively.

Since there was not at least one price fixing observable during all time intervals measured in minutes (e.g. only for 377 of the 425 disclosures in the first fifteen minutes following the event date), the sample size had to be adjusted as stated in Table 2.2. The period of analysis covers 120 minutes since longer analysis periods would have led to much smaller sample sizes.

Table 2.7: Intraday Price Reactions to Ad Hoc Disclosures According to Periods in Minutes (Parametric Test Statistics)

Interval (in minutes)	All disclosures Mean $CCAAR_{t1,t2}$ in %	All disclosures Student t-statistic	Disclosures of index members Mean $CCAAR_{t1,t2}$ in %	Disclosures of index members Student t-statistic	Disclosures of non-index members Mean $CCAAR_{t1,t2}$ in %	Disclosures of non-index members Student t-statistic
(1,15)	3.2620	8.17***	2.3666	10.05***	3.7444	6.24***
(16,30)	0.7642	3.41***	0.4661	5.06***	0.9233	2.72***
(31,45)	0.5439	1.49	0.2560	2.30**	0.6985	1.26
(46,60)	0.4017	1.81*	0.4136	3.68***	0.3951	1.17
(61,75)	1.3595	3.09***	0.6868	2.05**	1.7444	2.62***
(76,90)	0.5121	2.23**	0.1195	1.13	0.7298	2.07**
(91,105)	0.3673	1.45	0.1066	1.09	0.5092	1.32
(106,120)	0.1408	0.69	0.0696	0.81	0.1801	0.57

***, ** and * indicate significance at the 1%, 5% and 10% level respectively.

According to the analyzed time intervals in minutes reported in Table 2.7, significant price reactions can be shown to exist within the first 90 minutes following the event date for the whole sample and non-index members, with there being non-significant intervals in between (the (31,45) interval of all disclosures and the (31,45) and (46,60) intervals for non-index members). There is evidence that a shorter adjustment process of 75 minutes exists for index members as no significance can be found for later intervals.

2.2.5.2 Nonparametric Test Results

The nonparametric test procedure has been conducted with the Wilcoxon signed rank test for one sample. According to the parametric test procedure, it is hypothesized that the sample median of the $CAAR_t$ and $CCAAR_{t1,t2}$ samples, respectively, is zero.

$$H_0 : median(CAAR_t) = 0 \quad H_A : median(CAAR_t) \neq 0$$

and

$$H_0 : median(CCAAR_{t1,t2}) = 0 \quad H_A : median(CCAAR_{t1,t2}) \neq 0$$

Equations 2.14: Nonparametric Null Hypotheses

Like the Student t-tests, all Wilcoxon signed rank tests have been conducted using the statistical software package EViews 4.1. The following Table 2.8 summarizes the statistical significance of abnormal market behavior according to price fixings following the event date.

The nonparametric statistical tests yield results that are largely similar to those of the parametric tests. In the sample of all 425 disclosures significant abnormal market behavior can be observed for the first four price fixings and as well as for five other (the 9th, 15th, 16th, 18th and 19th) price fixings. The results of the analysis of price fixings intervals correspond with those obtained form the parametric test statistics, i.e. that the first three intervals (1,2), (3,5), and (6,10) are highly significant at the 1% level.

Table 2.8: Intraday Price Reactions to Ad Hoc Disclosures According to Price Fixings (Nonparametric Test Statistics)

Price fixing (or interval)	All disclosures ($I = 425$)		Disclosures of index members ($I = 140$)		Disclosures of non-index members ($I = 285$)	
	Median $CAAR_t$ or $CCAAR_{t1,t2}$ in %	Wilcoxon t-statistic	Median $CAAR_t$ or $CCAAR_{t1,t2}$ in %	Wilcoxon t-statistic	Median $CAAR_t$ or $CCAAR_{t1,t2}$ in %	Wilcoxon t-statistic
1	0.5516	12.07***	0.3082	8.14***	0.9198	9.80***
2	0.2236	7.71***	0.1374	6.22***	0.3361	6.01***
3	0.1572	5.44***	0.1765	7.76***	0.0573	2.91***
4	0.1103	4.85***	0.1076	5.79***	0.1153	3.39***
5	0.0118	1.03	0.0429	3.44***	-0.1211	0.09
6	0.0062	1.15	0.0385	4.19***	-0.0887	0.17
7	0.0087	0.66	0.0442	3.47***	-0.1306	0.16
8	-0.0119	0.57	0.0442	3.47***	-0.0853	0.74
9	0.0291	1.81*	0.0535	3.75***	0.0092	0.67
10	-0.0300	0.21	0.0327	2.92***	-0.1662	0.81
11	-0.0323	1.11	0.0108	1.55	-0.2186	0.90
12	-0.0300	1.60	0.0125	1.57	-0.1926	1.89*
13	-0.0200	0.28	0.0414	3.41***	-0.1802	0.97
14	-0.0227	0.74	-0.0052	0.84	-0.1033	0.79
15	-0.0845	3.81***	0.0075	1.08	-0.3440	3.91***
16	-0.0605	3.57***	-0.0011	1.41	-0.2415	4.02***
17	-0.0287	1.59	0.0007	1.09	-0.1876	2.61***
18	-0.0657	3.89***	-0.0085	1.22	-0.3028	4.17***
19	-0.0375	2.51**	-0.0052	0.45	-0.2052	2.71***
20	-0.0310	0.91	0.0161	1.89*	-0.2147	1.14
(1,2)	1.1489	13.58***	0.6382	9.26***	1.6865	10.93***
(3,5)	0.4908	7.11***	0.5071	7.89***	0.4141	4.34***
(6,10)	0.3721	4.20***	0.3918	6.43***	0.3596	2.34**
(11,15)	0.0940	0.74	0.1841	4.90***	-0.2984	0.76
(16,20)	0.0124	0.52	0.1454	3.58***	-0.4116	1.71*

***, ** and * indicate significance at the 1%, 5% and 10% level respectively.

In addition, the statistical results for the 140 index members are also largely similar to those of the parametric tests. Significance at a level of 1% can be found for the first 10 price fixings, the 13th price fixing, and all price fixing intervals. The latter interval analyses corroborate the results of the parametric test statistics.

For the 285 non-index members the Wilcoxon test statistic confirms significance for the first four price fixings and shows high significance at the 1% level. There is a remarkable significant interval between the 15th and 19th price fixing, which is not corroborated by the parametric test statistics. However, high significance levels were also found for the three first price fixing intervals (1,2), (3,5), and (6,10).

The analysis of intervals measured in minutes is done accordingly with the Wilcoxon test statistics. The empirical results of this analysis are summarized in the following Table 2.9.

Table 2.9: Price Reactions to Ad Hoc Disclosures According to Periods in Minutes (Nonparametric Test Statistics)

Interval (in minutes)	All disclosures		Disclosures of index members		Disclosures of non-index members	
	Median $CCAAR_{t1,t2}$ in %	Wilcoxon t-statistic	Median $CCAAR_{t1,t2}$ in %	Wilcoxon t-statistic	Median $CCAAR_{t1,t2}$ in %	Wilcoxon t-statistic
(1,15)	1.7075	11.65***	1.6299	8.85***	1.8951	8.34***
(16,30)	0.1125	2.47**	0.2963	4.65***	-0.0697	0.86
(31,45)	-0.0272	0.46	0.0471	1.57	-0.2313	1.25
(46,60)	-0.0930	0.88	0.1412	3.23***	-0.4225	2.38**
(61,75)	-0.1335	1.38	-0.0529	0.32	-0.3145	1.28
(76,90)	0.0020	0.31	0.0182	0.24	-0.0226	0.35
(91,105)	-0.1469	1.87*	0.0299	0.40	-0.3025	2.03**
(106,120)	-0.1513	2.06**	-0.0456	0.08	-0.2925	2.19**

***, ** and * indicate significance at the 1%, 5% and 10% level respectively.

According to the parametric test results, statistical significance can be found for all samples within the first thirty minutes except for non-index members were no significance can be found for the second interval. Furthermore, significance can be found during the last two intervals (91,105), and (106,120) for all disclosures and during the forth interval (46,60) for index members. In addition, stocks of non-index members show an abnormal behavior during the intervals (46,60), (91,105), and (106,120).

2.3 Conclusion of the Intraday Event Study

The event study presented in this chapter represents an analysis of intraday stock price effects on the German capital market following company announcements pursuant to article 15 of the German Securities Trading Act (WpHG). Section 2.1 introduced the event study methodology, which was applied in order to prove the existence and persistence of abnormal intraday stock price reactions.

Being theoretically derived form the efficient market hypothesis, the research hypotheses formulated in section 2.2.3 address possible opportunities arising form the observed price adjustment processes, which could be exploited with suitable information technology, especially, with mobile services.

Therefore, the *research hypotheses Ia* and *Ib* are formulated and tested in Section 2.2.3 and 2.2.5 using statistical analysis procedures. In order to achieve statistical robustness, parametric (Section 2.1.3.1) and nonparametric (Section 2.1.3.2) statistical test procedures were introduced and applied in Section 2.1.3 and 2.2.5.

The empirical results show that the significant abnormal price reactions can be corroborated by both test procedures, which substantiates the findings. As significant abnormal price behavior can be shown with both test procedures, *research hypotheses Ia* "Stock prices react after the publication of ad hoc disclosures" can be corroborated.

A more detailed analysis of the price adjustment process shows that the capital market reaction is not uniformly distributed during the event day. Rather, taking both test procedures into account, strong evidence can be found that there exists continuous abnormal stock price behavior during a short period following the event, which covers approximately a period of 30 minutes for non-index members and 60 minutes for index members, whereas the later abnormal price behavior can be observed at irregular intervals only. Analyzing the price adjustment process from a price fixing perspective provides evidence that the stock process reflect the information within the first ten price fixings following the publication date and that this process takes more price fixings for index members. Observed on a minute-by-minute basis, these price fixing intervals corresponds to a shorter (longer) interval in minutes for (non)-index members as price fixings can be observed more (less) frequently for (non-)index member. Therefore, *research hypothesis Ib* "*The observed price effects persist for a short period of time only (several minutes, up to a few hours)*" is also corroborated.

However, due to the restriction to 120 minutes following the publication of the ad hoc disclosures, no definite evidence can be delivered that the whole price adjustment process is completed within this timeframe. Nevertheless, the results are supported by the fact that the observed significance of abnormal price behavior is decreasing over the analysis intervals.

Furthermore, previous research has shown comparable price adjustment processed for similar event types. Compared to the results of previous non-domestic intraday event studies these price adjustment processes appear to be slower than the one for earnings and dividend announcements (Patell and Wolfson 1984), and the announcement of new equity issues (Barclay and Litzenberger 1988). A comparable adjustment process of approximately one hour was detected by Woodruff and Senchak (1988) for unexpected earnings releases. However, the observed price adjustment processes of this study appear faster than eight hours after the announcements of earnings (Jennings and Starks 1985), five hours after the announcements of takeovers (Smith et al. 1997), and four hours after trading halts (Lee et al. 1994).

Having established that continuous stock price adjustments on the German capital market can be observed for relatively short period of time only, these empirical results can contribute the understanding of the addresses problem space and the problem's relevance.

The empirical results in turn provide evidence for a window of opportunity provided to investors, which is addressed in the following chapter that introduces a mobile notification and decision support system concept. The concept aims to assist private investors to exploit the proven stock price effects.

3 Mobile Notification and Decision Support for Private Investors

Online brokers and banks have invested heavily into IT infrastructure in recent years involving a fundamental shift in sales channels towards online services (Beck et al. 2003; Minz et al. 2004; Meyer 2006). In parallel, previous research has shown that customers demand for better electronic banking services in terms of lower transaction costs (Polatoglu and Ekin 2001; Karjaluoto 2002; Howcroft et al. 2002), time and location independent service access (Polatoglu and Ekin 2001; Howcroft et al. 2002), high level of usability (Karjaluoto 2002; Pikkarainen et al. 2004), enhanced usefulness (Beckett et al. 2000; Howcroft et al. 2002; Wang et al. 2003) and increased transaction speed (Karjaluoto 2002).

So far, most existing financial information systems that support private investors in making their investment decisions are limited to conventional web-based services. Since the number of security types such as stocks, options and warrants, which can be traded online by private investors, has significantly increased in recent years, there is a growing demand for personalized financial information supply and for decision support. Web-based financial information systems on the one hand provide information for concrete investment decisions (so-called pull services). On the other hand, notification services triggered by certain events can support investors in making time-critical investment decisions (so-called push services). The preceding chapter has shown that particular events, such as the observed ad hoc disclosures, can cause significant stock price reactions and therefore call for prompt reaction. However, as private investors usually do not monitor their inbox status continuously, email based communication often does not reach the recipients in time, especially if the information provided becomes obsolete shortly. Mobile financial information and decision support systems should therefore support private investors in making time-critical investment decisions since enhanced time and place independent service access can be realized. The required mobile phone or PDA is generally a personal device, carried all the time, and not shared with others (Birch 1999). This promotes mobile devices as a suitable platform for financial services. In the mobile services domain, customers also demand for substantial benefits, in particular improved perceived usefulness or value which, for example, will affect positively investment performance (Lee et al. 2003; Luarn and Lin 2005; Laukkanen and Lauronen 2005).

The central goal of decision supports systems (DSS) is to process and provide suitable information in order support individuals or organizations in decision-making (Bonczek et al. 1981). Therefore, appropriate mobile decision support systems could bridge the gap and provide additional value to users as timely information supply and supported decision-making should provide a basis for more successful financial transactions.

The following chapter introduces an event-driven mobile financial DSS concept that should assist investors in identifying relevant ad hoc disclosures, which should significantly affect stock prices of the corresponding company. The subsequent Section 3.1 provides an introduction to decision support research and addresses types of decisions and dimensions of managerial control. Furthermore, it is illustrated which domains are addressed by decision support systems in general.

Then, Section 3.2 presents an expanded DSS classification framework originally presented by Power (2002 and 2004), which classifies decision support systems by their immanent characteristics. First, the *system purpose* (Section 3.2.1) classification criteria is determined, which ranges form general-purpose to task-specific depending on the domain's grade of specialization. Depending on the users addressed, the *target user group* criteria (Section 3.2.2) separates intra-organizational from inter-organizational DSS, whereas the latter includes customer decision support systems (CDSS), which play the major role in the following. *Enabling technologies* are then presented in Section 3.2.3, which represent the technological basis of deployed decision support systems. Then, Section 3.2.4 introduces different kinds of *DSS technology components*, which provide the system's core functionality.

Utilizing the presented DSS classification framework, the following section 3.3 introduces an event-driven mobile financial DSS concept. First, Section 3.3.1 summarizes the addressed application domain (*system purpose*) and the *targeted user group*. Then, Section 3.3.2 introduces mobile communication technologies such as mobile push message service and the underlying mobile communication infrastructure being the central enabling technologies for the proposed DSS concept. Therefore, it is explicated, how mobile communication technologies can support the whole investment process. A model-driven DSS approach is presented in Section 3.3.3, which shows how appropriate forecasting models can support investor's decision-making. Building the central DSS technology components of the proposed DSS concept, two such forecasting models are then presented in the following. First, a forecasting model is developed in Section 3.3.4 for estimating the price effect magnitude following the observed ad hoc disclosure. The temporal persistence of this price effect is then addressed in Section 3.3.5, which presents a corresponding forecasting model for estimating the duration of the price effect. Both forecasting models are econometrically estimated using an empirical dataset and statistical software packages. Finally, Section 3.4 concludes with a summary of the mobile financial DSS concept developed in this chapter.

3.1 Introduction to Decision Support Systems Research

Scott Morton introduced the term *management decision systems* in his widely cited work in 1971, which is often seen as the beginning of DSS research in general (Scott Morton 1971). In the same year, Gory and Scott Morton laid the basis for subsequent research including a definition of decision support systems (Gorry and Scott Morton 1971). Within the IS field, their work is probably the most highly regarded DSS framework that has been cited most frequently (Kirs et al. 1989).

Their framework is based on the idea to combine two different taxonomies for describing managerial activity within organizations. This is realized by integrating Anthony's (1965) work that categorizes different purposes of business activity (operational control, managerial control, and strategic planning) and Simon's (1960) concept of categorizing decisions by their grade of repetition, fuzziness, and novelty.

Figure 3.1: Classic Decision Support Framework[12]

	Type of control		
Type of decision	Operational control	Managerial control	Strategic planning
Structured	Accounts receivable, order entry, inventory control	Budget analysis, short-term forecasting, make or buy	Basic financial management, warehouse and factory location
Semi-structured	Production scheduling, inventory control	Budget analysis, project scheduling, credit evaluation	Advanced investment planning, mergers and acquisitions
Unstructured	Buying new software systems	Sales and production, recruiting an executive	R&D planning, new technology development

Gorry and Scott Morton's framework classifies decisions and task structures within organizations, which provides a perspective on the requirements and characteristics of appropriate information systems. Their classic framework is illustrated in Figure 3.1, where *type of decision* distinguishes from top to bottom grades of problem structure. The boundaries between the three types *structured*, *semi-structured*, and *unstructured* are often not clear (illustrated by the broken lines and the vertical double-sided arrow) and in reality, most decisions address semi-structured problems since they feature both structured and unstructured elements (Gorry and Scott Morton 1971). Gorry and Scott Morton (1971) adopted their problem 'structuredness' definition from a primal taxonomy proposed by Simon (1960) who defined the terms *programmed* and *nonprogrammed* problem types in order to describe the repetition and novelty of problems.

---

[12] Adapted from Gorry and Scott Morton (1971) and Turban et al. (2005).

Programmed decisions are repetitive and routine when a certain kind of decision recurs frequently. Consequently, suitable processes can be developed that operationalize this kind of decisions. *Nonprogrammed* decisions arise when a new type of novel problem is addressed. Typically, the different decision categories can be supported by different techniques, such as mathematical analysis for programmed decisions or heuristics for *nonprogrammed* decisions (Simon 1960).

Gorry and Scott Morton (1971) introduced the terms *structured* and *unstructured* problems since they describe the basic nature of the problem addressed, whereas *programmed* and *nonprogrammed* imply the grade of information processing performed by computers. There is also no explicit boundary between structured and unstructured decisions and most decisions have elements of both, which led to the term *semi-structured* decisions (Gorry and Scott Morton 1971). For structured decision making there usually exist standard solution methods, as such problems are typically repetitive. In contrast, unstructured decisions are characterized by fuzziness and novelty for which no standard solution is available (Turban et al. 2005). Examples for the different decision types are order quantity entry (structured), production scheduling (semi-structured), and R&D planning (unstructured) (Gorry and Scott Morton 1971).

Decision support systems provide primarily support for semi-structured and unstructured problems, whereas structured problems are usually addressed with Management Information Systems (MIS) (Laudon and Laudon 2006). The focus of Management Information Systems lies on the provision of routine business information, e.g. they assist managers with standardized reports (Turban et al. 2005).

Anthony's (1965) taxonomy for classifying managerial activity within organizations provides the basis for the second dimension of Gorry and Scott Morton's framework, which leads to the nine-cell DSS classification framework depicted in Figure 3.1. Anthony defines the three categories *operational control*, *management control*, and *strategic planning* that are used as classification scheme for planning and control information systems within organizations (Anthony and Dearden 1972).

Operational control is a process that assures that specific tasks such as inventory control can be fulfilled. Corresponding information systems provide support for solving such tasks as effectively and efficiently as possible. The time horizon of operational control is usually short, i.e. with a day-to-day focus and there is little judgment required by the user.

Management control addresses more general activities that ensure resources to be used efficiently. This requires a longer time horizon up to several years. Therefore, most management control systems are based on financial calculations which take output and resources (e.g. material quantities, working hours, etc.) into account (Anthony 1965). Furthermore, management control systems focus on the whole operation and not on single tasks. They support interpersonal interaction and demand for much more user judgment compared to operation control systems (Anthony and Dearden 1972).

Strategic planning addresses problems with the lowest degree of structure and therefore demands for the most creative and analytic activity (Anthony and Dearden 1972). The aim of strategic planning is to plan general objectives of an organization and to identify adequate activities for achieving these objectives. Strategic planning systems therefore provide support for forecasting and evaluating future scenarios of the organization development and its environment over a long-term time horizon.

Intuitively, there is no clear distinction between these three managerial activities since managerial decisions can have, for example, both management and operational control aspects (Anthony and Dearden 1972).

From a current point of view, this classic framework for classifying DSS is too narrow since it covers managerial decision making within organizations only. The increasing availability of computing power (e.g. server clusters, personal computers and mobile devices) and networking capabilities provide functionalities to design DSS that can be used across organizational boundaries such as between companies, or between companies and customers (Martin et al. 2005).

Both computer and management scientists are working in this area, which has become one of the major research field addressed by corresponding academic organizations (e.g. IFIP Workgroup 8.3 and Association for Information Systems SIG DSS). The design and evaluation of decision support systems continues to be a major stream in information systems and computer science research until today (Banker and Kauffman 2004).

There exist many different definitions for *decision support systems* covering a spectrum form narrow to broad and consequently, there exists no general and universally accepted definition of DSS (Sprague and Watson 1979; Turban et al. 2005). Ginzberg and Stohr (1982) show that definitions for decision support systems shifted from explicit statements of what DSS do (e.g. the definition of Keen and Scott Morton in 1978) to classification schemes that show how the objectives of the DSS can be addressed in a specific scenario (e.g. Power 2002). Turban et al. (2005), who criticize that the early formal definitions narrow down the scope of the individual parts of the DSS differently and therefore do not provide a consistent view, support this statement. Consequently, the focus of later DSS definitions shifted to DSS inputs such as components used by the system (Turban et al. 2005).

Alter (1977) summarizes that generally "DSS are designed to aid in decision making and decision implementation", and that their orientation "is more toward the overall effectiveness of individuals and organizations". Here, the DSS is defined in terms of usage patterns and system objectives.

According to Keen and Scott Morton (1978) DSS comprise computer systems, which "assist managers in their decision processes in semi-structured tasks" that "support, rather replace managerial judgment" and "improve the effectiveness of decision-making rather than its efficiency". Consequently, their approach addresses different types of problems and appropriate system functions needed to address these.

The widely cited definition by Sprague (1980) summarizes that "DSS is a class of information system that draws on transaction processing systems and interacts with the other parts of the overall information system to support the decision making activities of managers and other knowledge workers in the organizations". This definition combines both aspects of a DSS definition as it first describes what the objectives of a DDS are and second, how these objectives are achieved.

In a more recent definition, DDS are defined in more general terms as "interactive computer-based systems that help people use computer communications, data, documents, knowledge, and models to solve problems and make decisions" (Power 2002).

Turban et al. (2005) define DSS as "an approach (or methodology) for supporting decision-making", that "uses an interactive, flexible, adaptive CBIS especially developed for supporting the solution to a specific nonstructured management problem"[13].

These different definitions show that there is no generally accepted consensus how to define DSS and that the addressed scope of definition has changed over time. In the following, Power's (2002) definition is used as a working definition as it provides a broad definition that also covers most of the systems currently used in practice. Many other definitions such as those of Keen and Scott Morton (1978), or Turban et al. (2005) contain problematic limitations that for instance exclude user groups (e.g. customers) or decision types (e.g. non-managerial). Therefore they do not cover existing DSS concepts and implementations such as the popular web-based customer DSS (O'Keefe and McEachern 1998).

3.2   Characteristics of Decision Support Systems

There is a close relationship between DSS definitions and characteristics of DSS as many definitions are based on these characteristics (e.g. the focus on a management user group) and there exist several ways to group decision support systems in different types. An early framework has been developed by Alter (1977) who distinguishes between data-oriented and model-oriented decision support systems. These categories were derived empirically from fifty-six decision support systems, which were analyzed with the case study methodology. As a result of his study, Alter identifies these two categories by comparing the key issues across the analyzed systems (Alter 1980).

Sprague (1980) has developed a normative framework for categorizing decision support systems by three different characteristics. First, he defines four different technology components describing the software and hardware used. The second characteristic describes how the sys-

---

[13] In this work, CBIS is defined as *computer-based information system*.

tem has been developed (e.g. with an iterative design or as an adaptive system) and the third groups typical roles of people using the system, such as managers or technical staff.

Based on the previous DSS categorizations defined by Alter (1977) and Sprague (1980), Power (2002 and 2004) has developed an expanded conceptual model for classifying DSS. This framework does not take details such as the specific application domain into account.

Figure 3.2 illustrates Power's (2004) classification framework, which starts with a definition of the first dimension *dominant DSS technology component* listed in the left-hand column. The three secondary dimensions *target user*, *purpose*, and *deployment/enabling technology* are listed in the remaining columns. Each row presents a *dominant DSS technology component* and provides examples of secondary dimension attributes to be considered.

Figure 3.2: Expanded DSS Framework[14]

Dominant DSS Component	Target Users	Purpose	Deployment/ Enabling Technology
Communications Communication-driven DSS	Internal teams, now expanding to external partners	Conduct a meeting or help users collaborate	Web or Client/server
Database Data-driven DSS	Managers, staff, expanding to suppliers	Query a data warehouse, monitor performance indicators	Mainframe, client/server or web
Document base Document-driven DSS	Internal users, but the user group is expanding	Search Web pages or find documents	Web or client/server
Knowledge base Knowledge-driven DSS	Internal users, expanding to customers	Management advice or help structure decision processes	Client/server, web or stand-alone PC
Models Model-driven DSS	Managers and staff, expanding to customers	Crew scheduling, financial planning or decision analysis	Stand-alone PC, client/server or web

A large number of researchers and practitioners have used power's classification scheme to describe DSS concepts and systems (Power 2004) and it is used in the following as a conceptual basis to classify and describe a mobile financial DSS concept.

In contrast to the original *expanded DSS framework* by Power (2004), system characteristics are not categorized into two different dimensions here since this would place an emphasis on one (or more) of the characteristics. Furthermore, some classification characteristics (such as the enabling technology) were extended, since the original framework was not flexible enough.

---

[14] Adopted from Power (2004).

3.2.1   System Purpose

The central goal of a DSS is to improve the quality of decisions made or to decrease the time spent for making specific decisions. This can be achieved by improving the information supply or by changing the process of decision-making or by a combination of both (Gorry and Scott Morton 1971; Dhar and Stein 1997).

A decision support system can be built for different kinds of purposes depending on the application scenarios supported. Power (2002 and 2004) identifies three different kinds of system purposes that describe the application domain of a decision support system.

- General-purpose

  General-purpose DSS are built to support the user across a wide range of different tasks such as business planning or financial planning. The most general systems, the so-called DSS generators, are an example of general-purpose DSS. Such systems provide tools to design and build a specific decision support system (Sprague 1980). For example, Excel or special-purpose scripting languages can be used to specify or prove mathematical models, which are the basis component for a decision support system (Turban et al. 2005). Furthermore, DSS generator application systems can reduce or eliminate the need for time-consuming programming work that is required for developing a specific decision support system (Marakas 2002).

  On the other hand, concrete general-purpose decision support systems can provide support for a wide range of tasks within a specific application domain such as project management or business planning (Power 2001).

- Function-specific

  Function-specific DSS are designed for selected industry sectors and address specific business functions (Power 2004). For example, a DSS can be designed for business functions such as marketing and procurement within a specific industry, for example the financial sector or the automotive industry (Keen and Scott Morton 1978).

- Task-specific

  Task-specific DSS provide support for decision tasks that need to be addressed periodically such as the evaluation of the trade-off between risk and expected return in portfolio optimization. Compared to function-specific DSS, the application domain is much more focused, i.e. the restriction to a particular tasks leads to an increased specialization.

3.2.2   Target User Groups

Decision support systems address different decision-making processes and provide support for individuals, groups, or organizations depending on the task addressed (Hackathorn and Keen 1981). The target group categorization focuses on the relationship between the parties that are involved in the decision-making process. Individual decision support can be realized when the problem to be addressed and the decision process are independent form other organizations and persons. Such a system can for example support investment managers in making concrete investment decisions. Group decision support are needed when several individuals work on pooled tasks, i.e. the users work together on separate tasks such as standard office activities. Organizational support is provided when there are strong sequential interdependencies between the tasks performed, i.e. solving a problem depends on the collaboration between individuals. Organizational support is required in complex and communication intensive tasks such as R&D planning.

The distinction regarding the organizational level focuses on the affiliation of the parties involved and comprises intra-organizational and inter-organizational decision support systems (Power 2004).

- Intra-organizational DSS

  Intra-organizational DSS is the more common type of system, which supports enterprise-wide decision-making processes of individuals or groups within organizations such as companies and authorities. Typically, this type of DSS supports employees and managers of a company in doing their work. Common intra-organizational decision support tools include data warehouses, online analytical processing (OLAP) and data mining technologies, which for example integrate different data sources and separate relevant information for task-specific problem solving (Shim et al. 2002). As operations of companies are increasingly globally spread across different locations, centralized intra-organizational decision support systems have been developed which can be accessed via the cooperate Intranet (Ba et al. 1997).

- Inter-organizational DSS

  Inter-organizational DSS is a newer and less common type, which supports decision-making of external users such as customers und suppliers (Power 2000; Laudon and Laudon 2006). Web-based decision support systems provide external access to cooperate systems and databases. A prominent example of inter-organizational DSS are so-called customer decision support systems (CDSS), which assist existing or potential customers in decision making for complex products or services by providing access to company recourses (Martin et al. 2005; O'Keefe and McEachern 1998). The emergence of web-based decision support systems intensified the trend towards inter-organizational and customer decision support systems. Since many customers are familiar with internet- and web-based services, there exist many successful examples of CDSS such as web-based financial services provided by banks and online brokers that support private customers in developing personal investment plans (Grenci and Todd 2002).

3.2.3   Enabling Technologies

An enabling technology determines how a decision support system is deployed in reality (Power 2002). There exist several IT infrastructures and platforms, which can form the technological basis for a decision support system. These enabling technologies reflect the stages in which IT infrastructure evolved in the last couple of decades, and there is a trend from centralized to decentralized systems (Laudon and Laudon 2006).

- Mainframe computers

  This highly centralized infrastructure concept works with a central mainframe computer that supports several remote terminals. The processing power and business logic is provided by the mainframe and can be accessed from terminals that share the mainframe resources. Mainframe computers such as early airline reservation systems became commercially relevant in the 1950s and are still in use today (Laudon and Laudon 2006).

- Stand-alone PC

  Compared to mainframe computers and remote terminals, personal computers provide decentralized computing power and locally installed software that can be customized for businesses or individuals. Resources are not shared between individual personal computers. Instead, operation systems (e.g. Microsoft DOS or Windows) and software (e.g. office tools) need to be installed and maintained locally.

- Client/server

  The client/server paradigm is founded on the concept that clients (such as personal computers) and servers (e.g. mainframe computers or powerful personal computers) are both connected by a network enabling servers to provide different services for the clients. When a client sends a request to a server, this server processes the request and sends a response back to the client. Servers can provide different kinds of services such as providing access to centralized databases or business applications. Compared to mainframe computers, client/server architectures are highly scalable as computing work and service processing can be distributed across different servers that can be much cheaper than a centralized mainframe computer. Furthermore, additional servers can be added to the network e.g. when there is a bottleneck of processing power or new services are demanded. Client/server architectures can use different kinds of communication protocols that manage the communication between clients and servers.

- Internet and web-based systems

  The existence of different client/server communication standards hampered corporations to integrate their various local area networks. This problem was solved with the development of standardized network protocols such as Transmission Control Protocol/Internet Protocol (TCP/IP), which forms the basis for Internet communication today. This widely accepted und supported communication standard allows an integration of different platforms, hardware, and networks across departments, companies, and organizations. Utilizing Hyper-Text Transfer Protocol (HTTP) servers provide access to web pages that can be accessed from client computers having a web browser installed. Using these Internet standards, so-called web-based decision support systems can be deployed, which can be accessed easily by employees and customers (Bhargava and Power 2001; Power 2000).

- Mobile devices and services

    Current mobile devices, such as GSM or UMTS enabled phones or personal digital assis-tants (PDA's), provide different kinds of services that can be used for the design of deci-sion support systems. Data services such as GPRS, EDGE, or HSDPA can provide time and location independent access to web-based systems. Furthermore, different message services (e.g. Short Message Service, Multimedia Message Service, or WAP Push) provide push message functionality featuring different capabilities and constraints (Muntermann and Güttler 2004). Compared to traditional web-based systems, mobile devices and ser-vices offer ubiquitous access and additional messaging services, which suits the design of proactive decision support systems.

Compared to the DSS framework introduced by Power (2004) that comprises traditional IT infrastructures and platforms only, mobile devices and services were identified as addi-tional and important enabling information technologies that can provide the technological basis for the deployment of decision support systems. In the existing literature, this deploy-ment of mobile communications technologies has not yet attracted much attention. Even though it has been recognized that mobile technologies and services will play a major role in future DSS developments since they can provide additional capabilities such as ubiquitous access to information and decision support tools (Shim et al. 2002), location-based decision support (Basole and Chao 2004), or enhanced security features (Muntermann et al. 2005).

3.2.4 Decision Support Systems Technology Components

Alter (1977) explored the central technology components of existing decision support systems and developed an early categorization approach. He differentiates between data-oriented and model-oriented decision support systems. Based on these categories, Power (2002 and 2004) has identified five different system components that provide the system's functionality, in-cluding the underlying system technology component.

- Data-driven DSS

    This type of decision support system has its roots in Alter's taxonomy (1977 and 1980) and includes data retrieval and analysis systems such as file drawer systems (e.g. providing online access to available flight seats), data analysis systems (e.g. general financial analy-sis systems), and analysis information systems (e.g. online analytical processing (OLAP) systems). There are no clear boundaries between these system types and there exist sys-tems that were developed to support several functionalities.

- Model-driven DSS

  Alter (1977) also introduced the model oriented decision support systems type, which covers all systems that are designed to support decision-making within a specific field. Typical models are accounting models, representational models, optimization models, and suggestion models. The first two are characteristic planning and budgeting models providing support for evaluating the effects of specifics actions or conditions. Since the resulting consequences are estimated using the underlying model, they are called simulation models. The optimization and suggestion models produce suggestions how to decide in certain situations (Power 2000). As model-driven DSS support repetitive decision situations only, an appropriate set of models is needed.

- Knowledge-driven DSS

  These kinds of system provide support for specific problem domains as they propose or recommend concrete actions to decision makers. The problem-solving capabilities of such systems stem from the expertise of specialists in particular application domains including the capabilities of how to solve a set of problems within a given domain (Turban et al. 2005). Most of the problem-solving capabilities of such systems use artificial intelligence (A.I.) technologies, such as neural networks or genetic algorithms.

- Document-driven DSS

  Document-driven decision support systems are used for the retrieval of documents stored in an unstructured environment like the World Wide Web (Power 2002). These kinds of system grant access to a broad pool of information stored or managed within or outside the organization (Swanson and Culnan 1978). Typical document-driven DSS provide search engine functionalities, which empower users to efficiently discover documents such as relevant web pages from the Intranet or the Internet.

- Communication-driven DSS

  Communication-driven decision support systems are designed to support efficient communication and collaboration within an organization or a user group. So-called computer-supported cooperative work (CSCW) systems are one example for this type of DSS and they are usually used when group members work at different places or times, and for spontaneous communication, respectively (Turban et al. 2005). These systems provide functions such as electronic meeting and conferencing in order to support the decision-making process of teams.

A decision support system can work with more than one of these components. However, in practice, decision support systems are usually driven to a large extent by only one of these five components (Power 2002).

3.3   A Mobile Service Approach to Support Intraday Investment Decision Making

Most of the existing mobile financial services are modified versions of online banking services providing access to standard banking services such as presenting financial information, trading of stocks or conducting payments (Mallat et al. 2004).

Utilizing the DSS classification framework introduced in the previous sections, a novel task-specific mobile financial DSS concept is presented in the following, which supports an event-driven decision process via mobile communication infrastructures and mobile messaging services.

3.3.1   System Purpose and Targeted User Group

The purpose of the intraday decision support system is to support private investors when an ad hoc disclosure has been published which can significantly impact upon the investor's portfolio value or which opens a window of opportunity. Such a decision support system needs to be designed task-specific in order to provide detailed guidance and support during the decision process following such repetitive events.

In this process, investors are faced with decision problems in dynamic, complex, and unstructured situations (Heymann and Bloom 1988). The investment decisions that should be supported within a ubiquitous environment are similarly unstructured since the process of stock price adjustments to new information is complex as is evident from widespread research in this field in recent years (e.g. Carter and Soo 1999; Barclay and Litzenberger 1988; Muntermann and Güttler 2007). On the other hand, the observed events are repetitive and of the same type (ad hoc disclosures pursuant to article 15 of the German Securities Trading Law), and therefore the problem has also structured elements. Like in most other practical decision-support application domains, the addressed problem is consequently semi-structured featuring both structured and unstructured elements.

The goal of the DSS concept is to enable private investors to react quickly to relevant market events and to provide decision support such as evaluating the relevance of the event observed. Provision of decision support for private investors can be realized with the inter-organizational decision support system approach, more precisely with consumer decision support systems (CDSS). Private investors are seen as consumers of online banks and brokers, who demand useful (Beckett et al. 2000; Howcroft et al. 2002; Wang et al. 2003) financial information and decision support systems which provide notifications proactively and whose usage consumes as little time as possible (Karjaluoto 2002).

The providers of such services such as online banks and brokers aim to retain and built new relationships with customers and therefore offer personalized mobile financial services, usually free of charge (Pavich 2004).

3.3.2   Supporting Investors with Mobile Communication Technologies

Unlike typical CDSS that are usually web-based (O'Keefe and McEachern 1998; Turban et al. 2005), the CDSS concept proposed in the following utilizes mobile network infrastructures and services such as the Global System for Mobile Communications (GSM), General Packet Radio Service (GPRS), and Multimedia Message Service (MMS).

O'Keefe and McEachern (1998) present how financial decision-making can be supported with inter-organizational CDSS facilities on the basis of Internet and web technologies. This general CDSS framework bases on a generic model of the consumer decision process and exemplifies how CDSS facilities and corresponding application domains within the World Wide Web can support each of the customers' decision process tasks. In contrast to this web-based CDSS approach, the underlying enabling technologies of the novel CDSS concept are mobile devices and services offering near-ubiquitous reachability of and service accessibility for private investors.

Compared to the origin concept, which focuses on the impact of the Internet, especially the World Wide Web, the facilities of mobile telecommunication systems are addressed in the following.

The customer's investment process is divided into a decision support and a subsequent transaction service process, each consisting of a set of sub-processes, which are presented and described in the following Figure 3.3.

Figure 3.3: Mobile Investment Process Supported by GSM Facilities [15]

	Sub-processes	CDSS and Transaction Service Facilities	Mobile Communication System and Services Facilities
Decision Support Process	1.1 Need recognition	• Event observation and notification (publication of ad hoc disclosure)	• Event notification via mobile push services (e.g. SMS, MMS, etc.)
	1.2 Information search	• Provision of information regarding the event (announcement, affected stock, etc.) • Links to (and guidance on) on external sources	• Textual and graphical push message content (text, charts, etc.) • Links to external resources, such as company profiles, charts, etc.
	1.3 Evaluation	• Provision of evaluative models (event relevance, estimated price effect, etc.)	• Textual and graphical push message content (text, charts, etc.) • Push message meta information
Transaction Service Process	2.1 Transaction	• Settlement of portfolio transaction (such as buying or selling stocks of the company)	• Secure transactions via encrypted connection (SSL) • Transaction authorization via TAN or signature-capable SIM
	2.2 Transaction evaluation	• Customer communication and response	• Confirmation of transaction execution via mobile push services

---

[15] Based on O'Keefe and McEachern (1998).

For each sub-process, the respective facilities of a suitable intraday customer decision support system and the transactions service are presented. Each sub-process is supported to some extent by mobile communication system and services facilities. Therefore, relevant technical functionalities of the mobile communication infrastructure are presented. The mobile investment sub-processes are further explained in the following:

1.1 Need recognition

Private investors must recognize that a relevant market event (i.e. an ad hoc disclosure that most likely will affect the stock price of the respective company) has occurred and calls for a prompt reaction. By using messaging services provided by a mobile telecommunication system (e.g. GSM), the investor can be notified promptly on a corresponding personal mobile device.

1.2 Information search

The investor requires information regarding event details (e.g. the disclosure text), stock prices that might be affected or further information about the company before considering a securities transaction. Such information can be provided by the mobile push message that has informed the investor about the event.

There exists a wide range of different mobile push message services, which use the GSM telecommunication infrastructure, such as SMS and WAP Push, providing different capabilities and restrictions (Schiller 2003)[16]. Furthermore, the received push message can link to suitable external resources such as web sites that can directly be accessed via the mobile device. Mobile message services such as WAP Push provide corresponding facilities as they can link to external web sites to which the investor can be guided (WAP Forum 2001a).

1.3 Evaluation

The investor uses appropriate evaluation models that provide support for assessing the market situation. Suitable information aggregation methods can help to reduce the information available to a manageable dimension. The forecasting models presented in the following, as well as data processing techniques, or document retrieval methodologies that aggregate or select the relevant information can play a major role during the decision process. In the mobile investment decision scenario, the investor can for example be supported by calculated metrics providing information regarding the event relevance or graphical charts that illustrate the past and (forecasted) future stock price developments.

---

[16] Technical characteristics of different mobile messaging services are addressed in the following Chapter 4.

2.1 Transaction

The investor must perform a transaction in order to buy or sell a portfolio position. Performing transactions over wireless communication networks and using mobile devices requires appropriate security mechanisms. There exist different security requirements that need to be addressed by appropriate security mechanisms and technologies such as SSL encryption or digital signatures. However, existing concepts and implementations cannot yet fulfill all these requirements to realize secure and trustworthy transaction processing within mobile communication infrastructures (Muntermann et al. 2005).

2.2 Transaction evaluation

The investor should be informed whether or not the transaction has been performed including the buying or selling rate. Good experience made with the system will encourage the investor to use the decision support system in future or to recommend it to others. In the mobile brokerage scenario, investors can be notified via mobile push messages that contain a confirmation of the transaction performed including transaction details such as trading costs, execution price, and timestamp.

The mobile financial DSS concept presented in the following focuses on the on the decision support sub-processes, i.e. the sub-processes 1.1 to 1.3. The transaction-related sub-processes 2.1 and 2.2 are not considered since there is little decision support functionality involved and security questions become crucial here. Muntermann et al. (2005) and Muntermann and Roßnagel (2006) investigate the security requirements of the entire mobile investment process and provide a corresponding security analysis including possible solutions.

Compared to O'Keefe and McEachern (1998) and Turban et al. (2005), the proposed CDSS framework is adapted for the application domain of intraday financial decision support. Furthermore, it does not emphasize the impact and capabilities of generic Internet and World Wide Web facilities but focuses on the respective facilities of mobile communication technologies since these represent the major enabling technology of the proposed DSS concept.

3.3.3   Forecasting Models as Dominant DSS Component

Building forecasting models to estimate future developments on capital markets is a difficult task, as financial processes are complex and hard to model. Dhar and Stein (1997) identify four major difficulties when developing models for financial decision support systems:

- Due to the complexity of financial markets, the decision support system has to cover knowledge of financial relationships between variables where the type and intensity of the relationship can hardly be understood completely.

- In the financial domain, decision support systems usually have to process and analyze data series with highly complex behavior.

- Such systems have to deal with voluminous economic and financial data series. Especially when analyzing intraday market behavior, large amounts of data need to be processed automatically in order to extract comprehensible information for the investor.

- Since financial markets are non-stationary over time, the system needs to be flexible regarding model adjustments.

Thus, the design of a financial decision support system needs to deal with those difficulties and concerns. The analytical models presented in the following address these identified challenges. Analytical models comprise statistical models, data mining algorithms, financial models, forecasting models, and are typically expressed by formulas that are used for an analysis of datasets (Turban et al. 2005).

Chapter 2 has shown that there exist short-term price effects on the German capital market that might be exploited by investors. To enable private investors to tap these potentials they require not only timely information supply regarding intraday market events but also appropriate decision support to identify relevant events and to derive suitable investment decisions. The latter is addressed in the following by quantitative forecasting models, which are applied in order to forecast price effect magnitudes and price effect durations to assess the relevance of events and their temporal occurrence. An investor can use such forecasts for estimating the window of opportunity available. Forecasting methodologies are often applied in business and economic environments in order to evaluate uncontrollable external events and quantitative forecasting is feasible under several conditions (Makridakis et al. 1998): First, there is information available describing the addressed variable in the past. Second, this information is available in a numerical form and third, it is assumed that some of the information observed contains patterns regarding future developments.

Quantitative forecasting can be based on two different underlying models called explanatory and time series models (Harris and Sollis 2003; Makridakis et al. 1998). Explanatory models are based on the assumption that one or a set of independent explanatory variables can explain the dependent variable (that should be forecasted) to a certain extent. In contrast, time series models are based on the observation of past values of the variable to be forecasted and the discovery of some pattern (such as trends or seasonality) that might exist in the historical observations.

Financial speculation is one of the major areas were forecasting methodologies play an important role (Diebold 2001). However, their application in this field is discussed controversially, as even the most complex forecasting methodologies cannot cover all factors that influence asset prices. In the case of a new appropriate forecasting methodology to be found, it is furthermore agued that it can be utilized only within a short period until other market participants will use the same techniques. This critique does not apply to the forecasting approach presented in the following, as it does not predict positive or negative stock price developments, but the stock market abnormality and its temporal occurrence. The proposed forecasting models can be used to identify relevant, and to neglect irrelevant, market events, i.e. to provide potential windows of opportunity. An investment decision that is influenced by a corresponding forecast will still be based on the personal assessment of the individual investor. Therefore, identical forecasts can lead to different interpretations of the information that was not available to the private investor community before.

The following sections therefore describe two different forecasting models for estimating the magnitude and the duration of the expected stock price effect. While the empirical results of the event study analysis presented in the previous Chapter revealed different price behavior for index members compared to non-index members, general forecasted models are developed in the following. This was done for two reasons. First, the statistical results for the entire dataset including all events were highly significant and consistent using both parametric and nonparametric test procedures (significant abnormal price effects during the first ten price fixings following the event date). Second, it was not practical due to the available (sub-)sample sizes. Splitting the dataset would have not allowed subsequent model forecasting accuracy evaluations needed for assessing the model quality. Therefore, the models presented in the following focus on a pessimistic short time estimate regarding the price adjustment process. The empirical results of the previous chapter indicate that for this period highly significant abnormal stock price behavior can be expected with the utmost probability. This does not rule out the possibilities of later investment opportunities being not addressed in this study.

3.3.4 Price Effect Magnitude Forecasting

A suitable notification and decision support system has to inform about critical events, for which significant price effects can be expected (i.e. the need recognition sub-process). Therefore, a forecasting model providing information regarding these expected price effects can be a valuable tool for investors. Such a model can control a decision support system and can assist the investors in evaluating forthcoming price effects on the capital market.

3.3.4.1 Forecasting Object and Explanatory Variables

In order to design an easily controllable decision support system, a depended variable needs to be chosen as forecast object, which should be estimated with an appropriate forecasting approach.

Consequently, the variable $CCAAR_{i,3,10}$ has been selected as dependent variable, which corresponds to the *Corrected Absolute Abnormal Returns* of the stock affected by the corresponding ad hoc disclosure i cumulated over the third to tenth price fixing following the event date. In this analysis, critical events are defined as ad hoc disclosures that cause a significant price reaction lying above a critical value, which is defined as the mean of a price effect sample that has been observed during a period of two years. Other critical values such as the median or other sample percentiles are not explored in the following and represent a promising subject for further research.

If a decision support system can provide support for identifying events that cause price effects above this average, it can help investors to concentrate on these events only. Furthermore, an estimate of the price effect can support investors faced with an investment decision.

The period between the third and the tenth price fixing has been chosen for two reasons: First, the empirical results of the event study in Section 2.2.5 provided evidence that for the period of the first ten price fixings significant abnormal price effects can be proven with both parametric and nonparametric test procedures and for index and non-index members. Second, the first two *Corrected Absolute Abnormal Returns* ($CAAR_{i,1}$ and $CAAR_{i,2}$) were taken as independent variables and were therefore excluded from the period of time covered by the dependent variable.

Consequently, the price effect estimation is performed using a time series model that works with the assumption that the price behavior of the first two price fixings implies trend patterns. The dependent and independent variables used for the quantitative forecasting approach are summarized in the following Table 3.1 including hypothesized variable signs that indicate whether an independent variable is expected to have positive or negative impact on the dependent variable. As a positive correlation between the first two price effects and the following cumulative price effect is expected, positive variable signs are hypothesized for both independent variables.

Table 3.1: Variables for Intraday Price Effect Estimations

Dependent variable	Variable description	
$CCAAR_{i,3,10}$	Cumulated corrected absolute abnormal return between the third and tenth price fixing of the stock affected by event i following the event date.	

Independent variables	Variable description	Hypothesized variable sign
$CAAR_{i,1}$	Corrected absolute abnormal return of the first price fixing of the stock affected by event i following the event date.	Positive
$CAAR_{i,2}$	Corrected absolute abnormal return of the second price fixing following of the stock affected by event i following the event date.	Positive

As illustrated in Table 3.1, the expected price effect between the third and tenth price fixing should be explained by the price effects which correspond with the first two price fixings. The idea of this procedure is that the first two price fixings imply a trend that helps to estimate the further price development. The expected price effect can thus be estimated only subsequent to the first two price fixings following the event date. One could criticize that this approach is not adequate because valuable time of the window of opportunity is lost. This concern can be invalidated since there is a remaining window of opportunity of eight price fixings that correspond to an average of 15 minutes for index member and 43 minutes for non-index members.

3.3.4.2 Information and Forecasting Dataset

The forecasting model development is based on a primary dataset that has been introduced in Section 2.2.1, which covers 425 ad hoc disclosures and the corresponding intraday stock price series. The values of the dependent variable ($CCAAR_{i,3,10}$) and independent variables ($CAAR_{i,1}$ and $CAAR_{i,2}$) are calculated using these price series. The goal of the proposed decision support system approach is to identify ad hoc disclosures that cause significant price reactions lying above the average price reaction. Therefore, the primary dataset is sorted by value so each $CCAAR_{i,3,10}$ value lies either below or above the mean $CCAAR_{i,3,10}$.

The histogram depicted in Figure 3.4 shows the frequency distribution of the dependent variable $CCAAR_{i,3,10}$ and its segmentation into values below and above the frequency distribution mean. The mean of $CCAAR_{i,3,10}$ divides the dataset into unequally sized parts since the sample mean of 2.4694% is much larger than its median of 1.0500%, i.e. there are much more values lying below (282 values) than above (143 values) this mean. From this segmentation can consequently be expected that only approximately one third (143 of 425) of the events (with an expected price effect above average) are categorized as relevant which helps to control the level of user-intrusiveness.

Figure 3.4: Frequency Distribution of the Observed Price Reactions

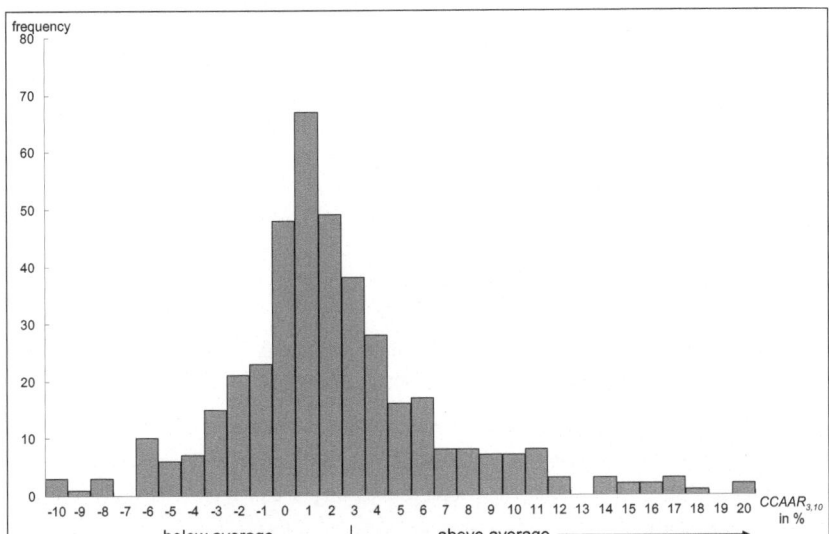

In the following, an information and forecasting dataset is introduced, which is used as data source for the construction and evaluation of a forecasting model aimed at estimating forthcoming price effect magnitudes.

The information dataset is defined as sample of historical observations that are used for developing a good forecasting model that allows good forecasts (Diebold 2001). In this analysis the information dataset Ω^I is multivariate as it comprises the dependent variable ($CCAAR_{i,3,10}$) and independent variables ($CAAR_{i,1}$ and $CAAR_{i,2}$).

$$\Omega^I = \left\{ CCAAR_{1,3,10}, CAAR_{1,1}, CAAR_{1,2}, \ldots, CCAAR_{200,3,10}, CAAR_{200,1}, CAAR_{200,2} \right\}$$

where

$CAAR_{i,t}$	=	corrected absolute abnormal return with indices i and t
$CCAAR_{i,3,10}$	=	cumulated corrected absolute abnormal return with indices i, $t1$, and $t2$
i	=	event index
$t, t1, t2$	=	price fixing indices

Equation 3.1: Multivariate Information Dataset

As illustrated in Equation 3.1, the information dataset contains 200 values each of the dependent and the two independent variables, i.e. 600 values in total.

Within the information dataset Ω^I there are exactly 100 $CCAAR_{i,3,10}$'s with a value above and below the sample mean of 2.4694% included. Otherwise, there might be a bias towards the more common category resulting in poorer forecasting accuracy for the rarer category (Groebner et al. 2001).

Outliers can negatively affect the results of the multiple regression methodology, which is introduced in the next section for building an appropriate forecasting model (Sprent 1996). In order to reduce this influencing factor, the information dataset is 5% trimmed, i.e. the top 2.5% and bottom 2.5% of the sorted dataset values were omitted from the information dataset (Sheskin 2004).

The forecasting dataset Ω^F, which is used for conducting and evaluating out-of-sample forecasts, includes the $CCAAR_{i,3,10}$, $CAAR_{i,1}$ and $CAAR_{i,2}$ values calculated for the remaining 225 ad hoc disclosures that were published later than those of the information dataset.

$$\Omega^F = \left\{ CCAAR_{201,3,10}, CAAR_{201,1}, CAAR_{201,2}, \ldots, CCAAR_{425,3,10}, CAAR_{425,1}, CAAR_{425,2} \right\}$$

Equation 3.2: Multivariate Forecasting Dataset

Consequently, information and forecasting dataset is defined in a way that the price effects are estimated with price behavior that has been observed before. The following table summarizes the characteristics of the datasets used.

Table 3.2: Information and Prognosis Dataset Characteristics (Price Effect Magnitude Model Construction)

	Sample size	$CCAAR_{i,3,10}$ mean	$CCAAR_{i,3,10}$ median
Panel I: Primary dataset Ω			
Total	425	2.4694%	1.0500%
$CCAAR_{i,3,10}$ below average	282	-0.9893%	-0.0491%
$CCAAR_{i,3,10}$ above average	143	9.2901%	5.8529%
Panel II: Information dataset Ω^I (5% trimmed)			
Total	190*	3.9162%	2.3796%
$CCAAR_{i,3,10}$ below average	95	-0.7527%	-0.0615%
$CCAAR_{i,3,10}$ above average	95	8.5851%	6.2385%
Panel III: Forecasting dataset Ω^F			
Total	225	0.6454%	0.4616%
$CCAAR_{i,3,10}$ below average	182	-0.8400%	0.0116%
$CCAAR_{i,3,10}$ above average	43	6.9325%	4.2439%

* The 2.5% extreme scores are removed from each of the dataset distribution tails.

The mean of the information (forecasting) dataset is larger (smaller) than the mean of the primary dataset, as it contains more (less) $CCAAR_{i,3,10}$ values lying above the primary dataset mean. One could argue that an information dataset having a $CCAAR_{i,3,10}$ mean that is much higher than the $CCAAR_{i,3,10}$ mean of the forecasting dataset is not appropriate. However, the alternative approach of constructing a forecasting model with an information dataset that has a similar distribution mean would result in a forecasting bias towards the more common category.

3.3.4.3   Model Construction

In the following section, a multiple linear regression model is applied in order to estimate the parameters of a forecasting model that can be used for estimating the intraday price effects following ad hoc disclosures. As described in Section 3.3.4.1 the dependent variable $CCAAR_{i,3,10}$ should be predicted with the two variables $CAAR_{i,1}$ and $CAAR_{i,2}$ using a linear forecasting model in the form of:

$$CCAAR_{i,3,10} = \beta_0 + \beta_1 \cdot CAAR_{i,1} + \beta_2 \cdot CAAR_{i,2} + \varepsilon_i$$

Equation 3.3: Linear Price Effect Forecasting Model

The minimization problem of the error term that needs to be solved to estimate the β_j-values is therefore defined as:

$$\min_{\beta} \sum_{i=1}^{190} \left[CCAAR_{i,3,10} - \beta_0 - \beta_1 CAAR_{i,1} - \beta_2 CAAR_{i,2} \right]^2$$

Equation 3.4: Multiple Linear Regression Model

> where
>
> | | | |
> |---|---|---|
> | β_j | = | model parameters with index j |
> | ε_i | = | error term with index i |
> | $CAAR_{i,t}$ | = | corrected absolute abnormal return with indices i and t |
> | $CCAAR_{i,3,10}$ | = | cumulated corrected absolute abnormal return with indices i, $t1$, and $t2$ |

By solving the minimization problem of the multiple linear regression model it is possible to estimate the model parameters. This is done using the statistical software package SPSS 11.5. The results of the regression including overall fit of the model and the estimated model parameters are summarized in Table 3.3.

The R-value of 0.604 shows the correlation between the observed values of $CCAAR_{i,3,10}$ and the corresponding values of $CCAAR_{i,3,10}$ calculated with the regression model, i.e. a large value of R indicates a high correlation between the observed values of the dependent variable and the same values predicted with the regression model[17]. A R-value of 1 would therefore stand for a model that can perfectly predict the observed $CCAAR_{i,3,10}$ values.

Having a R^2 of 0.365 the model can account for 36.5% of the variation of price effect $CCAAR_{i,3,10}$ that is explained by the price effects observed for the first two price fixings following the ad hoc disclosure. Obviously, other (unknown) factors have an effect on the dependent variable. The adjusted R^2 can be interpreted in the same way as R^2 but it is often denoted as more trustworthy goodness-of-fit measure as it includes adjustments regarding the degrees of freedom df used in the model fitting (Diebold 2001).

---

[17] R has a value between 0 and 1 indicating none or 100% correlation.

Table 3.3: Regression Results for the Price Effect Magnitude Forecasting Model

Model summary

	R	R^2	Adjusted R^2	Std. error of the estimate
	0.604(a)	0.365	0.359	0.057

ANOVA(b)

	Sum of squares	df	Mean squares	F-value	Significance
Regression	0.354	2	0.177	53.835	< 0.001(a)
Residual	0.615	187	0.003		
Total	0.969	189			

Coefficients(b)

	Unstandardized coefficients		Standardized coefficients		
	β_j-value	Std. error	Beta	t-value	Significance
(Constant)	0.013	0.005		2.561	0.011
$CAAR_{i,1}$	0.531	0.077	0.406	6.870	< 0.001
$CAAR_{i,2}$	1.366	0.209	0.386	6.531	< 0.001

(a) Predictors : (Constant), $CAAR_{i,1}$, $CAAR_{i,2}$
(b) Dependent Variable: $CCAAR_{i,3,10}$

Even though the forecast model is capable of covering approximately 36.5% of the price effect variation, the linear model can be an adequate forecast model for identifying events that cause price effects lying above the average. This question of forecast quality of the regression model is addressed in the next section.

The ANOVA (analysis of variance) is a statistical summary of the overall model fit regarding its prediction quality of the dependent variable (Field 2005). The F-value, which is the ratio of the regression mean square and the residual mean square, can be used for testing the statistical significance of the model. The F-value of 53.835 is calculated for testing the hypothesis that the predictors (i.e. $CAAR_{i,1}$, $CAAR_{i,2}$) have no predictive power. The corresponding significance level smaller than 0.1% indicates that this hypothesis can be rejected, and therefore a significant prediction power of the regression model is corroborated.

Whereas ANOVA provides information regarding the whole model, the coefficient section of Table 3.3 summarizes the details of the estimated model parameters including their significance. The β_j-values of the second column are the calculated parameter values for the linear price effect forecasting model. By replacing the β_j-values of Equation 3.3 with the calculated parameter values, the forecasting model becomes:

$$F\left(CCAAR_{i,3,10}\right) = 0.013 + 0.531 \cdot CAAR_{i,1} + 1.366 \cdot CAAR_{i,2}$$

where

$CAAR_{i,t}$ =   corrected absolute abnormal return with indices i and t

Equation 3.5: Price Effect Magnitude Forecasting Model

Equation 3.5 represents the forecasting model that can be used for evaluating upcoming price effects following the publication of new ad hoc disclosures. The regression model confirms a positive sign for both model parameters β_j and therefore, the empirical results corroborate the hypothesized positive impact of both independent variables on the dependent variable, which underpins the model validity.

Each β_j-value has a standard error, which is the standard deviation of the coefficient that shows whether a β_j-value is significantly different from zero, and is used for the calculation of the t-values in the fifth column.

Furthermore, the t-values and the significance columns in the coefficient section of Table 3.3 indicate whether each of the predictors (i.e. the constant, $CAAR_{i,1}$ and $CAAR_{i,2}$) makes a significant contribution to the forecasting model. Since all significance levels are less than 5%, all predictors have significant predictive power (Field 2005). The *Beta*-values (standardized coefficients) of $CAAR_{i,1}$ and $CAAR_{i,2}$ show how many standard deviations the dependent variable will change when exactly one of these predictors is changed by one standard deviation. Therefore, the *Beta*-values show how much each of these predictors contribute to the model. Having similar *Beta*-values of 0.406 and 0.386, the two predictors are of similar relevance.

3.3.4.4   Model Quality Evaluation

The forecasting quality of the price effect magnitude forecasting model introduced in the previous section is tested with the forecasting dataset introduced in Section 3.3.4.2. Therefore, the $CAAR_{i,1}$ and $CAAR_{i,2}$ values of this dataset and Equation 3.5 are used to forecast all corresponding $F(CCAAR_{i,3,10})$ values. Since the goal of the forecasting model is to identify events that cause price reactions lying above or below the sample mean $\mu(CCAAR_{i,3,10})$, the observed $CCAAR_{i,3,10}$ and the forecasted $F(CCAAR_{i,3,10})$ values are classified accordingly for each event i.

$$Z_i = \begin{cases} 0 & \text{if } CCAAR_{i,3,10} < \mu\left(CCAAR_{i,3,10}\right) \\ 1 & \text{if } CCAAR_{i,3,10} \geq \mu\left(CCAAR_{i,3,10}\right) \end{cases}$$

Equation 3.6: Observed Price Effect Magnitude Category

$$\hat{Z}_i = \begin{cases} 0 & \text{if } F(CCAAR_{i,3,10}) < \mu(CCAAR_{i,3,10}) \\ 1 & \text{if } F(CCAAR_{i,3,10}) \geq \mu(CCAAR_{i,3,10}) \end{cases}$$

Equation 3.7: Forecasted Price Effect Magnitude Category

where

$\mu(CCAAR_{i,3,10})$	=	mean of $CCAAR_{i,3,10}$
$CCAAR_{i,3,10}$	=	cumulated corrected absolute abnormal return with indices i and t
$F(CCAAR_{i,3,10})$	=	forecasted $CCAAR_{i,3,10}$ value
Z_i	=	price effect category of observed price effect magnitude with index i
$\hat{Z}_i$	=	price effect category of forecasted price effect magnitude with index i

By comparing the price effect categories Z_i and $\hat{Z}_i$ of the $CCAAR_{i,3,10}$ and $F(CCAAR_{i,3,10})$ values calculated for the forecasting dataset, it is possible to assess the forecast quality of the proposed price effect magnitude forecasting model. If an observed category corresponds with a forecasted category, this is added to the number of category hits and finally, a recognition rate is calculated for each category.

This is depicted in the following Figure 3.5 that illustrates the calculation of the observed and forecasted price effect categories of the forecasting dataset Ω^F. The upper (lower) figure area shows dataset elements where the observed price effect lies above (below) the average price reaction of $\mu(CCAAR_{i,3,10}) = 2.4694\%$.

Column 2 presents the symbol of the affected stock including the stock exchange identifier. The symbol NUW.ETR stands for example for the stock of MWG Biotech AG (NWU), traded on Xetra (ETR). When there was a higher trading volume (i.e. more price information available) on Frankfurt Stock Exchange (FSE) floor trading, these prices were taken for the price effect calculations.

The following two columns 3 and 4 show the corrected absolute abnormal return for the first ($CAAR_{i,1}$) and second ($CAAR_{i,2}$) price fixing following the event date, which are taken as input factors for the forecasting model in order to estimate the subsequent price reaction. The price reaction actually observed is shown in column 5 ($CCAAR_{i,3,10}$) followed by the forecasted price effect in column 6 ($F(CCAAR_{i,3,10})$). The calculation of the latter is illustrated by the note on the right of Figure 3.5. Since this calculation works internally with data having more than four decimal places, the presented formula exemplifies the calculation only, i.e. using the rounded four digit $CAAR_{i,1}$ and $CAAR_{i,2}$ values presented here would lead to slightly different $F(CCAAR_{i,3,10})$ values.

Figure 3.5: Quality Evaluation of the Price Effect Forecasting Model

	i	Symbol	$CAAR_{i,1}$	$CAAR_{i,2}$	$CCAAR_{i,3,10}$	$F(CCAAR_{i,3,10})$	Z_i	$\hat{Z}_i$	
Observed price reaction above average of 2.4694%	1	SMH.ETR	-0.0209%	1.4885%	4.1826%	3.3222%	1	1	
	2	NWU.ETR	20.0619%	-2.2133%	10.7602%	8.9295%	1	1	
	3	WCM.ETR	0.7027%	1.7635%	3.5499%	4.0820%	1	1	
	4	CWC.ETR	-0.2666%	2.7563%	5.9283%	4.9235%	1	1	
	5	TOI.ETR	0.3142%	0.0759%	2.6033%	1.5705%	1	0	Example calculation: $F(CCAAR_{8,3,10}) =$ 0.013 $+0.531 \cdot CAAR_{8,1}$ $+1.366 \cdot CAAR_{8,2}$ (internal calculation with more than four decimal places)
	6	VEC.FSE	0.0245%	4.0639%	5.7291%	6.8643%	1	1	
	7	MONT.FSE	1.1096%	1.2074%	4.2207%	3.5385%	1	1	
	8	MLP.ETR	0.9058%	0.7966%	3.3092%	2.8692%	1	1	
	9	SIS.ETR	2.0655%	-0.4123%	3.8150%	1.8336%	1	0	
	10	UUU.ETR	3.8773%	0.4200%	3.2492%	3.9325%	1	1	
	⋮	⋮	⋮	⋮	⋮	⋮	⋮	⋮	
Observed price reaction below average of 2.4694%	216	AAH.FSE	-0.4140%	-0.3655%	0.3400%	0.5809%	0	0	
	217	VSJ.ETR	1.4902%	0.6061%	1.7022%	2.9193%	0	1	
	218	PUM.ETR	1.0504%	0.0405%	1.6875%	1.9131%	0	0	
	219	ARL.ETR	0.5793%	0.0480%	1.2374%	1.6732%	0	0	
	220	NDX1.ETR	0.4340%	0.0765%	1.5313%	1.6350%	0	0	
	221	HEI.ETR	-0.0801%	-0.0775%	1.0523%	1.1516%	0	0	
	222	HLG.ETR	1.4204%	-0.1404%	1.1573%	1.8624%	0	0	
	223	PFD4.ETR	0.0335%	-0.0768%	1.5209%	1.2129%	0	0	
	224	BC8.ETR	0.7810%	0.9361%	1.0024%	2.9934%	0	1	
	225	PUS.ETR	0.4255%	-0.2328%	1.6598%	1.2080%	0	0	

The two last columns Z_i and $\hat{Z}_i$ show the price effect categories for the observed ($CCAAR_{i,3,10}$) and forecasted ($F(CCAAR_{i,3,10})$) price effects using Equation 3.6 and Equation 3.7. They indicate whether or not a price reactions lies above or below the mean price reaction. These price effect categories are compared in the following to asses the quality of the forecasting model.

The empirical results for this accuracy evaluation, including the recognition performance, are summarized in the following Table 3.4. If the forecasting model would not have been able to detect any patterns in the information dataset, a recognition rate of 50% can be expected on average. The average recognition rate (arithmetic mean) of 71.11% achieved by the price effect forecasting model is significantly higher that 50%, which provides strong evidence that the model used has recognized patterns in the information dataset. For ad hoc discloses that cause a price reaction lying above the average, nearly 75% were identified correctly.

Table 3.4: Forecast Accuracy of the Forecasting Model

Price effect category	Category frequency	Category hits $(Z_i = \hat{Z}_i)$	Recognition rate
Price reaction above $CCAAR_{i,3,10}$ mean	43	32	74.42%
Price reaction below $CCAAR_{i,3,10}$ mean	182	128	70.33%
		Weighted average	71.11%

Compared to previous studies working with data mining techniques (e.g. Schulz et al. 2003; Spiliopoulou et al. 2003; Mittermayer 2004), the proposed time series forecasting model features significant better forecasting quality.

3.3.5 Price Effect Duration Forecasting

The price effect magnitude forecasting model constructed in the previous section provides information regarding the expected price effect that can be observed between the third and tenth price fixing following the publication of an ad hoc disclosure. Since this period is measured in number of price fixings observed, it is not clear how many minutes will elapse during this period. This price effect duration is addressed in the following by a corresponding forecasting model that should provide information regarding the window of opportunity available to investors. Therefore, the price effect duration indicates after which period of time stock prices reflect most of the new information available.

3.3.5.1 Forecasting Objects and Explanatory Variables

The variable $\Delta t_{i,3,10}$ is defined as dependent variable, i.e. as forecasting object it represents the period of time (measured in minutes) that elapses between the third and tenth price fixing following event date. Consistent to the price effect magnitude forecasting approach the effect duration forecasting model addresses the question whether or not an effect period lies above its mean of $\mu(\Delta t_{i,3,10})= 34.61$ minutes. However, future research could address further forecasting objects being not addressed in the following.

If such a forecasting model is part of a decision support system, it can estimate whether or not the investor has more or less than the average of 34.61 minutes time to react. This information can be used by the system for calculating expiration dates of messages and by the user for evaluating the need for a prompt reaction.

According to the price effect magnitude forecasting model, which can be used for estimating the price effect between the third and the tenth price fixing, this period is chosen since first, the event study presented in Section 2.2.5 detects significant abnormal price effects during the first ten price fixings following the event date. Second, the time elapsed during the first two price fixings following the event date is taken as explanatory variable ($\Delta t_{i,1,2}$) and is consequently excluded from the period of time covered by the dependent variable. Finally, it is chosen because the price effect magnitude forecasting model presented previously provides information regarding expected price effects between the third and tenth price fixing. The price effect duration model evaluates the corresponding window of opportunity measured in minutes and should complement the decision support provided by the DSS concept.

The estimation of the price effect duration is based on a quantitative forecasting technique combining the time series and explanatory forecasting model approach. The period of time ($\Delta t_{i,1,2}$) elapsed during the first two price fixings following the event date represents the time series component. The assumption here is that this period implies a pattern that that is likely to continue during the following price fixings.

Furthermore, several explanatory variables are used as input for the explanatory forecasting model part. These comprise the three variables $TVol_{i,1,2}$, $Index_i$, and $\#Analysts_i$.

$TVol_{i,1,2}$ stands for the sum of trading volume (in 1,000 stocks) observed for the first two price fixings (observed on a minute-by-minute basis) following the event date and is taken from Deutsche Börse Group (Xetra or floor trading). Trading volume is an indicator for liquidity that should be negatively correlated with the time elapsed after which stock prices reflect new information available. Consequently, the hypothesized variable sign for $TVol_{i,1,2}$ is negative.

$Index_i$ is a so-called dummy variable having a value of "1" if the company is member of the DAX, MDAX, or TecDAX index or "0" if not. Dummy variables are used in order to include qualitative data in a regression analysis (Weiers 2005). The empirical results of the event study presented in Chapter 2 provide evidence that the price reaction is stretched over a longer period of time (measured in minutes) for non-index members than for index members and this findings holds for parametric (see Table 2.7) and nonparametric (see Table 2.9) test statistics. Therefore, the hypothesized variable sign for $Index_i$ is expected to be negative.

Stocks of companies whose shares are observed by more capital market participants should react more quickly to new information available. Assuming that the number of analysts covering a company ($\#Analysts_i$) can be interpreted as a proxy for the number of market participants observing this company in total, the hypothesized variable sign for $\#Analysts_i$ is negative, i.e. a higher number of analysts would shorten the period of time in which the third to tenth price fixing can be observed. This number of analysts covering a company is provided by *FactSet Research Systems Inc.* and this information is currently available for private investors on the websites of several German online banks and brokers.

All described variables are used as independent variables for the development of the price effect duration forecasting model, which are summarized in the following Table 3.5. This summary shows that the dependent variable ($\Delta t_{i,3,10}$) should be forecasted with the following four independent variables of which the first ($\Delta t_{i,1,2}$) represents a time series forecasting model part and the latter three ($TVol_{i,1,2}$, $Index_i$, and $\#Analysts_i$) are the explanatory model part.

Table 3.5: Variables for Intraday Effect Period Estimations

Dependent variable	Variable description	
$\Delta t_{i,3,10}$	Price effect duration measured in minutes, in which the third to tenth price fixings of the stock affected by event i can be observed following the event date.	

Independent variables	Variable description	Hypothesized variable sign
$\Delta t_{i,1,2}$	Period of time measured in minutes, in which the first two price fixings of the stock affected by event i can be observed following the event date. Values are calculated from transaction data taken from Frankfurt Stock Exchange Xetra or floor trading.	Positive
$TVol_{i,1,2}$	Sum of the trading volume measured in number of stocks traded (in 1,000 stocks) during the two first price fixings (on minute basis) following the event date. Values are calculated from transaction data taken from Frankfurt Stock Exchange (Xetra or floor trading).	Negative
$Index_i$	Index membership is a so-called dummy-variable that has a value of "1" if the stocks of the company who has published ad hoc disclosure are members of the DAX, CDAX, or TecDAX index. If not, $Index_i$ has a value of "0". Index membership is checked at the event date.	Negative
$\#Analysts_i$	Number of analysts covering the company that has published the ad hoc disclosure. This data is provided by FactSet Research Systems Inc.	Negative

3.3.5.2 Information and Forecasting Dataset

Consistent to the price effect magnitude forecasting model, a primary dataset is used which comprises a dependent variable ($\Delta t_{i,3,10}$) and independent variables ($\Delta t_{i,1,2}$, $TVol_{i,1,2}$, $Index_i$, and $\#Analysts_i$) for all observed 425 ad hoc disclosures.

Since forecasting the behavior of capital markets is complex and there are several difficulties to do so (Dhar and Stein 1997), it is not possible to build a forecasting model that is able to forecast capital market behavior in detail, the complexity of the price effect duration forecasting model is reduced to two broad categories. Similar to the price effect magnitude forecasting model it addresses the question whether or not the effect period $\Delta t_{i,3,10}$ of a price adjustment process lies above or below its mean.

Figure 3.6 depicts a histogram that illustrates the frequency distribution of the $\Delta t_{i,3,10}$ values, which should be forecasted. Furthermore, the arrows below the histogram indicate the sample segmentation into $\Delta t_{i,3,10}$ values below and above the sample mean of 34.69 minutes. Consequently, the sample is divided into two unequally large sub-samples with 288 members below and 137 members above the sample mean, whereas some extreme values (the highest value is 342 minutes) are truncated in order to ensure readability of the graph.

Figure 3.6: Frequency Distribution of the Observed Price Effect Duration

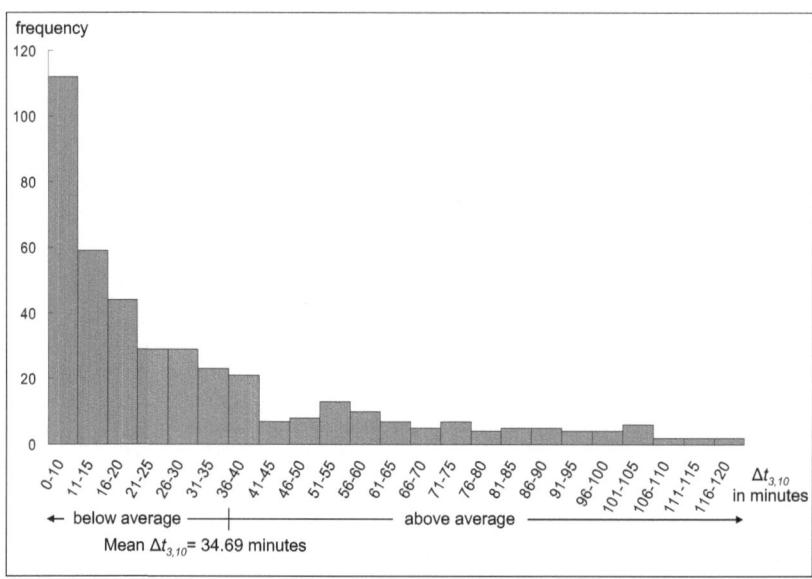

The frequency distribution further indicates that the underlying distribution of the $\Delta t_{i,3,10}$ population is highly positively skewed. There are seventeen extreme values with a $\Delta t_{i,3,10}$ between 121 and 341 minutes that lie beyond the $\Delta t_{i,3,10}$ axis presented.

Like in the previous section, the sample is divided in an information dataset Ψ^I and forecasting dataset Ψ^F both being multivariate since they contain the dependent variable $\Delta t_{i,3,10}$ and the independent variables ($\Delta t_{i,1,2}$, $TVol_{i,t-1}$, $Index_i$, and $\#Analysts_i$). The information dataset is used to build the forecasting model and the forecasting dataset is taken for proving the forecasting accuracy of the model.

$$\Psi^I = \left\{ \begin{array}{l} \Delta t_{1,3,10}, \Delta t_{1,1,2}, TVol_{1,1,2}, Index_1, \# Analysts_1, \ldots \\ , \Delta t_{200,3,10}, \Delta t_{200,1,2}, TVol_{200,1,2}, Index_{200}, \# Analysts_{200} \end{array} \right\}$$

where

$\Delta t_{i,t1,t2}$	$=$	period of time (in minutes) with indices i, $t1$, $t2$
$TVol_{i,1,2}$	$=$	trading volume with indices i, $t1$, $t2$
$Index_i$	$=$	index membership with index i
$\# Analysts_i$	$=$	number of analysts with index i
i	$=$	event index
t, $t1$, $t2$	$=$	price fixing indices

Equation 3.8: Multivariate Information Dataset

Equation 3.8 shows the information dataset that contains 200 values each of the dependent and the three independent variables and therefore comprises 800 values in total. In order to prevent a bias towards the more common category, there are exactly 100 $\Delta t_{i,3,10}$ values lying above and 100 $\Delta t_{i,3,10}$ values lying below its mean of 34.69 minutes.

The frequency distribution of the price effect duration (Figure 3.6) shows that the sample has many extreme values on the long right tail. In contrast to the information dataset of the price effect magnitude analyzed in the previous section, dataset trimming is not appropriate since the sample of the price effect duration shows extreme values on the right tail only. Dataset trimming can be applied on one tail of a sample distribution (asymmetric trimming) but this would lead to more $\Delta t_{i,3,10}$ values which can lead to a forecasting bias towards the more common category.

Therefore, the dataset has been winsorized asymmetrically, i.e. outliers on the long-tail side have been set to a specified percentile of the data, which is a common statistical procedure for treating long-tailed distributions (Sheskin 2004).

Since the distribution of the information dataset is a long-tailed distribution with many outliers lying several (up to 7.15) standard deviations[18] above the sample mean, the extreme values are winsorized and data above the 65th percentile set to the 65th percentile. The regression analysis presented in the next section has been performed with different numbers of scores that were trimmed (starting with no trimming down to the 60th percentile and by using the 65th percentile it was possible to increase the adjusted R^2 (measure for the regression goodness-of-fit measure) form 0.147 (no winsorization) to 0.305 (65th percentile winsorization).

---

[18] The standard deviation of the information dataset is 47.82.

The forecasting dataset Ψ^F comprises the $\Delta t_{i,3,10}$, $\Delta t_{i,1,2}$, $TVol_{i,1,2}$, $Index_i$, and $\#Analysts_i$ values for the remaining 225 ad hoc disclosures and is used for the forecasting model evaluation presented in the next section by conducting out-of-sample forecasts.

$$\Psi^F = \begin{Bmatrix} \Delta t_{201,3,10}, \Delta t_{201,1,2}, TVol_{201,1,2}, Index_{201}, \# Analysts_{201}, \ldots, \\ \Delta t_{425,3,10}, \Delta t_{425,1,2}, TVol_{425,1,2}, Index_{425}, \# Analysts_{425} \end{Bmatrix}$$

Equation 3.9: Multivariate Forecasting Dataset

From the 225 $\Delta t_{i,3,10}$ values of the forecasting dataset 32 values lie below and 193 above the sample mean. The ad hoc disclosures of forecasting dataset Ψ^F were published later than the ad hoc disclosures of the information dataset Ψ^I i.e. $\Delta t_{i,3,10}$ will be forecasted with a model that uses historical data. The characteristics of the primary dataset Ψ, the information dataset Ψ^I, and the forecasting dataset Ψ^F are summarized in Table 3.6.

Table 3.6: Information and Prognosis Dataset Characteristics
(Price Effect Duration Forecasting Model)

	Sample size	$\Delta t_{3,10}$ mean	$\Delta t_{3,10}$ median
Panel I: Primary dataset Ψ			
Total	425	34.62	20
$\Delta t_{i,3,10}$ below average	132	15.67	13
$\Delta t_{i,3,10}$ above average	293	76.66	61.5
Panel II: Information dataset Ψ^I (winsorized)			
Total	200	31.95	34.5
$\Delta t_{i,3,10}$ below average	100	15.69	13
$\Delta t_{i,3,10}$ above average	100	48.21	51
Panel III: Forecasting dataset Ψ^F			
Total	225	22.94	15
$\Delta t_{i,3,10}$ below average	32	15.66	13
$\Delta t_{i,3,10}$ above average	193	66.84	60.5

Due to the winsorization of the information dataset Ψ^I its median is larger than its sample mean. However, after the winsorization process the means of the information dataset (including the two sub-samples) are much more like those of the primary dataset (before the winsorization process the information dataset has a mean of 47.96 minutes).

3.3.5.3   Model Construction

According to the development of the price effect magnitude forecasting model presented in the previous section, a forecasting model is constructed in the following by performing a multiple linear regression analysis.

The result of this analysis should be a forecasting model that can be used for estimating the period of time measured in minutes ($\Delta t_{i,3,10}$) in which significant abnormal stock return can be expected. In detail, the dependent variable $\Delta t_{i,3,10}$ is estimated with a linear model using the independent variables $\Delta t_{i,1,2}$, $TVol_{i,1,2}$, $Index_i$, and $\#Analysts_i$, which is defined by the following Equation 2.1.

$$\Delta t_{i,3,10} = \beta_0 + \beta_1 \cdot \Delta t_{i,1,2} + \beta_2 \cdot TVol_{i,1,2} + \beta_3 \cdot Index_i + \beta_4 \cdot \#Analysts_i + \varepsilon_i$$

where

β_j	=	model parameters with index j
ε_i	=	error term with index i
$\Delta t_{i,t1,t2}$	=	period of time (in minutes) with indices i, $t1$, $t2$
$TVol_{i,1,2}$	=	trading volume with indices i, $t1$, $t2$
$Index_i$	=	index membership with index i
$\#Analysts_i$	=	number of analysts with index i

Equation 3.10: Linear Price Effect Period Forecasting Model

In order to estimate the listed β_j-values, the corresponding minimization problem of the regression model has to be solved.

$$\min_{\beta} \sum_{i=1}^{190} \left[\Delta t_{i,3,10} - \beta_0 - \beta_1 \cdot \Delta t_{i,1,2} - \beta_2 \cdot TVol_{i,1,2} - \beta_3 \cdot Index_i - \beta_4 \cdot \#Analysts_i \right]^2$$

Equation 3.11: Multiple Linear Regression Model

The results for this multiple linear regression model are calculated with SPSS 11.5 and the results of this analysis are presented in the following Table 3.7.

Table 3.7: Regression Results for the Price Effect Duration Forecasting Model

Model Summary

	R	R^2	Adjusted R^2	Std. error of the estimate
	0.561(a)	0.315	0.305	14.599

ANOVA(b)

	Sum of squares	df	Mean squares	F-value	Significance
Regression	19217.420	3	6405.807	30.054	< 0.001(a)
Residual	41776.080	196	213.143		
Total	60993.500	199			

Coefficients(b)

	Unstandardized coefficients		Standardized coefficients		
	β_j-value	Std. error	Beta	t-value	Significance
(Constant)	36.700	1.377		26.650	< 0.001
$\Delta t_{i,1,2}$	0.082	0.045	0.110	1.815	0.071
$TVol_{i,1,2}$	-0.018	0.006	-0.190	-3.149	0.002
$\#Analysts_i$	-0.681	0.088	-0.474	-7.783	< 0.001
$Index_i$	Not significant / removed from the model				0.419 (c)

(a) Predictors: (Constant), $\Delta t_{i,1,2}$, $TVol_{i,1,2}$ and $\#Analysts_i$

(b) Dependent Variable: $\Delta t_{i,3,10}$

(c) Calculated for a regression model including predictor $Index_i$

Compared to the price effect forecasting model (with an R^2 of 0.365) the calculated R^2 of 0.315 is lower for the price effect duration forecasting model, which should result in a poorer model forecasting quality.

However, the model ANOVA (analysis of variance) provides evidence that the model should have a significant prediction power, because with an F-value of 30.054 it is possible to reject the hypothesis that the model does not have any predictive power at a level of significance smaller than 0.1%.

With a significance level of 0.419 the independent variable $Index_i$ is not significant. There-fore, it has been removed from the regression model and Table 3.7 shows the results for a second regression analysis after removing this variable (the significance level for $Index_i$ stems from a first regression including this predictor).

Using the β_j-values calculated for the different predictors it is possible to define the linear function that represents the desired forecasting model (Equation 3.12).

$$F(\Delta t_{i,3,10}) = 36.70 + 0.082 \cdot \Delta t_{i,1,2} - 0.018 \cdot TVol_{i,1,2} - 0.681 \cdot \# Analysts_i$$

where

$\Delta t_{i,t1,t2}$	$=$	period of time (in minutes) with indices i, $t1$, $t2$
$TVol_{i,1,2}$	$=$	trading volume with indices i, $t1$, $t2$
$Index_i$	$=$	index membership with index i
$\# Analysts_i$	$=$	number of analysts with index i

Equation 3.12: Price Effect Duration Forecasting Model

This forecasting model provides support for identifying stock price adjustment processes ($\Delta t_{i,3,10}$) that persist longer or shorter than the mean effect duration of 34.69 minutes. This information can be valuable for private investors since it helps to estimate the window of opportunity available.

The results of the regression analysis (Table 3.7) indicate that three coefficients (constant, $TVol_{i,1,2}$, and $\# Analysts_i$) show a significance level of 1% and the forth coefficient ($\Delta t_{i,1,2}$) shows a significance level of 10%. Consequently, after removing $Index_i$ (due to lack of significance), all remaining coefficients have significant predictive power and therefore contribute to the forecasting model. Regarding the signs of the model parameters β_j that were hypothesized in Table 3.5 the regression results corroborate the positive or negative impact for all coefficients included. Therefore, these results provide further evidence for model validity.

The quoted *Beta*-values (standardized coefficients) indicate that the number of analysts ($\# Analysts_i$) have the most predictive impact on the model, followed by the trading volume during the first two price fixings following the event date ($TVol_{i,1,2}$) and the period of time consumed during these two price fixing ($\Delta t_{i,1,2}$).

3.3.5.4 Model Quality Evaluation

An assessment regarding the forecasting quality of the price effect duration forecasting model developed in the previous Section 0 is done by forecasting $F(\Delta t_{i,3,10})$ values for the forecasting dataset Ψ^F using Equation 3.12 and by comparing these values with the actually observed $\Delta t_{i,3,10}$ values. The objective of the forecasting model is to assign events and the corresponding price adjustment process to one of two categories. These categories define whether or not the period of time elapsed between the third and tenth price fixing ($\Delta t_{i,3,10}$) lies above the sample mean $\mu(\Delta t_{i,3,10})$ of 34.69 minutes. Therefore, actually observed $\Delta t_{i,3,10}$ and forecasted $F(\Delta t_{i,3,10})$ values are classified for each event i. To assess the forecasting quality, these classifications are then compared regarding their degree of conformity.

$$Z_i = \begin{cases} 0 & if \ \Delta t_{i,3,10} < \mu(\Delta t_{i,3,10}) \\ 1 & if \ \Delta t_{i,3,10} \geq \mu(\Delta t_{i,3,10}) \end{cases}$$

Equation 3.13: Observed Price Effect Duration Category

$$\hat{Z}_i = \begin{cases} 0 & if \ F(\Delta t_{i,3,10}) < \mu(\Delta t_{i,3,10}) \\ 1 & if \ F(\Delta t_{i,3,10}) \geq \mu(\Delta t_{i,3,10}) \end{cases}$$

Equation 3.14: Forecasted Price Effect Duration Category

where

$\mu(\Delta t_{i,3,10})$	=	mean of $\Delta t_{i,3,10}$
$\Delta t_{i,3,10}$	=	price effect duration with indices i, $t1$, $t2$
$F(\Delta t_{i,3,10})$	=	forecasted $\Delta t_{i,3,10}$ value
Z_i	=	price effect duration category of observed duration with index i
$\hat{Z}_i$	=	price effect duration category of forecasted duration with index i

After calculating the categories for the observed and forecasted price effect durations for all 225 elements of the forecasting dataset one can compare the categories and assess the forecasting quality (recognition rate) by dividing the number of category hits ($Z_i = \hat{Z}_i$) by the total number of observations. This is done separately for the price effect durations above and below the sample mean of 34.69 minutes, which is illustrated in the following Figure 3.7 where the upper (lower) area shows the elements with an observed price effect duration above (below) the sample mean. It furthermore illustrates how the price effect duration model can be applied to calculate the $F(\Delta t_{i,3,10})$ values.

Figure 3.7: Quality Evaluation of the Price Effect Duration Forecasting Model

	i	Symbol	$\Delta t_{i,1,2}$	$TVol_{i,1,2}$	#Analysts$_i$	$\Delta t_{i,3,10}$	$F(\Delta t_{i,3,10})$	Z_i	$\hat{Z}_i$	
Observed price effect duration above average of 34.61 minutes	1	PAQ.ETR	7	15.95	1	36	36.31	1	1	
	2	NWU.ETR	71	3.44	1	38	41.78	1	1	
	3	GCI.ETR	98	0.21	0	118	44.73	1	1	
	4	UTDI.ETR	7	0.97	13	37	28.40	1	0	
	5	VAB.FSE	51	0.57	0	36	40.87	1	1	
	6	IFQ1.ETR	13	19.18	1	37	33.08	1	0	Example calculation:
	7	FJH.FSE	116	4.88	5	37	42.72	1	1	$F(\Delta t_{8,3,10}) = 36.70$
	8	YSN.FSE	1	1.76	3	39	34.71	1	1	$+ 0.082 \cdot \Delta t_{8,1,2}$
	9	TVD.ETR	1	71.41	0	36	35.50	1	1	$- 0.018 \cdot TVol_{8,1,2}$
	10	IBB.ETR	26	1.18	1	76	38.13	1	1	$- 0.681 \cdot \#Analysts_8$
	:	:	:	:	:	:	:	:	:	(internal calculation with more than two decimal places)
Observed price effect duration below average of 34.61 minutes	216	VOW.ETR	1	96.19	35	8	11.22	0	0	
	217	VAB.ETR	60	0.08	0	22	41.62	0	1	
	218	DBK.ETR	1	375.72	32	8	8.23	0	0	
	219	ALG.ETR	7	3.74	0	32	37.21	0	1	
	220	VOW.ETR	1	293.37	34	8	8.35	0	0	
	221	DRN.ETR	1	4.74	10	32	29.89	0	0	
	222	CON.ETR	1	3.31	32	13	14.93	0	0	
	223	IXX.ETR	2	0.81	1	29	36.17	0	1	
	224	FAA.ETR	2	15.05	1	33	35.91	0	1	
	225	VOW.ETR	1	61.11	42	8	7.08	0	0	

Column 1 lists the sample element numbers i of the forecasting dataset Ψ^F with the first 32 rows exhibiting a price effect duration (i.e. the sixth column $\Delta t_{i,3,10}$) larger than the mean duration. The following rows 33 up to 225 show a duration smaller than these 34.69 minutes.

The second column shows the stock symbol, e.g. PAQ.ETR that is the identifier for the stocks of PARSYTEC AG (PAQ) traded on Xetra (ETR). The following three columns represent the values of the independent variables ($\Delta t_{i,1,2}$, $TVol_{i,1,2}$, and #Analysts$_i$) that are used by the price effect duration model.

Column 6 and 7 show the observed ($\Delta t_{i,3,10}$) and forecasted ($F(\Delta t_{i,3,10})$) price effect duration, which are used to define the corresponding duration categories in the following two columns. The values of the forecasted duration in column 7 are calculated with the price effect duration forecasting model (Equation 3.12) and the category values Z_i and $\hat{Z}_i$ are derived with Equation 3.13 and Equation 3.14. These last two columns show whether the observed and the forecasted price effect duration lies above or below the mean price effect duration. By counting the number of category matches, it is possible to evaluate the quality of the price effect duration forecasting model.

Table 3.8 presents a summary of the model accuracy evaluation that gives results for the two categories including category hits and the average recognition rate. If this rate lies above 50%, which can be expected when guessing the correct category by chance, the model should have derived successfully patterns from the information dataset.

Table 3.8: Forecast Accuracy of the Price Effect Duration Forecasting Model

Price effect category	Category frequency	Category hits $(Z_i = \hat{Z}_i)$	Recognition rate
Price effect duration longer than the $\Delta t_{i,3,10}$ mean	32	27	84.38%
Price effect duration shorter than the $\Delta t_{i,3,10}$ mean	193	110	56.99%
		Weighted average	60.89%

Compared to the recognition rate of the price effect forecasting model (71.11%) the achieved average recognition rate of 60.89% is significantly lower. However, an average overall recognition rate of more than 60% indicates that the forecasting model should provide limited predictive power whose forecasts should be used carefully and be marked accordingly. This limited forecasting quality also results form the unequal sub-sample sizes of the two price effect categories since the forecasting quality of the smaller sub-sample is much smaller and equally sized sub-samples would have lead to a recognition rate of 70.69%.

3.4 Summary of the Decision Support System Concept

Conceptual frameworks can be helpful for understanding new or complex subjects. Consequently, a DSS framework that provides the facility for classifying and describing decision support systems can be a valuable tool for describing and explaining a specific DSS and for distinguishing between the various types of decision support systems (Sprague and Watson 1996).

Therefore, Section 3.2 introduced an extended DSS framework originally presented by Power (2002) that summarized relevant DSS characteristics. The original framework has been expanded by an additional *enabling technology* "mobile devices and services" since the original version does not cover this increasingly important technology in the field of DSS research (Basole and Chao 2004; Padmanabhan et al. 2006). Section 3.3 introduced a novel concept of a mobile financial decision support system that should empower private investors to react promptly to critical market events. This proposed DSS was presented and described using the framework introduced in Section 3.2. The characteristics *system purpose*, *target user group*, *enabling technology*, and the *DSS technology component* of the proposed DSS are summarized in the following Table 3.9.

Table 3.9: Characteristics Summary of the Proposed Mobile Financial DSS Concept

	DSS characteristic			
	System purpose	**Target user group**	**Enabling technology**	**DSS technology component**
Description	Notifying users of relevant market event, financial decision analysis	Private investors (e.g. retail bank customers)	Mobile devices and mobile messaging services	Price effect and effect duration forecasting models
Category	Task-specific DSS	Inter-organizational customer DSS	Mobile devices and services DSS	Model-driven DSS

The proposed DSS concept describes a task-specific system that assists investors in a specific situation, i.e. when a relevant event has been observed by the system, which can significantly affect stock prices. The system provides support by evaluating this price reaction so that the investor is assisted in distinguishing between relevant and irrelevant events. For the latter there is a price effect expected lying below the average price effect.

The system addresses private investors as a particular *user group* since professional investors generally trade in the office using professional trading software such as Xetra Observer that can identify abnormal trading activity observed on the capital market. The approach aims at providing new opportunities for private investors and therefore represents an inter-organizational DSS for e.g. customers of online banks or online brokers (CDSS).

These new opportunities are addressed with a CDSSS concept that utilizes mobile communication infrastructures as technological basis, which represents the *enabling technology* for the DSS. The mobile communication infrastructures technologically consist of wireless networks, mobile devices, and mobile application architectures that provide the functions of the DSS (Mallick 2003). Compared to the widespread web-based system approach that has become a mainstream technological DSS basis, mobile communication infrastructures have not yet been established as a technological DDS basis. Web-based DSS are omnipresent today and can e.g. be found as intranet applications within companies or as website tools to support customers in making product selection (O'Keefe and McEachern 1998) or in planning investment strategies (Martin et al. 2005).

The presented DSS concept uses a price effect magnitude and a price effect duration forecasting model as central *DSS technology component* and therefore it is primarily model-driven. Both the system itself and the decision maker can utilize these estimation models. First, it can be used on the system side to identify relevant events that needs to be treated and processed in order to reduce the level of customer-intrusiveness. Customers would hardly accept a system that sends all published information to a mobile device without filtering and customizing information sources (McCrickard et al. 2003). Furthermore, the effect duration forecasting model can be used to specify expiration dates for messages sent to the user. If the user is not able to react within the specified period of time, the message can be identified as outdated or discarded automatically on the mobile device. Second, private investors can use estimated price effects for evaluating the impact of published ad hoc disclosures for which Chapter 2 has shown significant price effects. Consequently, these price effects represent an investment opportunity. The forecasted price effect duration can further be used to estimate the window of opportunity available but should be utilized carefully due to limited forecasting accuracy. The quality evaluation of the price effect magnitude forecasting model shows that it features a good forecasting quality that outperforms former text mining approaches (Mittermayer 2004; Schulz et al. 2003; Spiliopoulou et al. 2003). This forecasting model can therefore provide valuable support for investors in identifying relevant market events in the form of published ad hoc disclosures.

In the following chapter, the proposed decision support system concept is deployed and the design of a corresponding IT artifact is illustrated. This IT artifact comprises the setup of an appropriate system infrastructure (hardware) and a DSS server application (software) exploiting the presented advantages of these technologies.

4   Design of an IT Artifact for Intraday Decision Support

As illustrated in the introductory Chapter 1, the design science paradigm provides a framework for the prescriptive characteristics of this research field that focuses on the construction and evaluation of novel artifacts providing some kind of utility.

This chapter presents the design of a decision support system that informs investors about relevant market events and assists them in making better and timelier investment decisions.

This was motivated by existence of abnormal stock price behavior that might be exploited by investors following the publication of ad hoc disclosures, as shown in Chapter 2. Focusing on the private investor segment, a corresponding concept for a mobile notification and decision support system was presented in the previous Chapter 3.

In order to support the presented decision support process, this DSS concept is implemented by the design and deployment of an IT artifact that combines a prototypical software implementation and a system infrastructure setup.

Therefore, after introducing the role of IT artifacts in design science research (Section 4.1), Section 4.2 provides, in the form of a short literature review, a brief overview of current approaches to design science research.

The designed artifact is then presented in Section 4.3. After conducting a requirement analysis, technical details such as the technical infrastructure used and the implemented software are explained. Then, the system's functionality is presented in detail and limitations of the prototypical artifact implementation are discussed.

In the remainder of this chapter (Section 4.4), a conclusion of the IT artifact design is provided.

4.1   IT Artifacts in Information System Research

In research, there exist several definitions for the term *IT artifact*. This work uses as working definition the definition of Srinivasan et al. (2005) who define the IT artifact as a "combined hardware and software system that is designed and implemented within an organizational context and whose purpose is to collect, organize, and store data, and transform it into information needed for operating and managing the organization". The IT artifact that is presented in this chapter represents such a combination of technical infrastructure and prototypical software implementation that processes data in an inter-organizational context in order to provide utility to the parties involved.

A second and broader definition is provided by March and Smith (1995) who identify four different kinds of artifacts that can be the product of design science research. Thus, output of design science research can occur in the form of constructs, models, methods, and instantiations (March and Smith 1995), which are explained in the following.

Representing the vocabulary of a domain, new *constructs* provide the capability to describe and propose potential solutions to unsolved problems within this domain (March and Smith 1995). For example, the definition of normal forms for relational databases provides a useful formalism to describe and improve the structure of stored data, e.g. by reducing redundancy (Whitehorn and Marklyn 2001).

Models can be used for describing the relation between new or existing constructs in order to bring structure to problems, which can be useful for identifying and designing possible solutions. A well-known and widely used model is for example Chen's (1976) Entity-Relationship Model that provides a basis for unifying different data views (Chen 1976). Generally, models represent a tool that can be used to describe the nature of things or situations and therefore provide utility due to better understandability of the domain.

Using previously specified constructs and models, a *method* is a sequence of steps that are taken in order to perform a given task such as algorithms and practices (March and Smith 1995). The event study methodology presented in Chapter 2 represents an example of a widely used practice for analyzing the impact of unexpected events on security prices (Binder 1998). The design science research guidelines proposed by Hevner et al. (2004), which were presented in Chapter 1 provide a methodological basis for conducting design science in the realm of IS research. These are only two examples of methods and practices that are applied in this work.

Generally, *instantiations* are used to demonstrate the feasibility and applicability of designed models and methods (March and Smith 1995). The relevance of instantiations, such as system architectures, system designs or prototypical software applications, has been well recognized both in information system and computer science research. Newell and Simon (1976) argue that every new computer program in computer science research can be a valuable basis for discovering new phenomena or for exploring phenomena already known before.

Following this broader definition, the forecasting models developed in Chapter 3 would represent IT artifacts on their own since they have also been evaluated. In contrast, following the definition of Srinivasan et al. (2005), these forecasting models will be used in this chapter as an input for the design of an IT artifact (i.e. a combined hardware and software system).

4.2 Introduction to Design Science Research

In recent years, the design science research paradigm has been applied in information systems research in different application domains, where identified problems were addressed with respective IT artifacts.

Tiwana and Ramesh (2001), for example, deployed a prototypical application that supports teams in producing information products and created a knowledge management system, which supports collaborative work and decision-making. The designed IT artifact enables authors to deal with distributed authoring and synchronous deliberations that can be captured and linked to different versions of the information product. By designing and evaluating the IT artifact, they are able to explore the phenomenon of collaborative working environments.

Markus et al. (2002) designed and deployed a software tool TOP Modeler for developing information systems that support emerging knowledge processes such as new product development, strategic business planning, and organization design. They derived a design theory that provides principles to guide software developers, e.g. in specifying software feature lists.

Muntermann and Milic Frayling (2006) specified a recommender model for composed messages and showed how to choose the most appropriate communication channel, such as email, SMS or MMS, amongst the channels available. They furthermore built and evaluated a corresponding system infrastructure, and client applications, for mobile devices and desktop computers that can be used to compose generic message contents. After composing and sending a message to a central messaging server, users receive recommendations how these contents can be sent most suitably. Since the infrastructure supports cross-platform messaging, the deployed IT artifact empowers users to communicate across IP and mobile networks using different kinds of messaging services. In further research, they propose to address some of the questions posed by following the behavioral science research paradigm in order to evaluate the impact of the IT artifact designed within an organizational context.

However, it has also been criticized that within the IS community, compared to, for example, publications that utilize the behavioral science paradigm, there is less work published that applies the design science paradigm to considering the benefits of exploring IT artifacts for the development of new theories in IS research (Au 2001; Srinivasan et al. 2005). Orliowski and Iacono (2001) criticize that information system research in general has lost its focus on IT artifacts, which they consider to be the core object of investigation for IS research. To be able to understand their implications on individuals and organizations (e.g. by developing new theories about IT artifacts), IS researchers should therefore regard technological aspects of the IT artifacts involved in their research (Orlikowski and Iacono 2001).

Because existing methodologies and theories can often not adequately explain observations made, creative research paradigms such as design science are needed to reach beyond these limits. Markus et al. (2002) highlight that the descriptive and evaluative character of IS design research is not a shift from traditional and well established IS research paradigms, but rather an extension that provides the flexibility to explore new ideas, concepts, designs, and emerging technologies, which stimulates IS research in general. Using the mobile financial DSS concept presented in the previous chapter, such an IT artifact design is presented in the following.

4.3   The *MoFin DSS* IT Artifact: Mobile Financial Decision Support for Private Investors

The developed *Mobile Financial Decision Support System* (*MoFin DSS*) comprises a hardware infrastructure setup, and software components that provide the functionality to integrate different data sources, and to analyze the data processed, in order to provide decision support to investors. The data processed comprises ad hoc disclosure data, estimations of the stock price reactions and metadata about the companies having published the disclosure.

Starting with a requirement analysis (Section 4.3.1) of the IT artifact to be designed, Section 4.3.2 presents the underlying technical infrastructure. Then, Section 4.3.3 shows how the software components of the artifact were implemented. Section 4.3.4 illustrates the functionalities provided by the IT artifact addressing both server-side and client side view. Finally, Section 4.3.5 discusses conceptual and functional limitations, and security constraints, of the prototypical artifact design.

4.3.1   Requirement Analysis

This section describes functional and technical requirements that should be met by the system design. There exist many other software requirements such as performance or usability (e.g. see ISO/IEC 1991). Since the focus of the design is on functionality aspects, these are not addressed in the following. Starting with a description of the functional requirements in Section 4.3.1.1, the most relevant use cases and application activities are documented and illustrated. This functional requirement analysis comprises typical use cases for the different parties involved, as well as internal system processes that are needed in order to provide the functionalities demanded. A technical requirement analysis is presented in Section 4.3.1.2 addressing the technical aspects that need to be taken into account in order to achieve as much as possible of the functional requirements identified. This also includes a discussion of different technological options for the implementation of the system design.

4.3.1.1   Functional Requirements

In order to implement successfully the mobile financial decision support system, which has conceptually been introduced in the previous chapter, an assessment of functional requirements is needed. Therefore, it is important to identify and document these required functionalities that should be supported by the system. Consequently, both parties and systems involved need to be identified first to be able to recognize relationships and typical use cases in order to then identify the functionalities needed. First, the *private investor* and a *system operator* can be identified as human or organizational actors who use the developed system. The most relevant use cases from the users' perspectives are illustrated in the following Unified Modeling Language (UML) use case diagram (Figure 4.1).

Figure 4.1: Use Cases from the Users' Perspectives

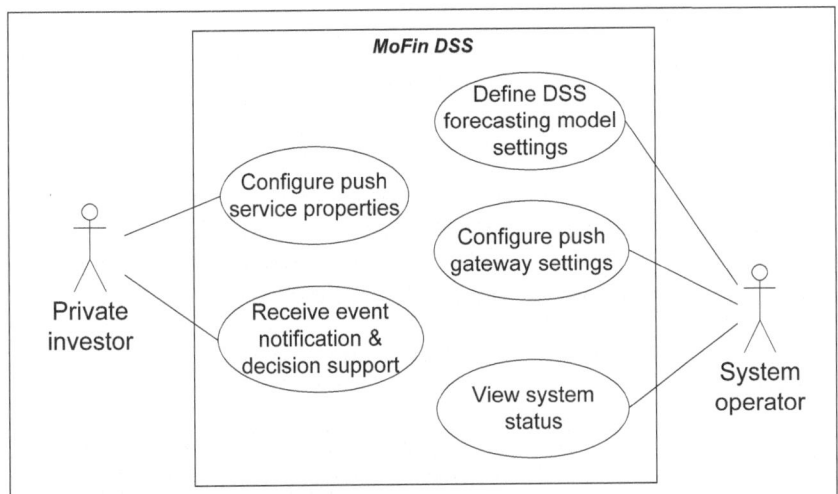

This kind of diagram provides a modeling framework for capturing the requirements of the system to be developed (Booch et al. 2005). The following functional requirement analysis defines actor (e.g. the private *investor*) and system roles (e.g. *MoFin DSS*), whereas the latter provide a basis for the technical infrastructure setup presented in Section 4.3.2.

Within this UML diagram, the private investor and system operators are defined as *actors*, who interact with *MoFin DSS* via so-called use cases. These use cases are represented by the ovals in Figure 4.1 within the system boundary of the *MoFin DSS*.

Since the private investor demands mobile financial decision support, it must be possible to configure the push service properties in order to realize ubiquitous reachability. These properties for example comprise the phone number of the private investor's mobile device and the preferred push message type (SMS, MMS, or WAP Push). Furthermore, *MoFin DSS* has to provide event notifications regarding relevant market events.

On the other hand, a system operator should be able to view the system status and to configure the system settings. The system status should inform the system operator about observed market events (i.e. published ad hoc disclosures) and forecasted price effects in order to understand whether or not, and why, a mobile message was sent.

The configuration of system settings comprises both technical and functional aspects. First, since the system should be flexible regarding changing forecasting model parameters (see Equation 3.10 and Equation 3.12), the system operator should be able to define and adjust the

DSS model settings. Second, it is necessary to configure the settings of a *GSM Push Gateway Server* via which the *MoFin DSS Application Server* sends mobile messages to the investor.

Actors within an UML Use Case Diagram need not necessarily be human and can for example be a system that contacts other systems (Stevens and Pooley 2006). In order to highlight their non-human character, such actors are typically represented with a rectangle labeled with the keyword «actor» (OMG Group 2005).

Since the designed IT artifact (i.e. *MoFin DSS*) needs to interact with other systems providing some kind of functionality, Figure 4.2 provides another perspective on use cases that need to be addressed by the system design. It therefore provides a detailed analysis of the *"Provide event notification"* use case presented in the previous use case diagram.

Figure 4.2: Use Cases from the IT Artifact Perspective

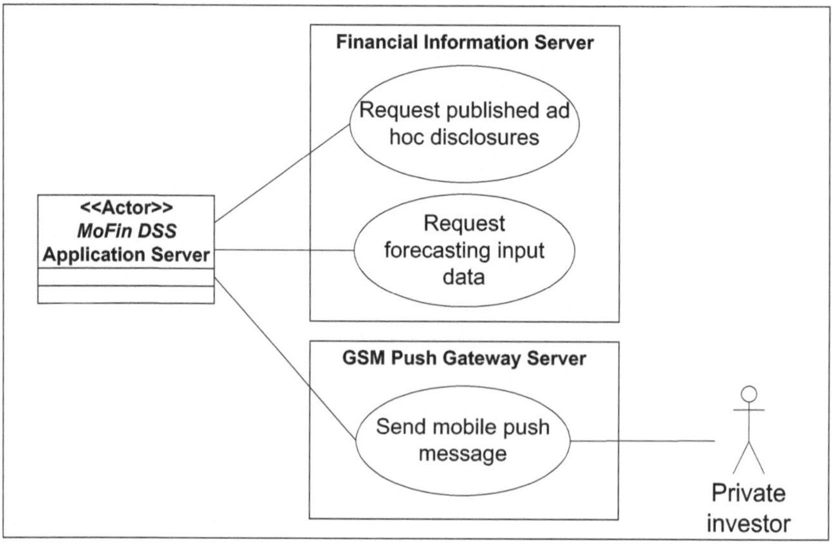

Here, the *MoFin DSS Application Server* is a non-human (system) actor, which accesses use cases provided by other systems. Since this server requires access to comprehensive data sources such as published ad hoc disclosures, company profiles and other financial data, appropriate data retrieval is required. The necessary data is provided by a system called *Financial Information Server*, offering two use cases being accessed by the *MoFin DSS Application Server*. These two use cases describe the requests made to a news feed, i.e. to ad hoc disclosures that were recently published. Furthermore, it grants access to financial data, which is needed as input for the forecasting models that were developed in Chapter 3 and are implemented in *MoFin DSS*. Depending on the event evaluation, the *MoFin DSS Application*

Server must be enabled to send mobile push messages to the private investors, for which it is supported by a second system called GSM *Push Gateway Server* providing the corresponding use case.

The event evaluation process decides whether and how a notification is sent to the mobile device of the investor. This evaluation and the compilation and delivery of the mobile push message calls for a sequence of actions including the communication between several systems and the investor.

Consequently, a detailed analysis of this interplay is required, as is done with the illustration of the activity flow (Figure 4.3) using an UML activity diagram.

UML activity diagrams can be used for describing and analyzing the sequence of lower-level behaviors and the conditions under which these occur (OMG Group 2005). This means that they represent a suitable framework for modeling the interplay of actions taken by the investor and the different systems involved.

The vertical lines (called swim lanes) in Figure 4.3 separate the four activity partitions (i.e. the *Investor*, *MoFin DSS Application Server*, *Financial Information Server*, and the *GSM Push Gateway Server*) and define the responsibility for the actions performed.

The diagram illustrates the control flow, which may result in a mobile push message notifying the investor about a relevant market event. This message contains further information in order to support the investment decision to be made. Since the observed ad hoc disclosures are published irregularly, the control flow needs to be reiterated periodically.

Figure 4.3: Activity Diagram of the Required Information Processing

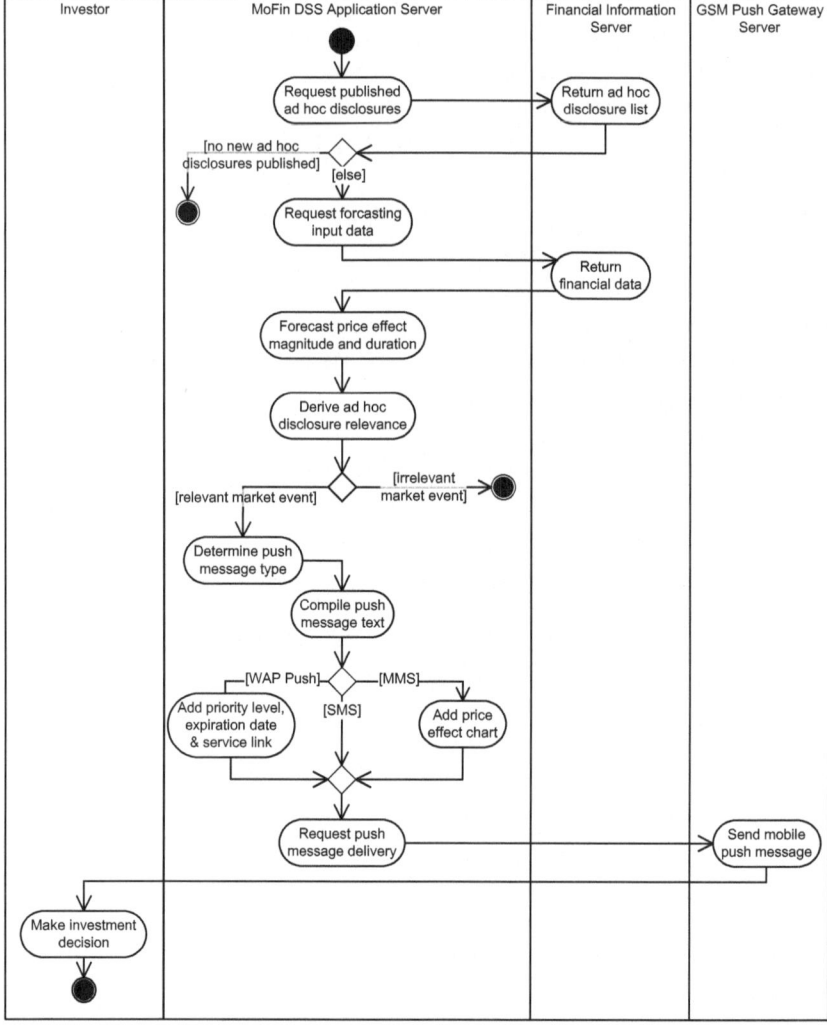

The activity diagram starts with a request of the *MoFin DSS Application Server* for a list of ad hoc disclosures that were published recently. After receiving this request, the *Financial Information Server* sends a response, which can contain one, several or none ad hoc disclosure. If there is no new ad hoc disclosure available, *MoFin DSS Application Server* stops the activity flow. Otherwise, input data is requested that is needed for the estimation of the price effect magnitude and duration according to the forecasting models that were introduced in the previous chapter. The forecasted price effect magnitude is then used to determine the relevance of the ad hoc disclosure. If this magnitude lies below the average price effect magnitude, the event is evaluated as an irrelevant market event, and the action flow is stopped. Otherwise, the mobile push message service is determined depending on the user settings. All mobile push messages contain message text that provides information regarding the ad hoc disclosure observed, the estimated price effect magnitude, and the estimated price effect duration. If MMS or WAP Push SI is chosen as messaging service, further information is added to the message. Whereas SMS does not provide the functionality to add such information, WAP Push SI messages contain an additional link that directly links to a trading or information service URL accessible via the WAP browser. Furthermore, a message priority level and expiration date is added to the message the latter being calculated using the ad hoc disclosure's publication date and the estimated price effect duration. As MMS features multimedia capabilities, a price effect chart is attached to the message that visualizes the observed and forecasted price effects following the publication date.

After compiling the message content, the *MoFin DSS Application Server* sends a push message delivery request to the *GSM Push Gateway Server*, which sends a mobile push message to the investor's mobile device. Consequently, the investor receives prompt notification regarding a relevant market event, including further financial information to support the investment decision. These mobile messaging services are further analyzed in the following.

4.3.1.2 Mobile Communication Requirements

The following analysis of mobile communication requirements focuses on the communication process between *MoFin DSS* and the investor, i.e. on the mobile messaging services, which are the technological basis (i.e. a part of the enabling technology of the presented DSS concept) for sending mobile push messages to the mobile device of the investor. In this section, characteristics of mobile messaging services are described and analyzed with regard to their appropriateness for delivering critical financial information to the investor. These characteristics are used later in section 4.3.4.2 for describing the artifact's functionality on the client-side.

Muntermann and Güttler (2004) discuss the properties of mobile push services regarding their technical appropriateness for sending financial notifications to mobile devices. Their message attribute set is the basis for the following requirement analysis.

Most fundamentally, it is required to send textual information with the mobile message, which contains information regarding the event being triggered by a published ad hoc disclosure for which a significant price reaction has been forecasted[19]. The message should also

---

[19] There exist mobile messaging services such as WAP Push Service Load (SL) that do not support this basic functionality.

inform about the price effect magnitude and duration forecasted by the system. Depending on the maximum message size available it can be useful to include (parts of) the original announcement published by the company. For the investor to be able to easily identify incoming messages sent by the system, it can be suitable to define a message subject, which helps to identify messages sent by *MoFin DSS* and that summarizes the message content.

Attached multimedia content can be useful in order to illustrate graphically the intraday price adjustment process including the forecasted price effect magnitude. Compared to a long message text and several figures that need further interpretation, a summarizing price adjustment chart can be quite self-explaining.

Since the observed market events usually demand prompt investor reaction, links to external information or transaction services can be useful for guiding the investor. Such links would direct the investors to a web page that provides further information regarding the observed market event or that allows to trade the stocks affected.

For the same reason it is important that the investor receives the mobile message within a short period of time after being generated, since the information provided becomes outdated quickly. Therefore, a guaranteed delivery time is of high relevance and should be supported.

Generally, automated message services can cause problems regarding user-intrusiveness caused by unwanted or outdated massages (McCrickard et al. 2003). This problem gets even more prominent when social and technical factors come into play (Sawhney and Schmandt 2000). For one, receiving unwanted messages can become socially intrusive in situations such as meetings. Also, technical constraints, such as limited device capabilities or low connection bandwidth, are critical issues with regards to user acceptance. Adding additional attributes to mobile messages can be a suitable approach to address these problems including security requirements that arise (Rannenberg 2000a). These security issues are not addressed in the requirement analysis here but are discussed in Section 4.3.5.3 that describes the limitations of the IT artifact designed. By setting a high priority level for the sent mobile messages it is possible to highlight these amongst other incoming messages. However, this requires that the priority level attribute is used carefully since it gets useless when too many incoming messages have a high priority flag.

The mobile messages sent to the investors become outdated within a short period of time in which stock prices almost reflect the information provided by the ad hoc disclosure. Therefore, a message expiration attribute can decrease the level of user-intrusiveness since outdated messages can be identified and deleted automatically on the mobile device.

In summary, the following technical requirements are defined for mobile messages to investors, which lay the technological basis for mobile decision support.

- Text content up to maximum message length
- Message subject

- Multimedia content attachments
- Link(s) to external services
- Guaranteed delivery time
- Notification lifetime control (expiration date)
- Priority levels of notifications

This mobile message attribute set is used in Section 4.3.4.2 to describe the artifact's functionalities from the client perspective.

4.3.2   Technical Infrastructure

The infrastructure that has been installed as technological basis for the IT artifact comprises a client/server architecture and a mobile communication infrastructure, which is illustrated in the following Figure 4.4.

Figure 4.4: Infrastructure Setup of *MoFin DSS*

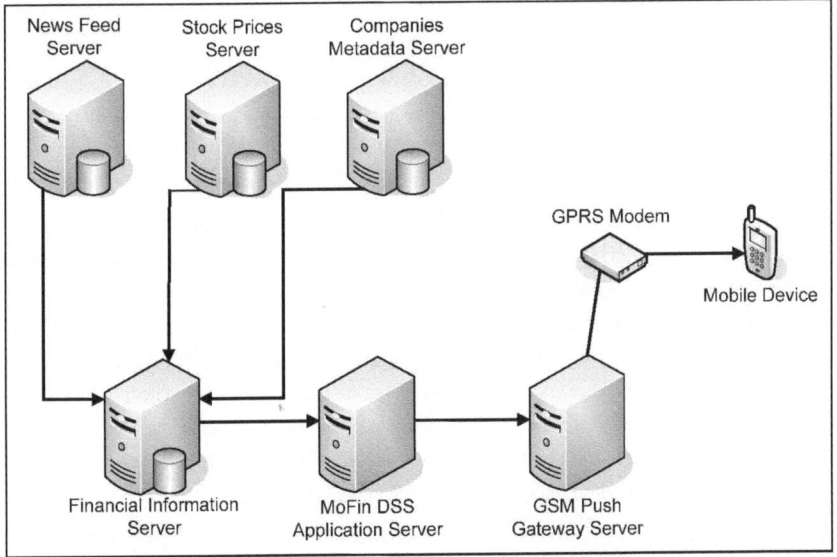

The central infrastructure component is the *MoFin DSS* Application Server, which manages and initiates all information flows. The communication between all servers involved is based on the client/server paradigm, and realized via standard Internet protocols, as specified in the following Section 4.3.2.1. The connection to the GSM network, which is needed for sending mobile messages to the users' mobile devices, is established with the help of a mobile communication infrastructure that is described in Section 0.

4.3.2.1 Client/Server Architecture

The client/server architecture comprises different servers of which some act as server and others act as both client and server. The three servers in the upper half of Figure 4.4 (News Feed Server, Stock Prices Server, and Companies Metadata Server) provide all market data, such as the ad hoc disclosures published, the stock prices and trading volumes of affected stocks, and further company figures. These data sources are accessed via a Financial Information Server that is operated and provided by the *Interactive Data Managed Solutions AG*.

The installed *MoFin DSS* Application *Server* receives required information from the *Financial Information Server*. This communication is based on the HTTP protocol using a standard TCP/IP Internet connection. The *Financial Information Server* stores and dynamically generates different documents defined in the Extensible Markup Language (XML), which can be accessed by the *MoFin DSS Application Server*.

The following Table 4.1 summarizes the data structures, i.e. the document type definitions (DTD), of the three XML documents that are provided by the *Financial Information Server*.

XML is a general-purpose markup language defined by the World Wide Web Consortium (W3C) to be used for describing datasets. Since XML documents have a well-defined document structure, they can easily be accessed and parsed with modern programming languages and with Microsoft's .NET framework that is used for this implementation.

A document DTD defines the markup declaration of an XML document, i.e. it specifies a grammar for a class of XML documents (W3C 2004). This declaration defines the structure and the content allowed within the XML document. For example, the DTD for the first document *getnews.xml* that is described in Table 4.1 defines that *news* is a valid element name, which must contain the four elements *nid*, *header*, *date* and *time*. The "***" at the end of the *news* element indicates there can be several *news* elements in series. The elements *nid*, *header*, *date* and *time* are valid and required element that contain character data (#PCDATA). The DTD's of the other two XML documents (*newsbody.xml* and *calceffects.xml*) have a simpler markup declaration without any nested or repeated elements.

When the *MoFin DSS Application Server* has initiated a request for an XML document, the *Financial Information Server* generates and sends back the requested XML document. This document is then parsed and the data included is processed and analyzed by the *MoFin DSS Application Server* in order to identify relevant company announcements and to calculate information that should be provided to the user.

Table 4.1: XML Documents provided by the Financial Information Server

	getnews.xml

DTD	`<!ELEMENT news(nid, header, date, time)*>`
	`<!ELEMENT nid(#PCDATA)>`
	`<!ELEMENT header(#PCDATA)>`
	`<!ELEMENT date(#PCDATA)>`
	`<!ELEMENT time(#PCDATA)>`

Parameter	*amount*
Description	The document contains a list of ad hoc disclosures that have been published recently. It provides information regarding unique keys (*nid*) for the identification of news, news headers (*header*), and the publication date exact to the second (*time*). The parameter *amount* specifies the number of news to be included in the document.

	newsbody.xml
DTD	`<!ELEMENT newsbody(#PCDATA)>`
Parameter	*Nid*
Description	The document contains the news body of a news item that is identified via the *Nid* parameter transferred, i.e. specified by the unique identification key of a news item.

	calceffects.xml

DTD	`<!ELEMENT ticks(#PCDATA)>`
	`<!ELEMENT caar1(#PCDATA)>`
	`<!ELEMENT caar2(#PCDATA)>`
	`<!ELEMENT deltaT01(#PCDATA)>`
	`<!ELEMENT deltaT12(#PCDATA)>`
	`<!ELEMENT TVol12(#PCDATA)>`
	`<!ELEMENT analysts(#PCDATA)>`

Parameter	*Nid*
Description	The document contains data of the independent variables required by the forecasting models defined in the previous chapter. These forecasting models are implemented in the *MoFin DSS* Server software. Element *ticks* show the number of price fixings observed following the event date. At least two price fixings must be available for the calculation of the next five document elements. The first two elements *caar1* and *caar2* are the *corrected absolute abnormal returns* of the first two price fixings and *deltaT01* and *deltaT12* determine the corresponding period of time elapsed (measured in minutes). *TVol12* is the sum of the trading volume (in 1,000 stocks) that has been observed during the two first price fixings following the event date. Finally, the *analysts* element defines the number of analysts covering the company that has published the ad hoc disclosure.

Depending on its configuration, the *MoFin DSS* Server can initiate a mobile message via the *GSM Push Gateway Server*, which is further described in the following section. Generally, this system architecture component provides the functionality to send messages from the Internet to mobile devices over the mobile cellular GSM network.

4.3.2.2   Mobile Communication Infrastructure

The GSM communication infrastructure comprises a *GSM Push Gateway Server* (hard- and software) and a *GPRS Modem* connected to the server. As server hardware, a standard Intel-based server is used running *Windows 2003 Server*. The utilized push gateway server software has been developed by *Now Wireless Ltd.* and is called *Now SMS/MMS Gateway 2006*. This server software provides an application programming interface (API) to send different kinds of mobile push messages such as SMS, MMS and WAP Push with HTTP requests via a standard Internet connection. Depending on this HTTP request, the gateway software compiles a mobile message, which is sent via a GPRS modem physically connected to the serial port of the server. For this communication infrastructure component, an external *Multitech Multi-Modem GPRS* is used, which provides dual-band 900/1800 MHz GSM/GPRS Class 10 connections and wireless packet data transfers up to 85.6K bps. To be able to send any mobile messages, the connection to the network operator's SMSC (Short Messaging Service Centre) and MMSC (Multimedia Messaging Service Center) needs to be configured. In this installation, the GSM network of T-Mobile Germany is used, i.e. the gateway server software is configured to work with T-Mobile's SMSC and MMSC. To prevent unauthorized connections to the *GSM Push Gateway Server*, requests were restricted both to authorized IP addresses and by an internal user management.

After sending an HTTP request to the *GSM Push Gateway Server*, requests are converted into a format that can be sent to the network operator's SMSC or MMSC. Short Message Services messages, including binary messages such as WAP Push (SI) are directly sent via the extended Hayes command set supported by the wireless modem. This command set is defined by the European Telecommunications Standards Institute in the GSM 07.05 Specification (European Telecommunications Standards Institute 1998).

Incoming MMS message requests that are initiated by the *MoFin DSS Application Server* are converted by the *GSM Push Gateway Server* to comply with the Multimedia Messaging Service Encapsulation Protocol defined by the Open Mobile Alliance (2004). Then, the MMS is uploaded to the mobile operator's MMSC using a GPRS connection established by the connected GRPS modem.

After sending a mobile message to the network operator's SMSC or MMSC, the message is delivered to the recipient's mobile device via the GSM network.

4.3.3   Software Implementation

Two different kinds of software components were implemented for the development of the IT artifact. These address the use cases from the IT artifact perspective that were presented in the functional requirement analysis (Figure 4.2). First, the server-side scripts that dynamically generate the XML documents that were presented in Table 4.1 were developed with a derivate of the server-side Tool Command Language (TCL), which was originally invented at the

University of California, Berkeley (Flynt 1999). When requesting one of the XML documents provided by the *Financial Information Server*, the programmed scripts request data from the different data sources and generate the content of the XML document. For example, the script that generates the *calceffects.xml* document requests data from the *Stock Prices Server* and the *Companies Metadata Server* in order to calculate and process the document element values.

The software component of the *MoFin DSS Application Server*, whose functionality is illustrated in the following section, was programmed with Microsoft Visual Basic 2005 and by using the .NET 2005 Framework 2.0. Compared to previous versions, Visual Basic 2005 has become a fully object-oriented programming language. It therefore provides the advantages of the object-oriented programming paradigm such as improved system modularity, an easier modeling process, or more effective code reuse (Johnson 2000). The following Unified Modeling Language (UML) class diagram describes the general structure of the implemented server software, and shows the implemented classes including most relevant methods and the relationships between the classes.

Figure 4.5: UML Class Diagram of the *MoFin DSS* Software Component

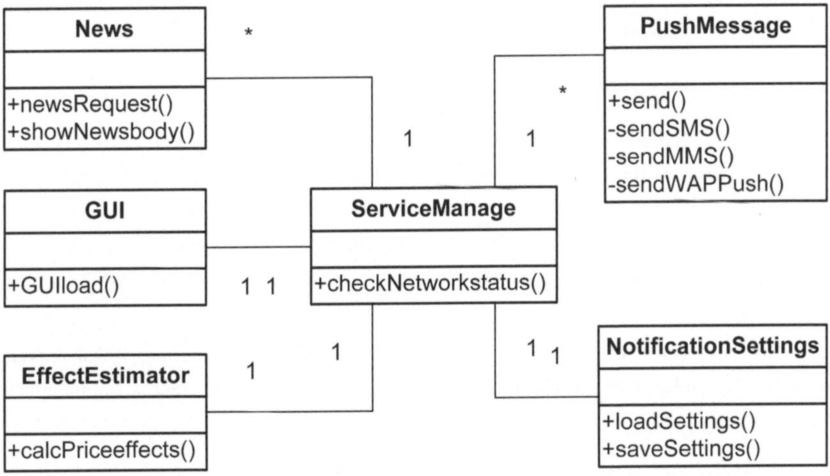

In reality, the developed software implementation is much more complex and consists of many more classes that are not presented in the UML diagram. This complexity is reduced since these classes are not essential for the understanding of the software component.

The central class *ServiceManager* is responsible for the entire server application management and continuously monitors the ad hoc disclosures published by companies. Therefore, HTTP requests are periodically sent to the *Financial Information Server* in order to check whether new ad hoc disclosures have been published. When new ad hoc disclosures were observed and received as XML document, new objects of the *News* class are created. *EffectEstimator* is responsible for estimating the price effect magnitude and price effect duration using the forecasting models that were defined in Chapter 3. This class provides methods for accessing the XML data documents that were presented in Table 4.1 in the previous section. This is technically realized by HTTP requests that are sent to the *Financial Information Server*. The *EffectEstimator* class uses this data for the forecasting of the $F(CCAAR_{i,3,10})$ (forecasted cumulated corrected absolute abnormal return between the third and tenth price fixing of the stock corresponding to event i) and $F(\Delta t_{i,3,10})$ (forecasted price effect duration of the stock corresponding to event i measured in minutes between the third and tenth price fixing following the event date) values. After comparing these forecasted price effects with the *NotificationSettings*, *ServiceManager* initiates a mobile *PushMessage* to be sent. This *PushMessage* can be a SMS, MMS, or WAP Push message depending on the user configuration. *ServiceManager* generates the message content using the estimated price effects for the observed ad hoc disclosure. Further message content such as a chart of the abnormal stock price movement or an expiration date is added to the push message. The message is finally sent via an HTTP request sent to the *GSM Push Gateway Server*. The *GUI* of the *ServiceManager* shows different status information, such as the configuration of the *NotificationSettings*, or a list of ad hoc disclosures that were monitored recently.

4.3.4   System Functionalities

The following sections describe the functionalities provided by the implemented *MoFin DSS* software component that address the use cases from the users' perspective as presented in the functional requirement analysis. First, this *MoFin DSS* software component is illustrated (Section 4.3.4.1), including its functionalities and configurations. It is shown how ad hoc disclosures are observed and identified as relevant market events initiating mobile push messages that provide decision support to investors.

Since there are different kinds of mobile push message services supported, which provide different capabilities and limitations, Section 4.3.4.2 present these differences from a client-side perspective.

4.3.4.1   Server-Side View

The *MoFin DDS* software component has a graphical user interface (GUI), which provides information to the system operator. Furthermore, it offers the capability to enter server configuration settings to adjust the system's behavior or its functionalities.

The GUI is subdivided into the three tabs *Market Events Overview*, *Notification Settings*, and *Push Service Settings*. The first of these tabs is depicted in Figure 4.6 and shows four different dialog sections. The top left-hand corner dialog (*Published Ad Hoc Disclosures*) shows a list of ad hoc disclosure headlines that were recently published, observed, and judged by the system. Clicking on one of these headlines causes the system to update the three other dialog sections, which all refer to the selected ad hoc disclosure.

Figure 4.6: *MoFin DSS* **Screenshot – Event Observation Dialog**

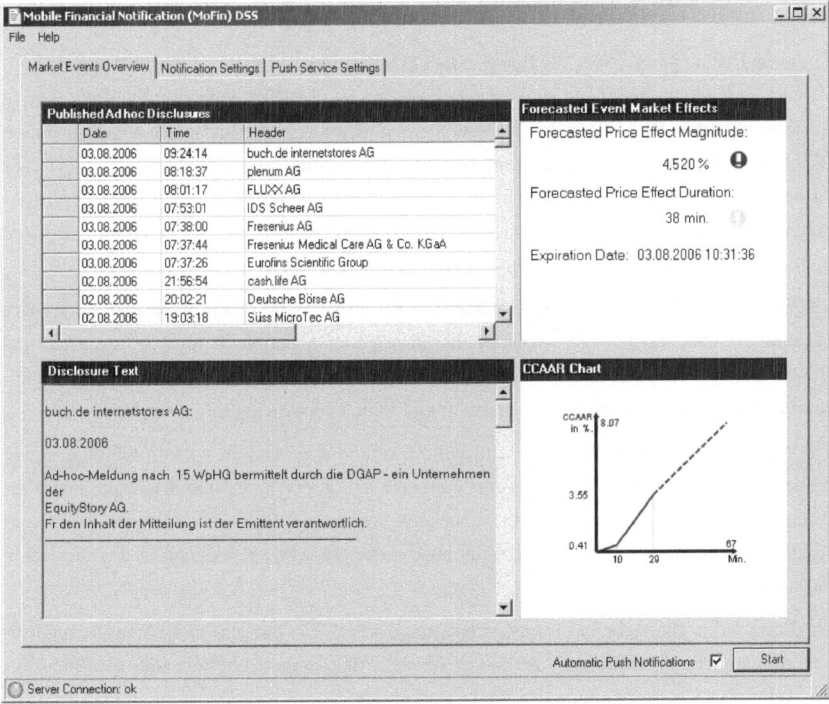

The bottom left dialog shows the corresponding ad hoc message text that was published by a company. Since the text of ad hoc disclosures is of variable length, the dialog features a scrolling capability that allows navigating through the ad hoc disclosure text.

In the top right dialog, several figures are shown that were calculated by the system. The forecasted price effect magnitude is shown in the first two rows, with the exclamation mark indicating a price effect magnitude above the average magnitude. The next rows show the forecasted price effect duration measured in minutes. Using this information and the publication date of the ad hoc disclosure an expiration date is calculated and shown, after which the stock price should reflect most of the new information available.

The price effect (*CCAAR*) chart on the right bottom graphically illustrates the observed and forecasted price effect magnitude (*CCAAR*-axis) in relation to the period of time elapsed

(*Min*-axis). Since the two first price fixings following the publication date are used as input factors for the forecasting model, *CCAAR* and Δt values can be calculated from the two observed price fixings and further explanatory variables.

Since the shown graph is drawn by using the four value pairs $(0, 0)$, $(CCAAR_{i,0,1}, \Delta t_{i,0,1})$, $(CCAAR_{i,0,2}, \Delta t_{i,0,2})$, and $(CCAAR_{i,0,10}, \Delta t_{i,0,10})$, it uses a linear approximation between these values.

These four value pairs divide the function into three segments illustrated by the two grey lines vertically plotted at the 10 and 29 minute values. The two first segments (ranging from 0 to 10 minutes and from 10 to 29 minutes) show the cumulated corrected absolute abnormal return (*CCAAR*) that were calculated from the first two price fixings following the publication of the ad hoc disclosure. The third segment, in which the dashed line is shown, illustrates the abnormal price movement for the following third to tenth price fixing that has been forecasted by the system using the presented forecasting models.

Since the event study performed in Chapter 2 has proven significant abnormal stock price behavior for the first ten price fixings, the corresponding period of time is forecasted and shown on the *Min.*-axis. The chart in Figure 4.6 for example illustrates that the forecast indicates a stock price reaction, which persists for 67 minutes following the event date.

The *Start/Stop* button on the right hand bottom can be used to start or stop the observation mode, i.e. whether or not the software is continuously observing ad hoc disclosure that were recently published. Furthermore, the checkbox *Automatic Push Notifications* determines whether or not *MoFin DSS* sends mobile push messages when a relevant ad hoc disclosure has been identified.

As illustrated in the technical infrastructure section (4.3.2.1) the *MoFin* DSS server application communicates continuously with other servers. An icon on the bottom status bar indicates that currently all server communication is working. In case of a communication problem (e.g. a network failure), this icon turns red and a failure description is shown.

The second tab of the user interface, *Notification Settings*, which is shown in Figure 4.7, provides the functionality to configure the forecasting models. When the impact of the function parameter changes over time, the system operator is able to adjust these factors. The shown empirical distribution histograms illustrate typical distribution histogram characteristics. The parameters of the empirical distributions will change over time (demanding adequate parameter adjustments). Since the shown empirical distribution histograms cover a timeframe of two years, a certain amount of robustness regarding the shape of the distributions can be expected.

Figure 4.7: *MoFin DSS* Screenshot – Notification Settings

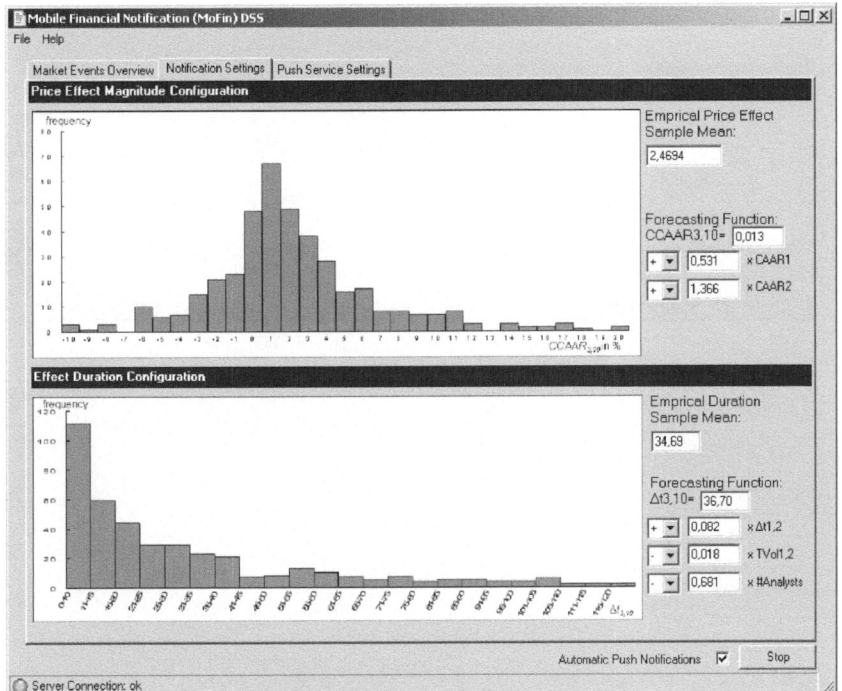

The notification settings presented in Figure 4.7 correspond with the forecasted model parameters that were determined with the linear regression models in Sections 3.3.4.3 and 0. Since *MoFin DSS* should inform about events for which price reactions lying above the average price reaction are forecasted, the system operator determines an empirical price effect sample mean being calculated from the empirical $CCAAR_{i,3,10}$ distribution. Consequently, this value implicitly defines the notification limit above which a forecasted $CCAAR_{i,3,10}$ value will trigger a mobile message to be sent.

The third tab, *Push Service Settings*, depicted in Figure 4.8 comprises all options and test functionalities of the system's capability to send mobile push messages via the GSM network. The *Gateway URL* defines the IP address and port number of the *GSM Push Gateway Server* on which the *Now SMS 2006* server software is installed and running.

Figure 4.8: *MoFin DSS* **Screenshot – Push Service Settings**

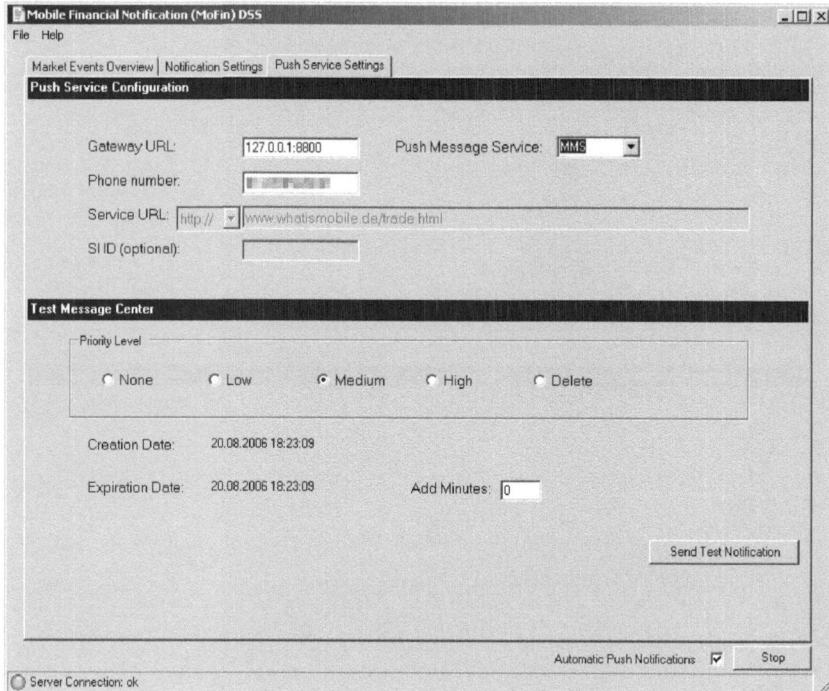

Here, the server is installed on the local host (IP address 127.0.0.1) on port 8800. When *MoFin DSS* triggers a mobile push message to be sent it will contact the *GSM Push Gateway Server* via this IP address. Alternatively, a standard domain name can also be used as uniform resource locator (URL). Furthermore, the *Phone Number* textbox defines the telephone number of a mobile device to which the mobile messages should be sent.

As already mentioned, *MoFin DDS* is able to send mobile push messages using different kinds of mobile messaging services (SMS, MMS, and WAP Push) providing different features and limitations. The messaging service to be used by the system is specified via the *Push Message Service* dropdown selection. In the configuration presented in Figure 4.8, MMS is chosen as active messaging service via which the investor will be contacted.

The following textbox *Service URL* is the URL to which WAP Push messages link, e.g. links to trading services or to websites, which provide further information, such as additional information regarding the ad hoc disclosure. Since in Figure 4.8 there is MMS selected as active push messaging service (which does not support links to external services), the text box *Ser-*

vice URL is not accessible. The same holds for the SI ID (service indication ID) textbox, which gives information regarding the provider of the service accessible via the service URL.

The lower half of the tab is the internal *Test Message Center*, which can be used for sending manually mobile push messages for experimental or test purposes. The system operator can configure manually some selected properties of the mobile message, which can be sent by clicking the corresponding button.

4.3.4.2 Client-Side View

The previous section has shown how and in which situations *MoFin DSS* sends a mobile push message to the investor. The actual financial information and decision support provided is illustrated in the following.

As presented in the previous sections, *MoFin DSS* is able to send mobile push messages via the three different kinds of mobile messaging services SMS, MMS, and WAP Push Service Indication (WAP Push SI) that provide different technological characteristics and limitations. On the basis of the work of Muntermann and Güttler (2004) a set of relevant mobile message service characteristics were presented for the focused application scenario in section 4.3.1.2. These are used in the following Table 4.2 for a brief description of the three messaging services supported by the system, which provides evidence to which extent *MoFin DSS* meets the communication requirements defined.

Table 4.2: Attributes of Mobile Message Services Supported by *MoFin DSS*[20]

	SMS	MMS	WAP Push SI Message
Textual content	Yes*	Yes	Yes
Message subject	No	Yes	No
Multimedia content	No	Yes	No
Link to external services	No	No	Yes
Message expiration date	No	No	Yes
Message priority	No	Yes	Yes
Guaranteed delivery time	No	No	No

*limited to 160 characters

From the three message services supported, SMS provides the least functionality, since it can send only textual content to a mobile device. However, a big advantage of SMS is that nearly

---

[20] Based on Muntermann and Güttler (2004).

all mobile devices currently in use support this messaging standard and most people are used to SMS since it is the most successful mobile messaging service with close to 2 trillion messages carried worldwide in 2005 (Short 2006).

Focusing on multimedia functionalities, MMS allows multimedia attachments such as graphic, animation, or sound files. Furthermore, as with standard email, a message subject field is supported. This and the message priory level can support the investor to appraise the relevance of incoming mobile messages.

Finally, WAP Push SI provides three additional features compared to SMS. From the three messaging services used, it is the only one that provides links to external services and an expiration date. Both are important to the user since the link capability can redirect her, or him, to additional information, or to transaction services, and therefore can save valuable time during the mobile investment process. The expiration date helps to identify outdated messages where (according to the system forecast) the price reaction is already completed. Like MMS, it supports message priority levels that can be used to mark the message importance.

Since all three types of message services follow a store-and-forward paradigm, they do not provide real-time messaging (European Telecommunications Standards Institute 1992; WAP Forum 2001b; WAP Forum 2001c).

In the following, the application of these three different message services that are supported by *MoFin DSS* is shown. Screenshots were taken form a Nokia 3650, which uses the Symbian OS v6.1 (Nokia Series 60 platform). This operation system was used by more than 55% market share of smartphones in 2005 (Brown et al. 2006).

The screenshots are presented in order to illustrate the different client-side functionalities and message type characteristics and their concrete impact on the information provided. The market event triggering all mobile push messages presented is an ad hoc disclosure published by *buch.de internetstores AG* on 2006-08-03, which was observed and evaluated by *MoFin DSS* as shown in Figure 4.6.

First, SMS-based information delivery is shown in Figure 4.9, which depicts three screenshots of an SMS message generated and sent by *MoFin DSS*.

Figure 4.9: SMS Message Screenshots

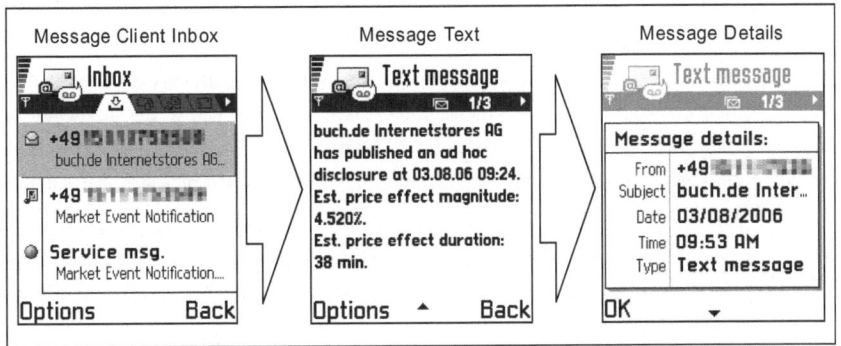

The screenshot on the left-hand side of Figure 4.9 depicts the message inbox of the used Nokia 3650 phone with the (marked) first message being the SMS message. The (intentionally) blurred telephone number belongs to the GPRS modem of the GSM Push Gateway Server via which *MoFin DSS* sends all mobile messages.

After selecting the SMS message, the second screenshot shows the message text received, in which the investor is notified about a relevant ad hoc disclosure that has been published by buch.de Internetstores AG at 2006-08-03 9:24 a.m. In order to support the investor to appraise the impact of the event on the stock of the company, the message provides information regarding the estimated price effect magnitude and its duration. These values are calculated for the remaining window of opportunity of 38 minutes. As shown in the screenshot on the right summarizing the message details, the message was sent (and received) at 9:53 a.m., i.e. 29 minutes subsequent to the event date. The forecasting models used cause this delay since they require the two first price fixings following the event date as calculation input. As illustrated in Table 4.2, SMS provides limited functionality and the shown text message of 156 characters is close to its limit of 160 characters. Furthermore, the investor needs to access a trading service such as telephone banking, or a mobile transaction service without any guidance. Nevertheless, the message provides prompt information delivery and basic decision support for the investor by presenting the relevance of the ad hoc disclosure that has been published recently.

The second message service supported by *MoFin DSS* is MMS, which provides additional functionalities, especially support for multimedia attachments. The following Figure 4.10 shows four screenshots of an MMS message that was triggered by the same ad hoc disclose that initiated the SMS message.

The comparison of the number of screenshots needed to depict the information provided by SMS (Figure 4.9 with three screenshots) and by MMS (Figure 4.10 with six screenshots) illustrates that the MMS is capable of providing much more information to the investor.

The first screenshot depicted in Figure 4.10 shows the message client inbox where the highlighted second message is the MMS message presented and explained in the following. In contrast to the SMS message, a message subject "Market Event Notification" is shown here including the sender's telephone number (blurred) and an icon, which indicates that a multimedia file is attached to the message.

Similar to the SMS message, the following two screenshots (Message Text (Page 1) and Message Text (Page 2)) show the textual content of the message including the message subject. Since MMS has no hard message length limit, the message has more characters and there is no need for abbreviating any words.

One could add the original ad hoc message text but this would be hardly readable on the small screen of the mobile phone.

Figure 4.10: MMS Message Screenshots

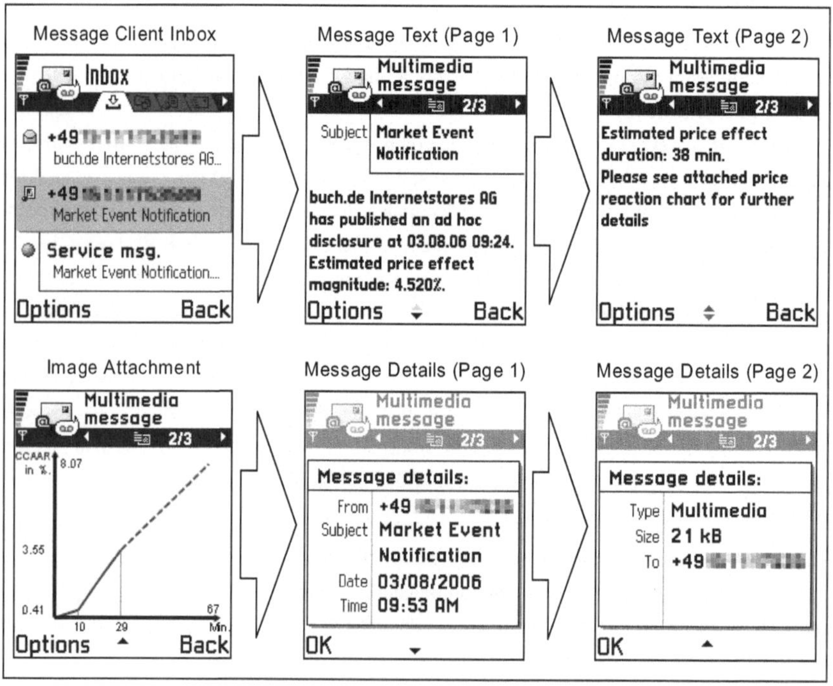

The most apparent difference is the image attachment shown in the first screenshot of the second row. This chart illustrates the price reaction process following the publication date of the ad hoc disclosure. Its interpretations correspond to those of the price reaction chart presented in the previous Section 4.3.4.1. The last two screenshots provide details regarding the message characteristics such as the date of receipt or the size of the attached image in kilobytes.

The third message service supported by *MoFin DSS* and presented here is WAP Push SI. This is a typical message service used for application-to-user communication and can usually not be composed and sent with the message clients installed on standard mobile phones.

Figure 4.11: WAP Push Message Screenshots

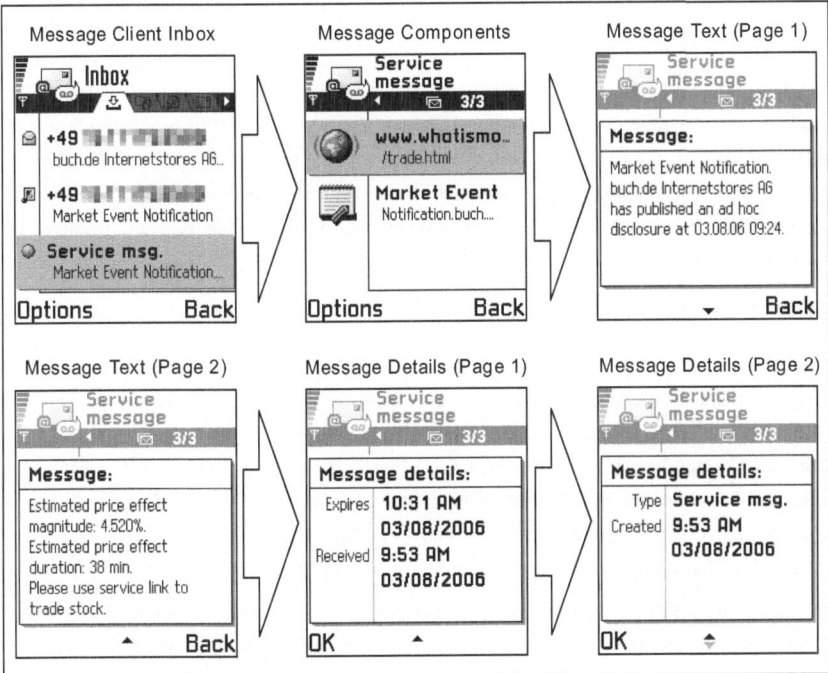

The first screenshot depicted on Figure 4.11 shows that the message client identifies the incoming (and highlighted) message as service message. By selecting the message, the user has access to the two message components.

One component is a link that provides access to an external service, which can be accessed via the internet. This service link can provide direct access to an external information or transaction service that provides further information and decision support, or which can be used to sell or buy the affected stock[21]. It therefore provides navigation guidance to the investor, which can be beneficial since valuable amount of time can be saved during the mobile investment process.

The second message component is a textual message part. In the same way as the SMS and MMS messages presented before, this text provides information regarding an ad hoc disclosure published and provides decision support to interpret the effects following the recent event. Additionally, the message text refers to the service link mentioned before.

Compared to the previous two message services, WAP SI provides details regarding message timing, which is illustrated in the two last screenshots (Message Details (Page 1)) and Message Details (Page 2)). This information can be utilized by both the investor and the mobile device. Most important, there is an expiration date, which is calculated using the publication date and estimated period of time for which abnormal price behavior can be expected. Depending on the mobile phone used (e.g. when using the Nokia 3650 from which all screenshots were taken), the device will automatically delete the message form the message client inbox when it has not been accessed by the user before the expiration date has passed. This prevents users from being bothered by outdated messaged because only relevant messages are presented to the user.

4.3.5   Limitations of the IT Artifact

The designed IT artifact addresses the functional requirements determined in Section 4.3.1 with a system infrastructure that integrates a set of different data sources and which provides access to mobile messaging services. The application logic uses the empirical results presented in Chapter 2 regarding the stock price adjustment processes following the publication of ad hoc disclosures on the German capital market. Furthermore, these findings are incorporated into a decision support concept developed in Chapter 3 that is implemented as a prototypical IT artifact comprising a hardware infrastructure and software components.

The artifact design and the prototypical implementation exhibit a set of limitations that will be considered in this section. This limitation analysis is divided into in three parts. First, conceptual limitations of the artifact design are addressed in Section 4.3.5.1. Then, Section 4.3.5.2 illustrates limitations of the deployed infrastructure design and the prototypical implementation.

Since incorrect processing or provisioning of financial information can result in financial losses, the application domain has some relevance to security that have not been addressed by

---

[21] The external service is not part of the implemented IT artifact since it should link to existing mobile brokerage information or transaction services provided by online banks or brokers.

the artifact design so far. Therefore, Section 4.3.5.3 provides a brief overview of security concerns involved that must be addressed by an operative system offered to customers.

4.3.5.1 Conceptual Limitations

Most of the conceptual limitations of the artifact design stem from the empirical analysis of the stock price adjustment process. On the one hand, the empirical results of the event study performed in Chapter 2 prove the existence of abnormal market behavior that could be exploited by customers. These findings provide a robust foundation for the addressed application domain of mobile financial information and decision support systems. On the other hand, this analysis focuses on the German capital market and on a specific event type. There is much evidence that similar price adjustment processes can be observed on other international stock exchanges such as the New York Stock Exchange (Woodruff and Senchak 1988). Nevertheless, corresponding intraday event study analyses are required when trying to adopt the artifact design to other stock markets than the German one. The same restriction holds for the type of event. The empirical analyses are based on the observation of ad hoc disclosures pursuant to Article 15 of the Securities Trading Act (WpHG) that were published by the Deutsche Gesellschaft für Ad-hoc-Publizität (DGAP). Article 15 obliges companies, which are listed for trading on German stock exchanges, to disclose any information, which could significantly affect the stock price of the company. There exist similar regulations in other countries such as Switzerland (Article 72 of the Swiss Stock Exchange's Listing Guidelines/Kotierungsreglement), Austria (Article 82 Stock Exchange Act/Börsegesetz), and the USA (Section 13 Securities Exchange Act of 1934), and similar price reactions can be expected for such company disclosures (e.g. Patell and Wolfson 1984). However, corresponding intraday event study analyses are required in order to adapt the artifact design to support other event types than the ad hoc disclosures pursuant to Article 15 of the Securities Trading Act (WpHG).

Another conceptual limitation of the artifact is the use of static forecasting models that were presented in Chapter 3. The prototypical implementation is flexible regarding new forecasting functions insofar as they can easily be adjusted by the system operator. However, the function parameters are determined manually with the linear regressions performed. A functionality of self-adjusting forecasting function could increase the system's flexibility regarding functional changes. Furthermore, iterative learning and adaptation functionality could be used to determine forecasting functions for other event types and other stock markets. Such functionalities are usually addressed with artificial intelligence (AI) approaches that involve iterative learning (Beale and Jackson 1990; Bishop 2004; van Eyden 1996). Furthermore, other non-linear forecasting models could provide more accurate price effect forecasts. Even though the artificial neural network approach presented by Muntermann (2005) does not provide evidence for a better forecasting accuracy compared to the linear forecasting models used here, this research field is far from settled. More accurate forecasting models could also be used for redesigning the notification process, which currently supports only binary relevance evaluations, i.e. the system differentiates between relevant and irrelevant market events only. Here, a more detailed distinction of evaluation categories is imaginable.

4.3.5.2 Functional Limitations of the Implementation

In the current version, *MoFin DSS* does not provide multi-user support, because one notification setting is configurable only. Furthermore, all incoming ad hoc disclosures are evaluated and might trigger a mobile notification message because no user specific filter rules, as defined, for example, by an individual portfolio setting, are supported. This limitation is of lower relevance because such a functionality would reduce only the number of events to be evaluated, and mobile messages to be sent, respectively.

Furthermore, there is no support for user profiles which enable users to define personal configurations. For example, the communication channel is defined on the server side and currently there is no support for user-defined channel selection. Moreover, there is only support for one mobile phone number to which all mobile messages are sent. It could also be feasible for the users to provide several phone numbers for different mobile message services, or for different periods of time, to enhance usability.

The current implementation supports the three standard mobile message services SMS, MMS, and WAP Push SI only. Since one goal of using mobile communication channels is to realize near-ubiquitous reachability, one could think of additional (non-mobile) communication channels such as instant messaging (IM) or classic email in order to approach this goal. However, these communication channels go beyond the scope of this work but they could be supported by a productive system.

This brief list of limitations of the artifact implementation illustrates its prototypical character. As for productive information systems, this description of functional limitations can address some of the most important aspects only. This discussion is not meant to be exhaustive since there is always room for improving an information system in different aspects, such as additional functionalities or human computer interaction (HCI) issues.

4.3.5.3 Security Constraints

The current artifact design does not take into consideration any security issues that would be relevant for a financial service that is offered to customers. Muntermann et al. (2005) explored security requirements of mobile banking services and proposed a security concept that is based on mobile electronic signatures.

The security constraints presented in the following concentrate on the proposed IT artifact design of *MoFin DSS* and therefore do not take any security requirements of mobile transaction services into account which are, for example, addressed by Muntermann et al. (2005).

From a technical perspective, four different security threats and protection goals can be identified for IT systems (Rannenberg et al. 1999; Rannenberg 2000b). Based on Rannenberg et al. (1999), these general protection goals and the corresponding threats are summarized in the following in order to evaluate their relevance for the proposed mobile notification and decision support system. This security evaluation focuses on the mobile communication channels used by *MoFin DSS* since the general infrastructure setup corresponds to those of classic client/server environments whose security properties have been for several years a subject matter in computer science and information systems research literature (e.g. Bishop 2004; Boockholdt 1989; Gollmann 2005).

- Confidentiality

  This protection goal describes the protection against unauthorized acquisition of information, i.e. that information becomes known to the wrong persons.

  In the presented scenario, confidentiality plays a minor role since little personal information is sent by *MoFin DSS* to the mobile device of the investor. When other people obtain access to the mobile message sent, they would gather information they could have received directly from the system. However, the more personal the sent information is, the higher the demand for confidentiality will be.

- Integrity

  A loss of integrity results from unauthorized modification of information, i.e. the information has been changed unintentionally or on purpose. Corresponding security mechanisms protect stored or transferred data from unnoticed modification.

  Potential attackers could alter the content of the mobile message that is sent to the investor. This may result in false investment decisions, i.e. in trading losses, for example, when the mobile message would misleadingly report that there is plenty of time available due to a long price effect duration supposedly calculated by the system. Therefore, integrity is of major relevance when designing a financial notification and decision support system that sends mobile messages to the users' mobile devices. Unfortunately, all message services used (SMS, MMS, and WAP Push) do not provide any protection of integrity. To ensure integrity of SMS messages, Muntermann et al. (2005) propose a solution that works with mobile signatures. Since this functionality needs to be supported by the Subscriber Identity Module (SIM) used, the service operator (e.g. the online bank or broker) must cooperate with the network operator and a corresponding SIM card needs to be provided.

- Availability

  A loss of availability can be caused by unauthorized, but noticed, influence on the system's functionality. The loss of availability can have significant impact because information or data required cannot or be accessed anymore. Furthermore, a loss of availability may result in delayed or partial information provisioning. Since current system infrastructures are based on subsystems such as hard- and software components and networks, the loss of availability can have manifold reasons. Focusing on the availability of the GSM network, redundant connectivity is realized in many regions due to several network operators. The loss of GSM connectivity is usually unintended and is due to shielded environments, such as underground garages, trains or during a flight. However, potential attacker can use so-called GSM jammers that disturb the connectivity by sending interfering signals (Ståhlberg 2000).

Availability is a highly relevant protection goal for the IT artifact proposed. Critical market events that trigger a mobile message, but then cannot be sent to the mobile devices of investors, may result in high trading losses. Investors will miss the opportunity to sell or buy any stocks subsequent to a market event for which highly significant price effects were forecasted by the decision support system.

Two of the mobile messaging services used by the system, SMS and WAP Push, do not provide any acknowledgements for delivered messages, i.e. availability cannot be guaranteed by the system design. One fundamental difference of MMS is that it supports delivery and read reporting to the sender. Once the multimedia message is delivered successfully, the sending device receives a corresponding message from the MMS Proxy Relay (Open Mobile Alliance 2004). When using a mobile phone, this delivery confirmation will also be displayed on the screen. Read reports are sent back by the recipient's message client when the user accesses the multimedia message received (Open Mobile Alliance 2004).

These additional functionalities provided by MMS can be useful since outstanding reports could initiate notifications sent via an alternative communication channel. Therefore, this message service provides enhanced security at higher costs compared to SMS and WAP Push[22].

- Accountability

   The loss of accountability is the consequence of unauthorized noncommitment, i.e. a responsible person or system cannot be identified definitely. Accountability is a relevant protection goal especially in business relations where all parties involved and all data, information and commitments that were electronically exchanged need to be identified without any doubt.

   The messaging services used do not provide any protection of authenticity and therefore potential attackers could pretend to act as *MoFin DSS* sending false notifications to the users. Accountability could also be achieved by the approach working with mobile signatures

---

[22] This cost ratio between MMS and SMS/WAP Push messages changes when the message needs to be split into several SMS messages (or binary SMS messages when sending a WAP Push message) since one MMS message can contain much more kilobytes of message content.

proposed by Muntermann et al. (2005) but this would demand particular SIM cards that provide signature functionality.

This analysis of protection goals shows that the proposed IT artifact design contains several security challenges, especially with focus on the communication channel used, i.e. the mobile message services via which the users receives decision support.

In particular, the integrity, availability, and accountability of the mobile messages received are required but can hardly be guaranteed. Muntermann et al. (2005) propose a solution that reaches the security goals of confidentiality, integrity, and accountability using mobile electronic signatures that need to be stored on the customer's SIM. Such SIM cards already exist, but they have not entered the market yet. However, the security problems identified are far from settled today demanding further research.

4.4 Summary of IT the Artifact Design

MoFin DSS addresses the different requirements that were developed in Section 4.3.1, which summarized functional requirements on the server side and the requirements for the mobile communication channels used for sending the information to the user. These requirements guided the design, setup, and implementation of infrastructure and server software that were presented in the following Sections 4.3.2 and 4.3.3. The IT artifact *MoFin DSS,* which comprises hardware infrastructure and server application software, is the result of this development process. It provides the functionalities determined and supports different mobile push message services that serve as mobile communication channels in order to achieve near-ubiquitous reachability and service accessibility for private investors.

Like all IT artifacts and prototypical implementations, *MoFin DSS* has some conceptual and functional limitations that were addressed in Section 4.3.5. Since the application domain of financial services has extensive requirements regarding security, this was also addressed in the limitations summary.

The designed IT artifact demonstrates the feasibility of the DSS concept and illustrates that the forecasting models developed in the previous chapter can be used in order to design a working system that provides decision support for private investors. Demonstrating feasibility is one major purpose of design science research since it supports researcher to understand the addressed problem domain. This includes suitable solutions to the problem and therefore extends the existing knowledge base (Nunamaker et al. 1991).

An evaluation of the designed IT artifact is a crucial part of the design science process. The following Chapter 5 introduces and applies a novel evaluation methodology in order to address this evaluation.

5   Evaluation of the IT Artifact

One central aspect of design science is the utility provided by the IT artifact designed. A utility evaluation of the artifact design is based on the development of appropriate evaluation criteria, and an assessment of the artifact against those criteria (March and Smith 1995). Therefore, appropriate metrics and methodologies need to be identified or developed. New evaluation criteria and evaluation methodologies are major research contributions to design science research since they extent the existing knowledge base of information systems research (Hevner et al. 2004).

Therefore, Section 5.1 provides an introduction to three *business value of IT* evaluation approaches, which are commonly applied in IS research (e.g. Brynjolfsson and Hitt 2003; Chircu and Kauffman 2000; Davern and Kauffman 2000; Hitt and Brynjolfsson 1996). Furthermore, the underlying theoretical basis for each of these approaches will be presented. Section 5.1.1 deals with productivity evaluations that can be applied for assessing how investments in information technology can impact on the firm's productivity. The second evaluation approach (Section 5.1.2) addresses the effect on a firm's profitability, i.e. it uses metrics for evaluating the impact on a firm's profits. Section 5.1.3 shows how an evaluation of the value provided to consumers can be a suitable approach for assessing the IT business value. Each of the three evaluation approaches presented address different aspects of business value, all featuring advantages and limitations. By comparing and considering these characteristics, a consumers' value evaluation approach is found to be most suitable for an *ex ante* evaluation of the business value provided by the IT artifact. Then, Section 5.1.4 provides in introduction to statistical hypothesis testing for two sample parameters. This lays the methodological basis for comparing different evaluation results.

Section 5.2 defines criteria used for the evaluation of the IT artifact *MoFin DSS* that has been designed in the previous Chapter 4. To be able to assess these, Section 5.2.1 describes its major contributions to consumers' value, which comprise the reduction of the investors' reaction time to relevant market events and the decision support provided. In order to evaluate these two contributions, two different metrics *realizable return* (Section 5.2.2), and *mean realizable yield* (Section 5.2.3), are introduced and defined in the following. The first metric is used for statistically corroborating the hypotheses that the artifact's two contributions significantly contribute to customers' benefits. The second metric measures the trading profits which can be realized by investors, and incorporates further factors such as trading costs, reaction time and trading volumes.

The following Section 5.3 introduces a novel simulation-based customers' value evaluation methodology. An earlier version of this approach has been presented by Muntermann and Janssen (2005), which lays the methodic basis for this chapter. The methodology is applied in order to assess the benefits of the reduction of investors' reaction time (Section 5.3.1) and the decision support (Section 5.3.2) provided by the IT artifact.

Using the evaluation metrics defined, as well as historical event observations and intraday stock price series, the simulations prove the statistical significance of the benefits provided. Furthermore, the simulation results illustrate the value provided to those investors supported by the *MoFin DSS* IT artifact. It is shown how the simulation-based evaluation methodology can be applied to different scenarios, and how the simulation results can support managerial investment decisions.

Finally, Section 5.4 summarizes the evaluation results and illustrates the relevance for, and contributions to, researchers and practice.

5.1   Theoretical Foundation and Statistical Foundations

Evaluating the impact of IT investments on a company's business success is an important consideration for researchers and managers. Therefore, the evaluation and measurement of the *business value of IT* has been addressed by the academic and the business community for several years with both qualitative and quantitative analysis approaches.

In recent years, several studies addressed the question how to measure this business value provided by investments in information technology. Whereas some of these studies confirm the value provided by IT investments, others such as Morrison and Berndt (1990), Loveman (1994) or Barua et al. (1995) come to contradictory results when analyzing the correlation between spending on information technology and the increase of business productivity. Brynjolfsson and Hitt (1996a) address this 'productivity paradox' of IT investments and analyze the impact of data sets used and evaluation methods chosen. Their results provide evidence that this paradox arises from the used evaluation methodologies and from aggregate statistics that cloud the real impact on business value.

Business value can be measured in several different dimensions that can be assessed by using different evaluation criteria. From existing IS literature, three major, related but separate, evaluation approaches can be identified, which address different questions whether or not IT investments provide any value (Hitt and Brynjolfsson 1996):

1. Do investments in IT increase productivity?

2. Do investments in IT improve business profitability?

3. Do investments in IT create value for consumers?

Furthermore, the aggregation level at which the evaluation is performed is an important issue when analyzing the IT business value. A meta-analysis performed by Chan (2000), reviewing articles on IT value published in leading IS journals during the period between 1993 and 1998, empirically derives six different aggregation levels from the papers analyzed (individual, group, organizational, industry, national and international level). The results show that most of the studies were performed on an organizational level and none of the articles analyzed addresses the question whether investments in IT create value for customers at an individual level on a quantitative basis (Chan 2000). Thus, metrics and methodologies addressing the evaluation of new products and services on an individual level that quantify the benefits or willingness to pay from customers' surplus, are not well developed.

Davern and Kauffman (2000) point out that there is a big difference between analyzing the *realized* and the *potential* value of IT investments. When IT budgets have been invested in the past, it is possible to perform an *ex post* analysis of the business value effect. In contrast, when assessing the business value of new, possibly competing innovations (such as *MoFin DSS*) or emerging technologies, an *ex ante* evaluation of the potential value is required. In this case, there is limited historical data available, which significantly limits the choice of evaluation methodologies available.

Depending on the research question addressed, aggregation-level chosen, and whether an *ex ante* or *ex post* evaluation is required, different IT business value analysis methods can be applied using different theoretical foundations. Based on Hitt and Brynjolfsson (1996), three classic evaluation frameworks frequently used in IS literature are presented in the following Sections 5.1.1, 5.1.2, and 5.1.3. This presentation comprises assumptions involved and each frameworks' appropriateness for evaluating the business value provided by an investment in the implementation of the IT artifact *MoFin DSS*.

Finally, Section 5.1.4 introduces statistical methods that can be used for statistical hypothesis testing of two samples. In this chapter, they are applied for comparing the results of the IT business value simulations and to statistically prove relative advantages provided.

5.1.1 Productivity Evaluations

The question of how IT investments can contribute to more production output and/or less production input is generally addressed with some kind of production function, which is derived from *production theory*. A production function f describes the dependency of the production output on the change of one or several input factors (Mankiw 2004). Generally, a production function of the form $f = \alpha e^{\lambda t} I_1^{\beta_1} I_2^{\beta_2}$ is used, where I_1 and I_2 represent the input factors (e.g. labor and IT investments) and β_j the elasticity of the output with respect to small changes in input factor j (Cobb and Douglas 1928).

IT business value evaluation approaches that refer to production theory and the production function approach are based on several assumptions that raise some drawbacks: First, a production function form needs to be assumed. This implicates further assumptions, e.g. constant returns to scale when choosing the Cobb-Douglas production function (Cobb and Douglas 1928). Second, function parameters have to be econometrically estimated (Fandel 1991), and third, the IT investments have to be correlated with some kind of measurable production or financial output.

Since productivity-related evaluation approaches focus on increased physical or monetary output, the reduction of costs or input factors, they are adequate evaluations for evaluating IT investments in the manufacturing sector. However, this kind of approach is usually inadequate for the service or finance sector where investments should provide enhanced customer service or better and timelier investment decisions, i.e. no direct correlation with output is measurable. Furthermore, it is not possible to evaluate other advantages like increased quality, variety, convenience, and timeliness, all being relevant business success factors.

Brynjolfsson (1993) argues that the traditional productivity related approach cannot be applied when analyzing the benefits of IT investments in new technologies or information systems since their potential impact might not be covered by a production function. Nevertheless, this output and productivity oriented approach can be suitable if input factors and output can be measured reliably, and the marginal contribution of each input factor to the output can be estimated and approximated by the production function form. For example on a higher aggregation level, such as unit-, firm- or branch-level, productivity function approaches can also be applied for assessing the impact of IT investments on non-production related output such as the firm's total revenue (Lichtenberg 1995). Consequently, production theory and production functions were applied by several researchers in the 1990s in order to assess the impact of IT investments (e.g. Brynjolfsson and Hitt 1993; Lichtenberg 1995; Loveman 1994; Morrison and Berndt 1991).

In an analysis performed by Brynjolfsson (1993), a Cobb-Douglas production function is applied on firm-level in order to econometrically estimate the output elasticity of the different input factors including computer capital and labor expenses. The results provide evidence that these two input factors have a significant higher impact on the output compared to other input factors since higher elasticity was econometrically estimated for these two factors.

Loveman (1994) analyzes the impact of several factors, including IT capital on physical output and revenues on a business unit level using a Cobb-Douglas production function. Remarkably, the author detects negative output elasticity for the IT capital factor and consequently, the results do not provide evidence for positive rate of return of IT investments in general.

Lichtenberg (1995) uses a log-linear production function approach in order to estimate the impact of capital invested in information systems, and IS employee expenses, on the firms' revenue, and detects a higher elasticity for the IS capital spent.

In an US-wide analysis, Morrison and Berndt (1991) use a cost function and a Leontief production function in order to assess cost-benefit ratios in the manufacturing industry. Their results indicate that the marginal benefits provided by IT investments are smaller than the marginal costs involved.

Consequently, production theory and production functions have successfully been applied to higher aggregation levels down to firm level in order to assess the productivity growth gained from IT investments. The evaluation framework is, however, hardly applicable for assessing the business value provided by specific IT investments such as the presented IT artifact design, or to compare different investments on product level. Moreover, it is remarkable that the different analyses performed do not provide a consistent view on how IT investments contribute to the productivity on firm-level.

Consequently, a productivity evaluation approach can hardly be applied for an *ex ante* evaluation of the business value provided by an investment in the *MoFin DSS* IT artifact since the shape of a corresponding production function, including its function parameters and a definition of appropriate input and output factors, is not available.

5.1.2   Business Profitability Evaluations

A second theoretical foundation for IT business value evaluation can be derived from microeconomics and the *theory of competitive strategy*, which says that companies are not able to capture the value of specific investments over time since all firms will invest the optimal amount in equilibrium (Porter 1980). The approach should provide insights into potential competitive advantage gained from IT investments such as increased profits or stock price evaluations.

Following the theory of competitive strategy, firms are not able to realize higher profitability in a competitive market, i.e. one without any barriers to entry. When new valuable technologies are available, market competition will attract other companies to use the same technologies, and therefore no competitive advantage can be realized in the long run. The key assumption is that companies are not able to capture the value of IT investments over time since all firms will invest the optimal amount of IT spending in equilibrium (Porter 1980). Clemons (1991) argues that investments in IT are required to retain competitiveness and that firms are unlikely to gain long-term profitability advantage since successful approaches will be copied by competitors.

On the other hand, entry barriers such as patents, capital intensive IT systems, and switching costs can lead to increased profitability when other companies are either not able to adopt the new technology, or there exists a market barrier that is too high for other companies to enter the market (Philip et al. 1995). Chen and Hitt (2002) analyze switching costs on the online brokerage market, which is the relevant market segment for the proposed IT artifact *MoFin DSS*. Their results provide evidence that there exist switching costs for customers, which vary across different online brokers and which depend on their investments in marketing programs.

In order to measure business profitability, general (e.g. growth in profits, market capitalization, etc.) or industry-specific (e.g. inventory turnover, mean time before failure, etc.) performance metrics are used for evaluating the correlation between IT spending and the profitability metric determined. Furthermore, the correlation to the profitability metric can be calculated for other factors (e.g. ratio of non-IT capital, marketing purchases, R&D purchases, etc.)

in order to compare different investments and their impact on business profitability (Barua et al. 1995; Sircar et al. 2000).

There are several studies analyzing the impact of IT investments on growth of business profitability. Whereas most studies performed in the 1980s and 1990s found little significant (e.g. Dos Santos et al. 1993; Hitt and Brynjolfsson 1996; Loveman 1994; Salerno 1985) or even negative (e.g. Franke 1987) correlation between IT investments and business profitability, more recent studies dispelled this paradox (Brynjolfsson and Hitt 2003; Lee 2001; Sircar et al. 2000). Evidence was found that the contradictory findings reported in earlier literature result from diverse measurement problems caused by cross-sectional analyses that fail to capture lag-effects (Kohli and Devaraj 2003; Lee 2001).

Business profitability evaluations can be a suitable approach for assessing the impact of IT budgets on business performance and has been applied successfully on a firm-, branch-, or industry-level in the past. However, it is inadequate for *ex ante* evaluations on product level, which are necessary for an evaluation of an investment in an IT product that currently exists as an IT artifact design only.

5.1.3   Consumers' Surplus Evaluations

A third evaluation approach for estimating IT business value considers the extent to which IT investments provide benefits to consumers. Evaluating the consumers' surplus is based on the idea that this criterion is a good proxy for the real value created. Brynjolfsson and Hitt (1996) found that companies that focus IT investments on customer service improvement are significantly more productive than their competitors.

Corresponding evaluation approaches are mostly based on the microeconomic *theory of the consumer* and the consumer demand curve (Bresnahan 1986; Brynjolfsson 1996; Brynjolfsson et al. 2003). Therefore, the parameters of, and the area under, the consumers' demand curve have to be estimated. This area can be appraised for different aggregation levels using econometric methods or index-number techniques (Bresnahan 1986). Given the shape of the demand curve and the product price, it is possible to calculate the consumers' surplus.

Evaluating the benefits of IT investments by measuring consumers' surplus overcomes several problems involved with the production function and the business profitability approach (Brynjolfsson 1996). The latter tend to underestimate the real value of IT investments since they do not cover the total benefits. The consumers' surplus, however, measures the customers' value for the considered product and can therefore be applied to new products, where the elasticity of productivity function parameters or the contribution of IT to the performance metric can hardly be econometrically estimated. Consequently, the approach is adequate for supporting managerial decisions because investments into new IT products and services can be evaluated. Nevertheless, the approach requires some assumptions. The shape of the demand curve needs to be assumed or estimated for the evaluated product, which is problematic in case of an emergent technology for which no empirical data is yet available. Furthermore, the aggregated demand curve is based on the assumption that consumers choose the most beneficial amount of product units given the product price and the consumers' income. This, however, can not be determined for information products or services where the splitting into product units is not possible.

Typically, a standard log-linear demand function of the form $d(p,y) = Ap^{\alpha}y^{\beta}$ is used, where p is the price of the product, y is the income and α, β are the elasticity of the parameters (Brynjolfsson et al. 2003).

Subramanyam and Krishnan (2001) address this problem when assessing business value in the context of investments into customer call centers. They choose the time in which a given customers' problem is solved as proxy for the consumers' value, i.e. the business value of the IT investment. Their approach works with this proxy in order to evaluate potential productivity gains but it is not appropriate for evaluating the provided customers' benefits resulting from lower expenditure of time.

Assessing IT business value evaluation with the value provided to customers' appears to be an approach flexible enough for valuations on product level. However, suitable metrics and evaluation methods need to be developed that allow a quantitative evaluation on the product-level. This problem is addressed in Sections 5.2 and 5.3.

5.1.4 Statistical Hypothesis Testing for Two Sample Parameters

Before introducing novel evaluation metrics and methodologies, this section provides an introduction to statistical hypothesis testing for two sample parameters. This lays the methodological basis for statistical analyses of the evaluation results presented in the remainder of this chapter.

The statistical tests procedures presented in the second chapter addressed the question whether a sample parameter such as the mean or median lies significantly above a certain value. In order to assess different evaluation results, it is necessary to compare two sample parameters.

5.1.4.1 Paired Differences t-Test

A paired sample test is appropriate when each data from the first sample is related to the corresponding data value from the second sample (Groebner et al. 2001). This can, for example, be the case when two identical sample observations (with the same sample size) were made under different conditions or at different time intervals. Then, the samples are not independent and need to be treated as paired samples. After formulating a null hypothesis H_0 (e.g. that the sample means are equal) and the alternative hypothesis H_A (e.g. that the sample means are unequal), the paired difference pd need to be calculated for all values of the two samples:

$$pd = x_1 - x_2$$

> where
>
> pd = paired difference
>
> x_s = values from sample s

Equation 5.1: Paired Difference

After calculating the paired difference sample, the paired differences t-test statistic is given as (Groebner et al. 2001):

$$t = \frac{\overline{pd} - \mu_0^{pd}}{s_{pd}/\sqrt{I}}$$

> with
>
> df = $I-1$
>
> where
>
> $\overline{pd}$ = mean of paired difference sample
>
> μ_0^{pd} = hypothesized paired difference
>
> s_{pd} = standard deviation of paired difference sample
>
> I = number of paired differences (sample size)
>
> df = degrees of freedom

Equation 5.2: Paired Differences t-Test Statistic

Like for the Student t-test for one sample, critical values can be obtained from the Student t-distribution for a specified level of significance α and the degrees of freedom df. The null hypothesis H_0 can be rejected when the calculated t-value lies outside these critical values.

5.1.4.2 Unequal-Variances t-Test

The unequal-variance t-test is applied when the two samples are not dependent and the standard deviation is not equal. The test is also robust with sample sizes smaller than 30. It provides a test statistic for comparing the means of two independent samples for which the standard deviation in unknown. A null hypothesis H_0 (e.g. that the two sample means are equal) and an alternative hypothesis H_A (e.g. that the two sample means are not equal) need to be formulated and the corresponding test statistic is defined as (Weiers 2005):

$$t = \frac{(\bar{x}_1 - \bar{x}_2) - \mu_0^{sm}}{\sqrt{\dfrac{s_1^2}{I_1} + \dfrac{s_2^2}{I_2}}}$$

with

$$df = \frac{\left[\left(s_1^2 / I_1\right) + \left(s_2^2 / I_2\right)\right]^2}{\dfrac{\left(s_1^2 / I_1\right)^2}{I_1 - 1} + \dfrac{\left(s_2^2 / I_2\right)^2}{I_2 - 1}}$$

where

$\bar{x}_s$	=	mean of sample s
μ_0^{sm}	=	hypothesized difference between sample means
s_s^2	=	variance of sample s
I_s	=	size of sample s
df	=	degrees of freedom

Equation 5.3: Unequal-Variances *t*-Test Statistic

After defining a level of significance α, the null hypothesis H_0 can be rejected when the calculated *t*-value lies outside the critical values obtained from the *t*-distribution.

5.2 Definition of the Artifact Evaluation Criteria

The question of whether and to which extent investments in emerging products and services create value at low aggregation levels is far from settled and metrics and methodologies addressing an *ex ante* evaluation quantitatively are not well developed yet (Muntermann and Janssen 2005).

The presentation and analysis of the different IT business value evaluation approaches has shown that customer benefit assessments (being based on the consumers' value provided) have several advantages, especially for evaluations on a process- or product-level when suitable metrics for the consumers' value can be defined (Subramanyam and Krishnan 2001). Therefore, the following valuation approach aims at assessing the value that is provided by the *MoFin DDS* IT artifact to consumers, i.e. to potential private investors, which are supported by a corresponding information system.

5.2.1 Major Contributions of the IT Artifact to Consumers' Value

In order to evaluate quantitatively the benefits provided, it is required to identify in which ways *MoFin DSS* contributes to consumers' value. Based on the findings presented in Chapters 2 and 3, the evaluation of the IT artifact should address two contributions. It is hypothesized that *MoFin DSS* improves the following aspects of the investment decisions of private investors: (1) prompt information supply resulting in timelier investment decisions (reduction of reaction time) and (2) identifying those market events, which will have significant impact on the customer's portfolio value or open up a window of opportunity (decision support). Therefore, two research hypotheses are formulated addressing these artifact contributions:

Research hypothesis Va: *Reduction of the investors' reaction time leads to transactions that are more profitable on average.*

Research hypothesis Vb: *Investors supported by the IT artifact can realize transactions that are more profitable on average.*

The research hypotheses do not address the second decision support model developed, which addresses the duration of the possible price effects, since r*esearch hypothesis Va* states, as will be statistically tested in the following, that a shorter reaction time leads to higher trading profits on average. Therefore, forecasted price effect durations indicate priorities of events and call attention to these market events but play a secondary role when evaluating how *MoFin DSS* can contribute to transactions that are more profitable.

Chapter 2 and 3 have provided strong evidence that the capital market reflects new information provided by an ad hoc disclosure published within a short period of time and that the significance of abnormal price behavior decreases with the time elapsed. Since event studies address the level of price abnormality only, these results provide no insights into benefits for customers' that are interested in investment returns. The same holds for the decision support model presented in the previous chapter including its forecasting evaluation. The two major contributions were formulated as research hypotheses that are addressed in the following sections with statistical hypothesis testing procedures that were introduced in Section 5.1.4. Figure 5.1 summarizes how the IT artifact's contributions to customers' benefits are categorized and how each contribution is addressed by a corresponding research hypothesis.

Figure 5.1: Major Contributions of *MoFin DSS* to Customers' benefits

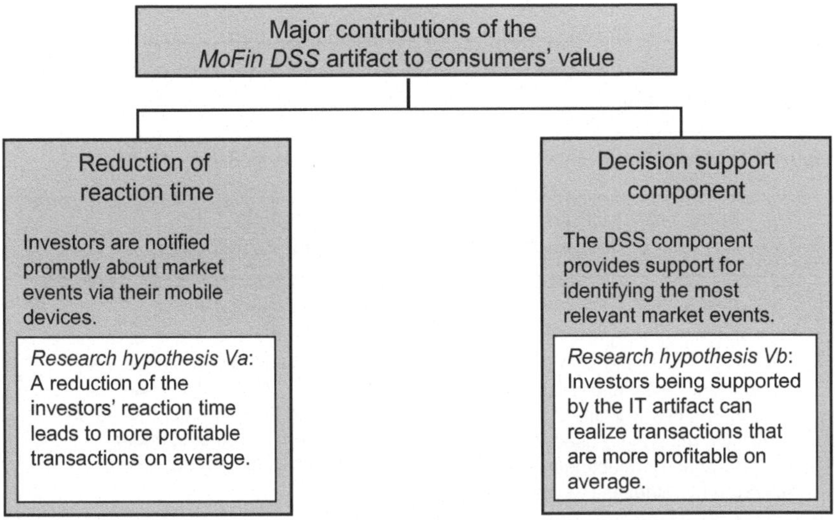

Major contributions of the *MoFin DSS* artifact to consumers' value

Reduction of reaction time	Decision support component
Investors are notified promptly about market events via their mobile devices.	The DSS component provides support for identifying the most relevant market events.
Research hypothesis Va: A reduction of the investors' reaction time leads to more profitable transactions on average.	*Research hypothesis Vb*: Investors being supported by the IT artifact can realize transactions that are more profitable on average.

First, the impact of a reduction of the investors' reaction time should be covered, and second, the impact of decision support provided by *MoFin DSS* should be addressed by the evaluation approach. Compared to the evaluation approach presented by Muntermann and Janssen (2005) who concentrate on the reduction of reaction time only, this IT business value assessment comprises two different dimensions.

A metric called *realizable return*, which is presented in the following Section 5.2.2, covers the impact of different reaction delays on returns that can potentially be realized by the investor. Furthermore, this metric is used for evaluating the value provided by the decision support with which investors are enabled to focus on those market events that were identified as most relevant by the system. Therefore, the metric can be used for calculating and statistically prove the benefits provided by *MoFin DSS*, i.e. corroborating or rejecting the two research hypotheses *Va* and *Vb* by simulating and statistically evaluating the positive impact of the two major contributions of *MoFin DSS* on consumers' value.

A second evaluation metric *realizable yields*, that is introduced in Section 5.2.3 supports managerial decision-making and can be used for simulation-based customer value evaluations taking into account company specific settings such as observed trading volumes and trading fees. Therefore, it is suitable for individual value analyses that include a company's present state of business or future scenarios.

These two metrics are used Section 5.3 for the evaluation of the two major contributions of *MoFin DSS* to consumers' value, as illustrated in the following Figure 5.2.

According to Davern and Kauffman (2000) both approaches address the *potential* value provided by the IT artifact and therefore allow an *ex ante* evaluation of the IT investment. Since the proposed *MoFin DSS* system design is not in operation yet, the evaluation of the potential (or realizable) value of the IT investment can be valuable for the evaluation of a corresponding product implementation.

Figure 5.2: Metrics for Evaluating the Consumers' Value Provided by *MoFin DSS*

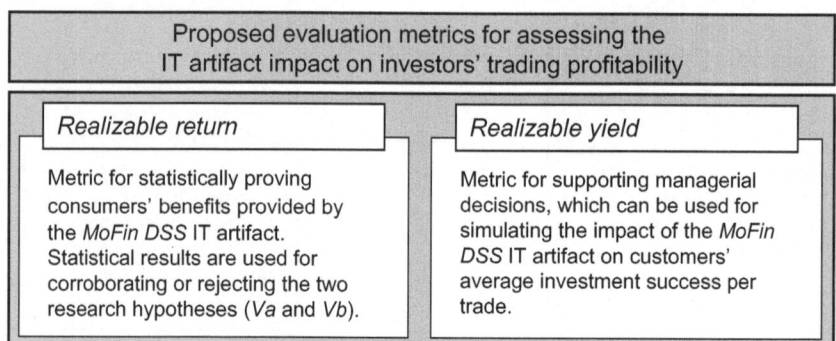

Whereas IT investments into transaction services are usually evaluated on the basis of increased transaction numbers and transaction costs, the evaluation of new information and decision support services and their potential benefits resulting from better or timelier information supply is difficult to quantify. This problem is addressed in the following.

5.2.2   Realizable Return Calculation

In order to compare potential trading profits, which can be realized following the publication of an ad hoc disclosure that has been observed by *MoFin DSS*, the metric *realizable return* $|r_{di}|$ is defined by Equation 5.4.

The calculation of absolute values is done since *realizable return* is used for evaluating the potential trading profit realizable by investors. Consequently, the evaluation metric is based on the assumption that company announcements that cause falling (increasing) stock prices will prompt investors to sell (buy) the affected stock. This approach can be interpreted as measuring the width of the opened window of opportunity.

$$\left| r_{i,d} \right| = \left| \frac{p_{i,t_c} - p_{i,t_d}}{p_{i,t_c}} \right|$$

with $d = (0,15,30,45,60,75,90,105,120)$

where

d =   delay level

i =   event index

p_{i,t_c} =   closing price of stock with index i

p_{i,t_d} =   first observable stock price, d minutes subsequent to the event date

$\left| r_{i,d} \right|$ =   realizable return of the stock affected by with indices i and d

Equation 5.4: Realizable Returns

The evaluation metric *realizable return* is flexible for assessing the impact of the two factors that contribute to consumers' value. First, it considers different delay levels, which represent a reduction of the investors' reaction time. By calculation *realizable returns* at different delay levels, it is possible to address *research hypothesis Va*.

Second, by adjusting the event sample for which the metric is calculated, it is possible to incorporate the decision support provided when relevant events are taken into account only. A comparison of *realizable returns* calculated for events that were identified as relevant with the *realizable returns* values of all events observed lays the basis for addressing *research hypothesis Vb*.

The results of corresponding statistical test statistics can then be used for corroborating or rejecting the two research hypotheses.

5.2.3 Mean Realizable Yield Calculation

For evaluating the IT artifact's impact in concrete business scenarios, another valuation metric is required that takes into account additional factors, such as trading volumes and trading costs.

These additional factors are covered by a second evaluation metric *mean realizable yield* (Equation 5.7) via which one can calculate trading profits that can be realized by investors per transaction. Therefore, *realizable trading returns* and *trading costs* have to be determined, which are given by Equation 5.5 and Equation 5.6.

$$\left| tr_{i,d} \right| = \left| v \cdot \frac{p_{i,t_c} - p_{i,t_d}}{p_{i,t_c}} \right|$$

where

$\left| tr_{i,d} \right|$ =   realizable trading return with indices i and d

v =   trading volume (in €)

Equation 5.5: Realizable Trading Return

$$c_i = \begin{cases} c_{Min} & v < v_{Min} & \text{lower bound trading costs} \\ c_{Fi} + c_v \cdot v & v_{Min} < v < v_{Max} & \\ c_{Max} & v > v_{Max} & \text{upper bound trading costs} \end{cases}$$

where

c_i =   total trading costs with index i

c_{Fi} =   fixed trading costs

c_v =   variable trading costs

c_{Min} =   minimum trading costs of a stock transaction

c_{Max} =   maximum trading costs of a stock transaction

v_{Max} =   maximum trading volume (in €)

v_{Min} =   minimum trading volume (in €)

Equation 5.6: Trading Costs

For trading costs, there exists a minimum (maximum) trading volume below (above) which fixed minimum (maximum) trading costs are involved.

The *realizable trading return* (Equation 5.5) and *trading costs* (Equation 5.6) can then be used for calculating the *mean realizable yield*:

$$\overline{y_d} = 1/I \sum_{i=1}^{I} |tr_{i,d}| - c_i$$

where

$\overline{y_d}$ =   mean realizable yield at delay d

$|tr_{i,d}|$ =   realizable trading return of the stock affected by event i

at delay level d

c_i =   total trading costs

Equation 5.7: Mean Realizable Yield

Using Equation 5.7, it is possible to evaluate the mean of potential intraday trading profits per trade, which can be realized subsequent to the publication of an ad hoc disclosure. The calculation is suited for evaluations of specific scenarios, such as at different delay levels, trading volumes, or trading costs, and for data samples that do incorporate the decision support provided by the IT artifact. Since the metric is used for *ex ante* evaluations addressing the potentials provided, it is assumed that if a published ad hoc disclosure causes stock prices to fall the held amount v can be sold and if it causes prices to rise, stocks with the trading volume v can be bought. A variation of the delay level d allows an evaluation of the impact of the timelier information supply realized by the mobile notification service. If the reduction of d involves a significant higher *mean realizable yield*, one can evaluate the customers' value by comparing *mean realizable yields* affected by customers trading behavior.

This evaluation approach implies some assumption regarding the investor and the capital market. First, it is assumed that the investor maximizes returns and minimizes costs. Secondly, it assumes market clearance if the investor sells or buys any stocks, which also implies that orders will not be executed partly.

5.3 Simulation-based Empirical Evaluation Results

Hevner et al. (2004) summarize different kinds of IT artifact evaluation methods that are presented in Table 5.1.

Table 5.1: IT Artifact Evaluation Methodologies[23]

Observational	
Case study	studies artifact in depth in business environment
Field study	monitors use of artifact in multiple projects
Analytical	
Static analysis	examines structure of artifact for static qualities (e.g., complexity)
Architecture analysis	study how artifact fits into technical IS architecture
Optimization	demonstrates inherent optimal properties of artifact or provides optimality bounds on artifact behavior
Dynamic analysis	studies artifact in use for dynamic qualities (e.g., performance)
Experimental	
Controlled experiment	studies artifact in controlled environment for qualities (e.g., usability)
Simulation	executes artifact with artificial or historical data
Testing	
Functional (black box) testing	executes artifact interfaces to discover failures and identify defects
Structural (white box) testing	performs coverage testing of some metric (e.g., execution paths) in the artifact implementation
Descriptive	
Informed argument	uses information from the knowledge base (e.g., relevant research) to build a convincing argument for the artifact's utility
Scenarios	construct detailed scenarios around the artifact to demonstrate its utility

The evaluation methodology introduced in the following is not based on traditional consumer demand curves due to the already highlighted problems. Since a product like *MoFin DSS* has not been offered to customers yet, the shape of the demand curve could only be assumed, which bears the problems pointed out.

Therefore, a novel evaluation methodology is presented in the following, which is working with simulations of potential investor transactions incorporating the impact of the *MoFin DSS* IT artifact, which supports private investors during their investment process. Hence, an experimental evaluation approach is chosen that simulates the impact of the IT artifact with artificial and historical data.

---

[23] Adopted from Hevner et al. (2004).

Therefore, this methodology is applied in order to assess the two major contributions to customers' value provided by the IT artifact. First, the reduction of investors' reaction time (Section 5.3.1) is evaluated. Then, Section 5.3.2 shows how to assess the decision support provided.

The simulation of trading profits is based on the two metrics *realizable trading return* and *mean realizable yield* taking different delay levels and investor behavior into account.

First, the two *research hypotheses Va* and *Vb* are statistically tested with the results of *realizable return* simulations. Second, the simulation of *mean realizable yields* provides support for managerial decision making since this method enables investors to assess the consumers' value provided within different scenarios such as the current business situation or the business outlook.

5.3.1 Reduction of Reaction Time

The impact of a reduction of the investors' reaction time is explored in the following subsections. First, the simulation setup and datasets used are introduced in Subsection 5.3.2.1, followed by a statistical analysis of simulated realizable returns (addressing *research hypothesis Va*) in Subsection 5.3.2.2).

Finally, in Subsection 5.3.2.3 a simulation illustrates a reduction of the reaction time impacts on the consumers' value, which represents a tool for managerial decision-making how to evaluate the investment in financial information and decision support systems.

5.3.1.1 Simulation Setup and Dataset

The consumers' value simulation approach uses the primary dataset that was introduced in the event study analysis presented in Chapter 2 and comprises a set of 425 ad hoc disclosures, which have been published during stock exchange trading hours between 2003-08-01 and 2005-07-31. The event study has shown that this kind of event causes significant abnormal stock price reactions on an intraday basis. However, since event study analyses apply adjusted returns (e.g. by general market trends), the event study results cannot be used for value assessments when these price effects are exploited by investors.

For each of the 425 ad hoc disclosures, there is a publication date available exact to the second and the stock symbol of the corresponding company. Given this stock symbol, the corresponding intraday stock price series during the publication date were taken as input factors for the simulation.

5.3.1.2 Realizable Return Simulation

In order to corroborate the *research hypothesis Va* that timelier information supply (resulting form the proposed mobile notification service) opens a window for private investors, it is necessary to compare the realizable returns $|r_{i,d}|$ at different delay levels. For each delay level, the realizable returns can be interpreted as a population of returns.

The realizable returns $|r_{i,d}|$ are calculated for each stock affected by event $i = 1,...,425$ and delay level $d = (0, 15, ..., 120)$. The returns of a delay level can be interpreted as return population $|R_d|$, whose center parameters are summarized in Table 5.2.

Table 5.2: Center Parameters of the Realizable Return Populations

	$|R_0|$	$|R_{15}|$	$|R_{30}|$	$|R_{45}|$	$|R_{60}|$	$|R_{75}|$	$|R_{90}|$	$|R_{105}|$	$|R_{120}|$
Mean	6.35%	4.47%	3.98%	3.66%	3.32%	2.98%	2.79%	2.51%	2.36%
Median	2.94%	2.05%	1.63%	1.51%	1.43%	1.30%	1.07%	0.97%	0.93%

The means of the realizable return populations indicate that the observed market events open a window of opportunity for private investors, since average return rates around 5% can be achieved when reacting promptly to the market event.

Since for all populations the mean is larger than the median, all populations feature a right-skewed data distribution. Furthermore, as the population means decrease with increasing delay level, a first (weak) indicator has been found corroborating the *research hypothesis Va* that a reduction of the reaction delay tends to result in higher realizable returns on average (for further details regarding the population distributions see Appendix B). The differences between the population means provide evidence about which returns can be realized (on average) if the reaction delay of the investor can be reduced by mobile services supported by the proposed IT artifact design.

Since the samples at different delay levels can not be assumed to be independent, paired samples hypothesis testing is applied. Therefore, paired differences $pd_{i,d1,d2}$ are calculated for the 425 values of all sample values and delay levels according to Equation 5.1 (Groebner et al. 2001).

$$pd_{i,d1,d2} = |r_{i,d1}| - |r_{i,d2}|$$

with $(d1,d2) = (0,15), (15,30), (30,45), (45,60), (60,75), (75,90), (90,105), (105,120)$

where

$|r_{i,d}|$ =   realizable return with indices i and d

Equation 5.8: Paired Difference of Realizable Returns

The *research hypothesis Va* "*Reduction of the investors' reaction time leads to transactions that are more profitable on average*" can be tested with a corresponding statistical hypothesis test that addresses the question whether or not the reduction of the reaction delay from level

$d2$ to $d1$ significantly increases the *realizable returns*. Therefore, sequential test statistics can be calculated for the different reaction delay levels d addressing, for example, the question whether or not the mean of the realizable returns 15 minutes subsequent to the event date is larger compared to the one 30 minutes subsequent to the event date (i.e. $(d1,d2) = (15,30)$). The corresponding null and alternative hypotheses are stated as follows:

$$H_0 : \mu\!\left(pd_{d1,d2}\right) \le 0$$

$$H_A : \mu\!\left(pd_{d1,d2}\right) > 0$$

with $(d1,d2) = (0,15), (15,30), (30,45), (45,60), (60,75), (75,90), (90,105), (105,120)$

If the null hypothesis for two sequential delay levels can be rejected, it can be shown that a decrease of reaction delay allows higher realizable returns at a given level of significance (e.g. the mean of the *realizable returns* 15 minutes after the announcement is significant higher than after 30 minutes).

Using the t-test statistic for the paired differences (Equation 5.2) of the neighboring realizable returns regarding the delay levels $(d1,d2) = (0,15), (15,30), (30,45), (45,60), (60,75), (75,90), (90,105), (105,120)$ it is possible to corroborate the research hypothesis that the mean of realizable returns is the higher the shorter the delay level.

Table 5.3: Test Statistic for Paired Difference of Realizable Returns

	Delay levels $(d1,d2)$ in minutes							
	(0,15)	(15,30)	(30,45)	(45,60)	(60,75)	(75,90)	(90,105)	(105,120)
Mean	2.77%	0.48%	0.32%	0.34%	0.34%	0.19%	0.28%	0.14%
t-value	4.37***	2.92***	2.77***	2.95***	1.92**	1.55*	3.21***	1.62***

***, ** and * indicate significance at the 1%, 5% and 10% level respectively.

Given the results of the test statistics in Table 5.3 it is possible to reject the null hypotheses H_0: $\mu(pd_{d1,d2}) \le 0$ for all sequential delay levels at significance levels of 1% (for six paired differences), 5% and 10% (for one paired difference each) respectively. Within the first 120 minutes following the announcement, each reduction of reaction time increases the rate of return which can be realized on average. These empirical result provide strong evidence that *research hypothesis Va* can be corroborated, i.e. that "*Reduction of the investors' reaction time leads to transactions that are more profitable on average*". Therefore, investment in a mobile notification service providing a reduction of investors' reaction time can provide significant value for customers, which illustrates the business value of the proposed IT artifact *MoFin DSS*.

5.3.1.3   Mean Realizable Yield Simulation

For a simulation of *mean realizable yields* the two central parameters v (trading volume in €)
and d (delay level) need to be controlled. All stock prices parameters are based on empirical
intraday stock price series. The trading cost parameters c_{Fi}, c_i, c_{Min}, and c_{Max} were taken from
comdirect bank AG, one of the largest online brokers in Germany (Comdirect Bank 2005), but
other online brokers and banks operate with comparable cost functions and charge similar
trading fees. In order to evaluate the impact of the reaction time and the investment volume
on the realizable yields, corresponding transactions are simulated using Equation 5.5 to
Equation 5.7 with the parameters $v = (50, 100, \ldots, 1000)$ and $d = (0, 15, \ldots, 120)$.

Table 5.4: Simulated Mean Realizable Yields per Trade (in €)
with $d = (0, 15, \ldots, 120)$ and $v = (50, 100, \ldots, 1000)$

v in €	Delay level d in minutes								
	0	15	30	45	60	75	90	105	120
50	-6.73	-7.67	-7.91	-8.07	-8.24	-8.42	-8.51	-8.65	-8.72
100	-3.55	-5.44	-5.92	-6.25	-6.59	-6.93	-7.12	-7.40	-7.54
150	-0.38	-3.21	-3.93	-4.42	-4.93	-5.45	-5.73	-6.15	-6.37
200	2.80	-0.98	-1.95	-2.59	-3.28	-3.96	-4.34	-4.90	-5.19
250	5.97	1.25	0.04	-0.77	-1.62	-2.48	-2.95	-3.65	-4.01
300	9.14	3.47	2.03	1.06	0.04	-0.99	-1.56	-2.40	-2.83
350	12.32	5.70	4.02	2.89	1.69	0.49	-0.17	-1.15	-1.65
400	15.49	7.93	6.01	4.71	3.35	1.98	1.22	0.10	-0.48
450	18.66	10.16	8.00	6.54	5.00	3.46	2.61	1.35	0.70
500	21.84	12.39	9.99	8.37	6.66	4.94	4.01	2.60	1.88
550	25.01	14.62	11.97	10.20	8.31	6.43	5.40	3.85	3.06
600	28.19	16.85	13.96	12.02	9.97	7.91	6.79	5.10	4.24
650	31.36	19.08	15.95	13.85	11.63	9.40	8.18	6.35	5.41
700	34.53	21.31	17.94	15.68	13.28	10.88	9.57	7.60	6.59
750	37.71	23.54	19.93	17.50	14.94	12.37	10.96	8.85	7.77
800	40.88	25.77	21.92	19.33	16.59	13.85	12.35	10.10	8.95
850	44.06	27.99	23.91	21.16	18.25	15.33	13.74	11.35	10.13
900	47.23	30.22	25.90	22.98	19.91	16.82	15.13	12.60	11.30
950	50.40	32.45	27.88	24.81	21.56	18.30	16.52	13.85	12.48
1000	53.58	34.68	29.87	26.64	23.22	19.79	17.91	15.10	13.66

Divided by the number of events taken into account, $\overline{y_d}$ is normalized and can consequently
be easily compared with other simulations that use different datasets. The results of the performed trading simulation are given in Table 5.4.

The simulation results provide evidence that (1) a decrease of the delay level d causes an increase of realizable yields and (2) depending on the reaction time elapsed a trading volume

limit exists under which the transaction costs will exceed any yields that could be realized by the investor. The customers' value of the proposed mobile information service cannot be evaluated generally, as it depends on the trading behavior of customers and the realized reduction of the reaction delay. Therefore, the simulation approach provides valuable information regarding the interdependences of trading volume, reaction delay, and realizable yields. If, for example, an online broker analyzes their customers' trading volume behavior and considers different implementation alternatives (e.g. a highly integrated mobile information service providing a higher reduction of the reaction delay compared to a simpler implementation) the customers' value can be evaluated for different IT investment strategies and customer segments.

The empirical results of the *mean realizable yield* simulation are graphically illustrated in the following Figure 5.3.

Figure 5.3: Simulated Mean Realizable Yields per Trade (in €) with
$d = (0, 15, ..., 120)$ **and** $v = (50, 100, ..., 1000)$

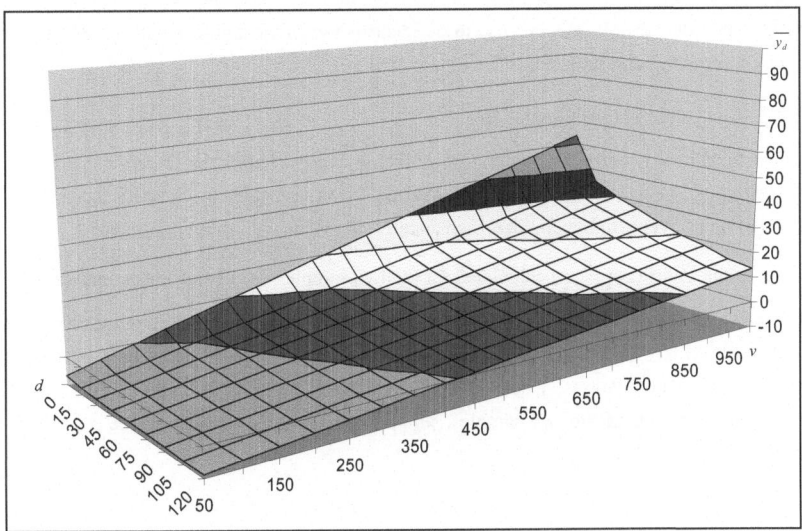

5.3.2 Decision Support Model

The second value evaluation focuses on the decision support provided by *MoFin DSS* and addresses the research hypothesis whether or not investors can make more profitable transactions when concentrating on those events that were identified by the DSS model while reducing the total numbers of transactions processed.

The datasets used are described in Subsection 5.3.2.1 followed by simulations that compare realizable returns for supported and unsupported decision making in Subsection 5.3.2.2. Finally, Subsection 5.3.2.3 presents simulations illustrating the impact of the provided decision support on the mean realizable yields.

5.3.2.1 Simulation Setup and Dataset

Since parts of the original dataset of 425 events and the corresponding intraday price series were used as input for the development of the price effect forecasting model (information dataset) that was introduced in Chapter 3, this data is not adequate for assessing the consumers' value of the decision support provided. Therefore, the value assessment of the decision support model is based on the forecasting dataset defined in Section 3.3.4.2 comprising only 225 events and the corresponding intraday stock price series on the events' publication date. Otherwise, if the dataset includes the information dataset, it will not be possible to assess the real benefits provided since the evaluation would partly be based on in-sample forecasts, i.e. there would be an overestimate of the value provided. 86 of the 225 events from the forecasting dataset were identified by the DSS model implemented in *MoFin DSS* as relevant market events. Therefore, the simulations use these identified events (sample 1 with $I = 86$) and the original forecasting dataset (sample 2 with $I = 225$)

5.3.2.2 Realizable Return Simulation

In order to address *research hypothesis Vb "Investors supported by the IT artifact can realize transactions that are more profitable on average"*, it is necessary to compare the realizable returns of those events that were identified as relevant events with those of all events.

The realizable returns $|r_{i,d}|$ are calculated for the two samples $s = 1$ (relevant events) and $s = 2$ (all events), each event $i = 1, ..., 86$ (for relevant events) and $i = 1, ..., 225$ (for all events), and delay level $d = (0, 15, ..., 120)$. The returns of a sample s and a delay level d are interpreted as return populations, whose sample parameters are summarized in Table 5.5. For comparing the means of the two samples, suitable statistical hypotheses can be expressed as follows.

$$H_0 : \mu\left(\overline{|r_{1,d}|} - \overline{|r_{2,d}|}\right) \leq 0$$

$$H_A : \mu\left(\overline{|r_{1,d}|} - \overline{|r_{2,d}|}\right) > 0$$

with $(d1,d2) = (0,15), (15,30), (30,45), (45,60), (60,75), (75,90), (90,105), (105,120)$

where

$$\overline{|r_{s,d}|} \quad = \quad \text{mean of realizable return with indices}$$

$s = 1$ (relevant events), $s = 2$ (all events), and d

For comparing two samples with different sample sizes where the variances s^2 are unequal, the unequal-variances t-test is appropriate (Equation 5.3). The test results of these tests are also summarized in Table 5.5.

Table 5.5: Sample Parameters and Test Statistic for Comparing Realizable Returns of Unsupported vs. Supported Decision Making

	Delay level d in minutes								
	0	15	30	45	60	75	90	105	120
	Sample $s = 1$: Simulated realizable return sample for events that where identified as relevant events ($I = 86$)								
Mean	9.24%	4.83%	3.67%	3.72%	3.66%	3.65%	3.51%	2.84%	2.71%
Median	3.79%	2.34%	1.87%	1.63%	1.85%	1.32%	1.22%	1.03%	1.03%
s^2	0.1174	0.0081	0.0035	0.0035	0.0034	0.0037	0.0039	0.0034	0.0035
	Sample $s = 2$: Simulated realizable return sample for all events ($I = 225$)								
Mean	2.48%	1.94%	1.81%	1.72%	1.58%	1.43%	1.33%	1.26%	1.20%
Median	1.44%	1.29%	0.75%	0.74%	0.71%	0.65%	0.53%	0.44%	0.48%
s^2	0.0461	0.0036	0.0018	0.0019	0.0017	0.0018	0.0018	0.0016	0.0016
df	111	115	120	121	119	118	117	116	116
t-value	1.71**	2.76***	2.68***	2.85***	3.05***	3.11***	2.97***	2.30**	2.20**

*** and ** indicate significance at the 1% and 5% level respectively.

The statistical results, i.e. the t-values in the last row, show that it is possible to reject the formulated null hypothesis $H_0 : \mu\left(\overline{|r_{1,d}|} - \overline{|r_{2,d}|}\right) \leq 0$ for all delay levels at significance levels of at least 5%. Consequently, this indicates that the decision support provided enables investors to make, on average, significant higher realizable returns, when concentrating on those events that were identified. This result holds for all delay levels, i.e. the mean realizable return is always significant higher when relying on the DSS model implemented in *MoFin DSS*. Therefore, these findings corroborate *research hypothesis Vb* that "*Investors supported by the IT artifact can realize transactions that are more profitable*". This means that the proposed IT artifact *MoFin DSS* does provide significant consumers' value.

5.3.2.3   Mean Realizable Yield Simulation

The method of simulating the impact of the decision support model on *mean realizable yields* is similar to the simulation presented in the previous section. Again, the parameters v (trading volume in €) and d (delay level) are controlled and the trading cost parameters c_{Fi}, c_i, c_{Min}, and c_{Max} were retained. In contrast, two simulations were conducted and compared using two samples. The first sample is taken for a simulation of *mean realizable yields* for those events that were identified by the DSS model. The corresponding simulation results are given in Table 5.6.

Table 5.6: Simulated Mean Realizable Yields per Trade (in €) for Sample 1 (Forecasted Relevant Events) with d = (0, 15, ..., 120) and v = (50, 100, ..., 1000)

v in €	Delay level d in minutes								
	0	15	30	45	60	75	90	105	120
50	-5.28	-7.49	-8.06	-8.04	-8.07	-8.08	-8.15	-8.48	-8.54
100	-0.66	-5.07	-6.23	-6.18	-6.24	-6.25	-6.39	-7.06	-7.19
150	3.96	-2.66	-4.39	-4.32	-4.40	-4.43	-4.64	-5.65	-5.83
200	8.57	-0.25	-2.55	-2.46	-2.57	-2.60	-2.89	-4.23	-4.48
250	13.19	2.17	-0.71	-0.60	-0.74	-0.78	-1.13	-2.81	-3.12
300	17.81	4.58	1.12	1.26	1.09	1.05	0.62	-1.39	-1.77
350	22.43	6.99	2.96	3.12	2.93	2.87	2.37	0.03	-0.41
400	27.05	9.41	4.80	4.98	4.76	4.70	4.13	1.44	0.94
450	31.67	11.82	6.64	6.84	6.59	6.52	5.88	2.86	2.30
500	36.29	14.24	8.47	8.70	8.42	8.35	7.64	4.28	3.65
550	40.91	16.65	10.31	10.56	10.26	10.17	9.39	5.70	5.01
600	45.52	19.06	12.15	12.42	12.09	12.00	11.14	7.12	6.36
650	50.14	21.48	13.99	14.28	13.92	13.82	12.90	8.53	7.72
700	54.76	23.89	15.82	16.14	15.75	15.65	14.65	9.95	9.08
750	59.38	26.30	17.66	18.00	17.59	17.47	16.40	11.37	10.43
800	64.00	28.72	19.50	19.86	19.42	19.30	18.16	12.79	11.79
850	68.62	31.13	21.34	21.72	21.25	21.12	19.91	14.20	13.14
900	73.24	33.54	23.17	23.58	23.08	22.95	21.66	15.62	14.50
950	77.86	35.96	25.01	25.44	24.92	24.77	23.42	17.04	15.85
1000	82.47	38.37	26.85	27.30	26.75	26.60	25.17	18.46	17.21

The highlighted *mean realizable yields* values in the upper rows indicate the limits of trading volume below which intraday trading can not be profitable due to the trading costs involved that exceed the profits realized. These trading volume limits increase with a higher delay level d (only the mean realizable yields at the 30-minute reaction delay level are not in line with this trend). Figure 5.4 graphically illustrates these findings.

Figure 5.4: Simulated Mean Realizable Yields per Trade (in €) for Sample 1 (Forecasted Relevant Events) with d = (0, 15, …, 120) and v = (50, 100, …, 1000)

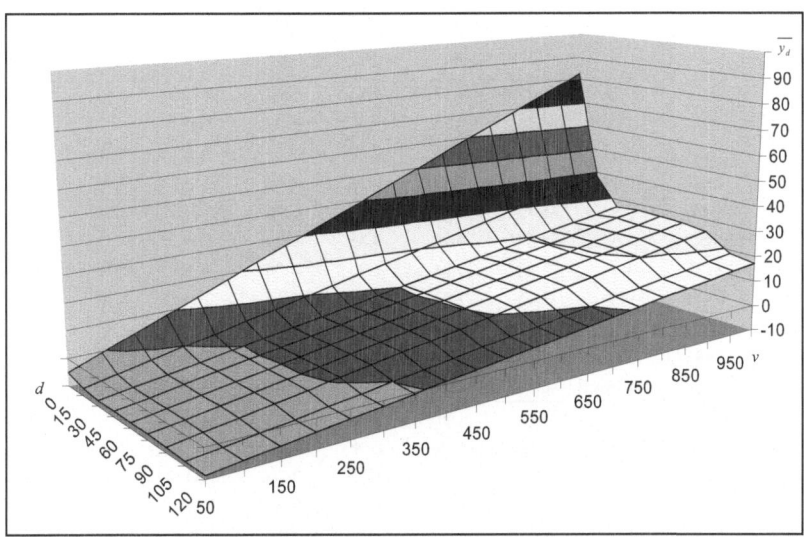

The graphical illustration (Figure 5.4) of the simulation results shows that there are high *mean realizable yields* at the $d = 0$ minutes level, which significantly decrease with the time elapsed. The mean realizable yields between the reaction delays of 30 to 90 minutes stay nearly constant at a comparably high level with more that 25 € for a trading volume of 1,000 €.

The results for the second simulation using the second sample with all 225 events are presented in Table 5.7. The highlighted area indicating negative *mean realizable yields* values is much larger compared to the results of the first simulation, which was based on the sample including those ad hoc disclosures that have been identified by the DSS forecasting model.

The simulations have therefore confirmed that investors concentrating on those events that are identified by the *MoFin DSS* IT artifact can perform more profitable intraday transactions while reducing the total number of transactions made.

Table 5.7: Simulated Mean Realizable Yields per Trade (in €) for Sample 2
(All Forecasted Events) with d = (0, 15, …, 120) and v = (50, 100, …, 1000)

v in €	Delay level d in minutes								
	0	15	30	45	60	75	90	105	120
50	-9.11	-9.38	-9.47	-9.52	-9.58	-9.67	-9.72	-9.75	-9.77
100	-4.93	-7.66	-8.38	-8.35	-8.38	-8.39	-8.48	-8.90	-8.97
150	-2.33	-6.42	-7.49	-7.45	-7.50	-7.51	-7.65	-8.27	-8.38
200	0.28	-5.18	-6.60	-6.55	-6.61	-6.63	-6.81	-7.64	-7.80
250	2.89	-3.93	-5.72	-5.65	-5.73	-5.76	-5.98	-7.01	-7.21
300	5.50	-2.69	-4.83	-4.75	-4.85	-4.88	-5.14	-6.39	-6.62
350	8.10	-1.45	-3.94	-3.84	-3.96	-4.00	-4.31	-5.76	-6.03
400	10.71	-0.20	-3.06	-2.94	-3.08	-3.12	-3.47	-5.13	-5.44
450	13.32	1.04	-2.17	-2.04	-2.20	-2.24	-2.64	-4.50	-4.85
500	15.93	2.28	-1.28	-1.14	-1.31	-1.36	-1.80	-3.88	-4.26
550	18.53	3.53	-0.39	-0.24	-0.43	-0.48	-0.97	-3.25	-3.68
600	21.14	4.77	0.49	0.66	0.46	0.40	-0.13	-2.62	-3.09
650	23.75	6.01	1.38	1.56	1.34	1.28	0.70	-2.00	-2.50
700	26.36	7.26	2.27	2.46	2.22	2.16	1.54	-1.37	-1.91
750	28.96	8.50	3.15	3.36	3.11	3.03	2.37	-0.74	-1.32
800	31.57	9.74	4.04	4.26	3.99	3.91	3.21	-0.11	-0.73
850	34.18	10.99	4.93	5.16	4.87	4.79	4.04	0.51	-0.14
900	36.79	12.23	5.81	6.06	5.76	5.67	4.88	1.14	0.44
950	39.40	13.47	6.70	6.96	6.64	6.55	5.71	1.77	1.03
1000	42.00	14.72	7.59	7.86	7.53	7.43	6.55	2.40	1.62

The corresponding graphical illustration of the simulation results for sample 2 uses the same $\overline{y_d}$ scale as the illustration for sample 1 (Figure 5.4) and can therefore be compared directly. One can, for example, easily deduce that at a trading volume of 1,000 € and the reaction delay between 30 and 90 minutes, intraday profits per trade on average more than double when investors use the decision support provided by *MoFin DSS*.

Also for sample 2, the *mean realizable yields* between the reaction delays of 30 to 90 minutes stay nearly constant around 7.50 € for a trading volume of 1,000 €. Compared to sample 1 (relevant events), this is approximately only one forth of the mean realizable yields, which could be taken when being supported by *MoFin DSS*, i.e. when concentrating on those event that have been identified as relevant. Figure 5.5 provides a graphical illustration of these findings.

**Figure 5.5: Simulated Mean Realizable Yields per Trade (in €) for Sample 2
(All Forecasted Events) with d = (0, 15, …, 120) and v = (50, 100, …, 1000)**

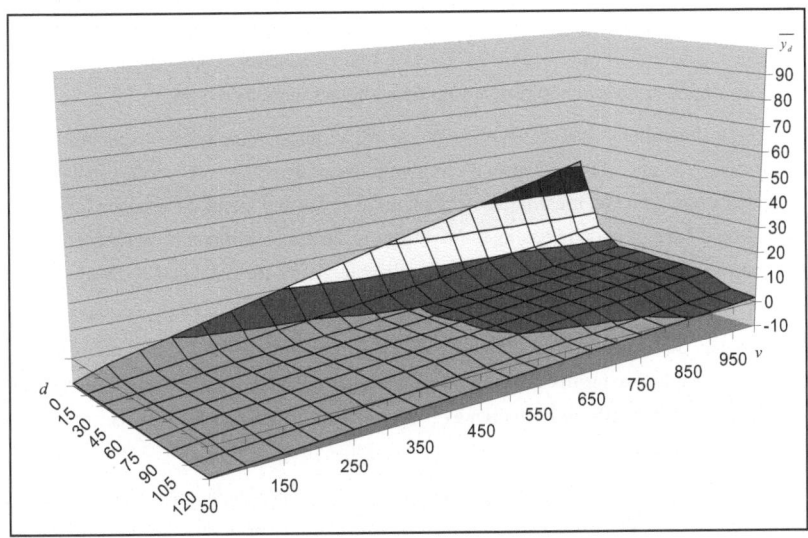

5.4   Conclusion of the IT Artifact Evaluation

The evaluation of the business value of IT provided by the *MoFin DSS* IT artifact has been addressed with a simulation approach that assesses the value provided to customers, who could benefit from the system's usage. This evaluation approach has been chosen since other approaches, which are based on production theory or the theory of competitive strategy and which evaluate the impact on productivity or profitability are not suitable for *ex ante* evaluations of the business value provided. These cannot be applied when evaluating new product and services being not yet available on the market (Brynjolfsson and Hitt 1996). Compared to previous consumers' value assessments that mostly estimate the parameters of a consumers' demand curve using historical data, the presented evaluation approach applies a novel simulation approach that is capable of simulating the impact on the benefits provided to potential customers who will use the IT artifact. It is therefore suitable for *ex ante* evaluations of the IT business value, as it indirectly addresses the customers' willingness to pay (Brynjolfsson 1996).

The results of the consumers' value simulations show that this approach is appropriate for assessing the business value provided by the two major contributions of the *MoFin DSS* IT artifact, i.e. the reduction of the investors' reaction time and the decision support provided.

The simulation-based evaluation has been separated into two different simulation techniques. First, simulations measure the impact of the two IT artifact contributions on the defined metric *realizable return*. The results of these simulations are used for a statistical evaluation of the two research *hypotheses Va* and *Vb*. The results indicate that a reduction of reaction delay and the decision support provided by *MoFin DSS* open a window of opportunity for investors since both empower investors to realize significant higher intraday returns.

Second, the simulations of *realizable yields* address virtual trading scenarios taking into account further relevant factors, such as trading volumes and trading costs. Both simulation approaches are based on historical intraday stock price series and therefore simulate how the IT artifact would have provided benefits to investors during the corresponding period. To be able to compare simulation results, the means of realizable yields are simulated so that results are comparable amongst datasets from different periods.

The empirical simulation results show that the IT artifact empowers investors to realize significant higher intraday profits per trade. This provides evidence that the capital market does not react efficiently to new information available, which contradicts the efficient market hypothesis.

Depending on the dataset used and parameters defined, this simulation approach is highly flexible regarding a given business situation or future scenarios, and can therefore support managerial decision-making, for example for selecting the most beneficial investment among competing IT projects.

Like all IT business value evaluation approaches, the presented methodology is based on different assumptions. First, it is assumed that the transactions performed by the investors using the mobile information service will not influence the stock price development itself. However, since only a minor percentage (15% in 2004) of all stocks on the German capital market are held by private investors (von Rosen 2004), this constitutes only a marginal problem. Furthermore, since the trading volume per order of private investors should be (depending on the segment and category) below average (Glaser and Weber 2004), and as only a subset of all private investors will use such a system, the interdependency should be almost negligible. Otherwise, the designed IT artifact will positively affect the efficiency of the capital market when stock prices reflect new information available within a shorter period of time.

There is a limitation regarding the second *mean realizable yield* simulation since the used dataset of the second simulation (sample 2) could influence the business value calculated. This stems from the forecasting dataset used, which is the basis of the simulations that evaluate the benefits provided by the DSS model. Compared to the original dataset where 143 of 425 (33.65%) of the observed price effects lie above the mean observed price effect, the used forecasting dataset contains 86 of 225 (38.22%) observed price effects above the mean. In fact, this is not a methodological problem and could be addressed by the use of larger sample sizes or further simulations that are based on adjusted input data.

In summary, the presented consumers' value simulation approach is a novel and highly flexible methodology for performing *ex ante* evaluations of the IT business value. It can be applied to new products or emerging technologies such as the presented IT artifact *MoFin DDS*. It further supports managerial decision-making since managers can use the simulated consumers' value to estimate customers' willingness to pay (Brynjolfsson 1996). Furthermore, the simulation results can assist managers when selecting the most promising investment (Brynjolfsson and Hitt 1996).

6 Summary and Further Research

This interdisciplinary thesis has provided new findings in the field of mobile financial research. It provides insights into relevant financial market behavior, presents new forecasting models and an IT artifact, and applies a newly developed methodology for IT investment evaluations aimed at helping to inform managerial decision-making.

The following Section 6.1 summarizes the general approach of this work. Then, major research contributions are presented in Section 6.2. Due to the interdisciplinary focus of this work, contributions are made in different research directions ranging from empirical financial studies to design science research. Section 6.3 illustrates practical implications of the approach presented. Finally, Section 6.4 points out how this work can stimulate future academic endeavors.

6.1 Summary of the Approach

Once titled as possible killer applications, mobile financial services have not yet lived up to expectations. Therefore, discrepancy between characteristics of mobile financial services that positively affect the value gained by customers and existing mobile financial services is addressed in this work. The design science research paradigm has been chosen as research foundation with the aim of extending existing boundaries of mobile financial services addressing both practical and academic issues. Following this paradigm, the design, implementation, and evaluation of an appropriate IT artifact can provide new knowledge that contributes to the understanding and solution of the addressed problem domain (Srinivasan et al. 2005).

Starting with an analysis of the application domain in Chapter 2, the efficient market hypothesis was identified as relevant theoretical foundation. The semi-strong form of the efficient market hypothesis, after which stock prices adjust efficiently to new information available to the market, is addressed here.

An analysis of intraday price effects following the publication of ad hoc disclosures explores a promising domain for mobile financial services since previous research provided evidence for significant abnormal intraday stock price behavior. The analysis was performed in the form of an intraday event study, a standard empirical analysis methodology in financial research, which is applied for evaluating the impact of unexpected events on security prices. Using high-voluminous intraday stock price series, it was possible to address the following two research hypotheses that provide a motivation for providing mobile decision support to private investors:

- *Research hypothesis Ia: Stock prices react after the publication of ad hoc disclosures.*

- *Research hypothesis Ib: The observed price effects persist for a short period of time only (several minutes, up to a few hours).*

The empirical results of the intraday event study corroborated both research hypotheses, which have illustrated the business relevance since investors could exploit these price effects when being supported appropriately. These findings provide a motivation for the following research approach because they show a window of opportunity for investors when being notified and supported with a ubiquitous mobile financial service.

After introducing a DSS classification framework originally defined by Power (2002 and 2004) and based on a set of distinctive system characteristics, a corresponding mobile financial notification and decision support system concept was explored and developed in Chapter 3. The DSS concept utilizes mobile communication technologies and addresses the question how to provide event-driven ubiquitous decision support to private investors when a relevant ad hoc disclosure has been observed by the system. Therefore, two econometrical forecasting models were developed for estimating the price effect magnitude and price effect duration following the event date. These represent the dominant components of the DSS concept, which aims to provide customers a relative advantage compared to traditional online banking services. An evaluation of out-of-sample forecasts has shown that the chosen approach achieves superior forecasting quality compared to previous approaches working with text mining techniques (Mittermayer 2004; Spiliopoulou et al. 2003).

This DSS concept laid the basis for the following Chapter 4, which presented the design of an IT artifact labeled *Mobile Financial DSS* (*MoFin DSS*) that demonstrates the feasibility of the DSS concept utilizing mobile communication infrastructures and services.

Following the definition in Srinivasan et al. (2005) of the IT artifact as a "combined hardware and software system that is designed and implemented within an organizational context and whose purpose is to collect, organize, and store data, and transform it into information needed [...]", *MoFin DSS* was designed as such a combined hardware and software system, and comprises a complex infrastructural setup and prototypical software implementations. The research approach was founded on the design science research paradigm, which focuses on the development and evaluation of novel IT artifacts that should empower individuals or organizations to extend their abilities. Even though the value of design science is well recognized in information systems (IS) research, it is less commonly applied than the behavioral science paradigm, which focuses on the development and verification of theories about the behavior of individuals and organizations (Srinivasan et al. 2005).

The hardware component of *MoFin DSS* comprises a client/server and a mobile communication system architecture integrating different data sources and providing the functionalities to send mobile push messages via a GSM network.

The prototypical *MoFin DSS* software component was implemented using VB.NET 2005 and operates on a Microsoft Windows Server 2003. The software is able to observe and evaluate ad hoc disclosures being published during stock exchange trading hours. The implemented forecasting models are used for identifying relevant events enabling investors to receive prompt decision support via mobile push messages. The software supports different kinds of push message types providing different functionalities und limitations. A selection of the most appropriate push message type is not a simple task since technical limitations, personal preferences, and costs involved need to be considered. For example MMS provides a graphical illustration of the observed and forecasted stock price adjustment process that can be interpreted easily by the investor. On the other hand, WAP Push provides a smart integration of external services such as trading services which could reduce the time needed by the investor to react. SMS, for example, is supported by nearly all mobile GSM devices and people are used to this service.

Finally, Chapter 5 explored an *ex ante* evaluation of the IT artifact's business value that could be provided by a product making use of the *MoFin DSS* design. A summary of existent evaluation approaches and underlying theories (Section 5.1) has shown that on product-level there is no appropriate quantitative evaluation methodology available. An assessment of the customers' value was found to be the most appropriate evaluation approach. First, two research hypotheses were formulated addressing the relative advantage provided by the IT artifact:

- *Research hypothesis Va: Reduction of the investors' reaction time leads to transactions that are more profitable on average.*

- *Research hypothesis Vb: Investors supported by the IT artifact can realize transactions that are more profitable on average.*

Evaluation criteria and metrics were developed to test these hypotheses. These metrics were utilized in the following by a novel simulation-based evaluation methodology for assessing the impact of the artifact on investors' trading success. The empirical results corroborated both research hypotheses and illustrated the relative advantage of the mobile notification and decision support functionality provided by the IT artifact designed.

Furthermore, the simulation approach was developed and applied to assess the provided IT business value for given business scenarios that incorporate factors such as trading behavior, trading costs, and reaction delays. The results provided evidence that customers can realize higher trading profits when being supported with *MoFin DSS*, and showed how the concrete business scenario affects evaluation results. The novel simulation-based evaluation methodology can therefore provide managerial decision support for selecting the most promising investments in novel information systems.

Finally, coming back to the efficient market hypothesis that was a starting point of this work, it has now become clear that even the weak form of the efficient market hypothesis does not hold for the analyzed event type and the subsequent price adjustments. The weak form states that stock prices always reflect the information available to market participants to such an extent that investors reacting to public news will not be able to realize trading profits that exceed trading costs (Jensen 1978). This work has shown that this hypothesis does not hold on the German stock market for ad hoc disclosures and the corresponding stock price effects. The *MoFin DSS* artifact provides evidence that private investors can exploit these market inefficiencies.

6.2 Research Contributions

The design science research paradigm applied in this work aims to solve an identified problem within an organizational context by creating and evaluating novel and innovative IT artifacts (Hevner et al. 2004). Theoretical foundations and research methodologies were used in order to achieve research results that contribute to the understanding of the problem's knowledge base and to exhibit research rigor (Lee 1999).

The major research contributions of this work can be summarized as follows:

- The intraday event study analysis of the German capital market (Chapter 2) has proven the existence of abnormal stock price behavior following the publication of ad hoc disclosures pursuant article 15 of the German Securities Trading Act (WpHG). Compared to the study presented in this work, previous intraday studies were conducted on a lower level of detail than the one-minute intervals or for an analysis period shorter than two years. The empirical results therefore significantly contribute to the understanding of the problem field addressed. A continuous price adjustment process was observed for the period of ten price fixings (on a one-minute basis) and the first 30 minutes following the publication date of the ad hoc disclosure, with this price behavior usually persisting longer for index members than for non-index members.

- In the field of decision support systems research, Power's (2002 and 2004) widely cited DSS classification framework has been extended (Section 3.2.3). The characteristic enabling technology has been supplemented by mobile devices and services. So far, existing DSS literature has not yet paid much attention to these emerging technologies. However, this work, and other recently published literature presented in this work, show that a corresponding framework adjustment is sensible and more research in this direction can be expected in the future. Taking into account these publications, one can add mobile devices and services as DSS enabling technology to the classification framework. The extended framework can be used by researchers for classifying or analyzing their DSS concepts.

- The forecasting models presented in Sections 3.3.4 and 3.3.5 represent a novel approach to estimate the magnitude and persistence of abnormal price behavior following the publication of ad hoc disclosures. The explanatory and time series models used provide higher recognition rates compared to previous approaches working with text mining techniques.

- The *MoFin DSS* IT artifact, whose design and implementation have been documented in Chapter 4, demonstrates the feasibility of the newly-developed mobile DSS concept, including the forecasting models. The proof of concept is an important research contribution of design science research since foundational IT artifacts represent research contributions to the IS knowledge base (Hevner et al. 2004; March and Smith 1995). An extended knowledge base can be a necessary requirement for subsequent behavioral science research. Corresponding research can, for example, analyze the impact of the system on the behavior of private investors.

- The simulation-based customers' value evaluation methodology (Chapter 5) represents a novel approach for assessing the business value provided by IT investments. The existing evaluation approaches were not able to cover quantitatively customers' value on product level for novel products and services, for which a customers' demand curve cannot be estimated econometrically. Furthermore, the approach is capable of assessing the customers' value of information products offered free of charge, which can hardly be addressed with previous approaches. For evaluating the IT artifact designed, two new evaluation metrics were developed. Both the developed evaluation methodology and the defined metrics represent typical design science research contributions (Hevner et al. 2004).

- The empirical simulation-based trading profit analysis (Chapter 5) has shown that *MoFin DSS* provides functionalities that enable investors to realize intraday profits that exceed trading costs. This is an important result since this contradicts the weak form of the efficient market hypothesis. This states that stock prices always reflect all information available to market participants in a way that trading costs involved exceed realizable profits when an investment strategy is based on public information (Jensen 1978). The findings have uncovered market inefficiencies that can obviously be exploited by private investors.

6.3 Practical Implications

The design science research paradigm aims to provide new knowledge to people and organizations regarding novel technologies (Hevner and March 2003) and therefore, this work has a special focus on practical relevance. It has been criticized that much behavioral IS research lacks relevance to practice since it overemphasizes research rigor (Benbasat and Zmud 1999; Lee 1999). Considering empirical results and research contributions presented in this work, there a several implications to practice, which are summarized in the following:

- The proven intraday stock price reactions following published ad hoc disclosures, and persisting for a short period of time, confirm that observing, and reacting to, these events represents a promising opportunity for investors. Online banks and brokers can use this knowledge for the design and implementation of novel financial services. This involves both information and transaction services that empower investors to be promptly notified about the event, to receive information providing decision support, and to place a stock trade, preferably without changing the device and application used. The *MoFin DSS* IT artifact presented in this work is one possible example of such an application scenario but one can think of other service concepts utilizing different infrastructures or providing decision support in one way or another. The empirical results presented in Chapter 2 are therefore valuable to people (e.g. investors), organizations (e.g. online banks and brokers) and technology (e.g. infrastructures and applications).

- The developed DSS forecasting models represent a novel approach for identifying relevant market events. Service providers, such as online banks and brokers can develop new services utilizing this concept. These can be integrated into their existing information services in order to support decision-making of their customers. When offering such DSS services, service providers have to consider legal regulations that exist for consultancy services to private investors such as in Germany (Krammer 2002).

- The IT artifact designed and prototypically implemented illustrates that it is feasible to realize an event-driven mobile DSS that utilizes an existent mobile communication GSM infrastructure. Due to high market penetration of mobile communication channels, such as a rate of 96% in Germany (Bundesnetzagentur 2006), service providers are able to offer new services to most of their customers via an as yet unexploited communication channel. When service providers succeed in pointing out the relative advantage of these novel mobile services, they should be able to increase the number of transactions performed by customers, which is generally a major business goal.

One could argue that the relative advantage provided to customers will persist only for a given period of time until all investors will use the service. Following this argument, the diffusion of a mobile financial information service would have significantly increased the efficiency of the capital market since stock prices would reflect the new information available more quickly. It is quite unlikely that all investors will behave the same way and adopt the service. When the service will be used by private investors only, trading volumes usually below 7,500 € per trade can be assumed (European Commission 2005). This should have only a minor impact on the stock price development, which depends on other factors such as the market segment. Furthermore, the DDS component does not provide any information whether to sell or buy the affected stock and how much to trade, i.e. the users of the service will not trade equally. Therefore, significantly increased market efficiency due to an implementation of the *MoFin DSS* is rather improbable because of a presumable adoption rate significantly below 100%, diverse trading behavior, and the expected trading volumes.

- The developed metrics and methodology for evaluating the customers' value of the IT artifact can be applied by companies planning investments into financial information and decision support services such as the presented IT artifact. The simulation-based evaluation methodology addresses the relative advantage provided by financial services often neglected in the past. The approach is flexible for customization such as different trading volumes and trading costs. Applying the simulation-based evaluation approach to *MoFin DSS* (Section 5.3) has proven significant IT business value provided to customers under several assumptions (e.g. specific trading cost function and minimum trading volumes).

This result raises the question why there is no corresponding product available on the market yet. Typical for an IT artifact and its innovative character, the *MoFin DSS* concept and the prototypical implementation has a set of limitations (presented in Section 4.3.5) that call for further research and developments before it can be offered to customers. This constitutes the difference between design science and routine design (Hevner et al. 2004). Some of the limitations that need to be addressed before bringing a corresponding financial service onto the market comprise unsolved security issues, more sophisticated forecasting models, and automated model adjustments. Some of these issues are addressed in the following section presenting research questions that can be addressed by further research.

The presented implications of the finding to practice can be fruitful to the practitioner in the field. However, investment into applications and services offered to customers need to be based on conventional analyses, such as *net present value* (NPV) calculations, since the investment profitability depends on business situations and many other factors, which are not the subject matter of this work (Bodie and Merton 2000).

6.4 Further Research

The preceding sections have summarized the general approach, major research contributions, and the practical implications of this work. Keeping the presented limitations in mind, the findings provide opportunities for further research not yet addressed in this work. New avenues for future research also arise due to the research contributions such as the event study results and its implications on the efficient market hypothesis, the IT artifact designed, and the simulation-based consumers' value evaluations for assessing the IT business value provided. The research opportunities, which have now opened up, are presented in the following including brief discussions of possible research approaches.

- Generalization of the intraday event study findings regarding other event types

  The event study presented in Chapter 2 analyzed the intraday stock price adjustment process following the publication of ad hoc disclosures pursuant to article 15 of the German Securities Trading Act (WpHG). The empirical results provided evidence for significant abnormal stock returns following the publication date of the disclosures. These results made this kind of event an interesting candidate to focus on. The DSS concept and IT arti-fact design developed in the subsequent chapters were motivated by the knowledge that observing and reacting to this kind of event offers an opportunity to investors. With regard to a broader, more international focus, the presented concept could gain more flexibility when other kinds of events could be integrated. There is a wide range of potential candi-dates of events that could also provide opportunities to investors both on the German and on other international stock markets. As there exist similar regulations to article 15 WpHG in other countries such as Switzerland (Article 72 Kotierungsreglement), Austria (Article 82 Börsegesetz), and the USA (Section 13 Securities Exchange Act of 1934), similar intra-day event study analyses could provide insights into the corresponding stock price adjust-ments on those capital markets. Furthermore, other event types such as analyst reports or changes in credit ratings are promising event types that should be subject of future analy-ses.

So far, there exist several intraday event studies analyses addressing the intraday speed of stock price adjustments following different kinds of event types. However, these analyses do not comply with the requirements needed, since they use highly aggregated stock price series. The intervals of analysis are longer than the one-minute intervals used in this work and therefore do not provide detailed insights into the adjustment process of intraday stock prices. Thus, there exist opportunities and challenges for identifying relevant market events and the detailed analysis of subsequent stock price adjustments using voluminous intraday stock price series. To be able to process such data volumes, corresponding analyses can be methodologically addressed with an approach that realizes automation of data processing (Section 2.2.1.3).

- Further development of highly sophisticated forecasting models

The forecasting models developed in this work (Chapter 3) represent a novel approach to identifying relevant market events for which price effects lie above the effect that can be expected on average. This also includes the corresponding period of time, for which these price effects can be expected. Being based on an explanatory and time series model ap-proach, these forecasting models significantly differ from existing approaches in this field, which work with text mining techniques (e.g. Mittermayer 2004; Schulz et al. 2003). While the presented models feature superior forecasting quality, there is still room for im-provements, in particular through the development of enhanced forecasting models.

In a first step, specific forecasting models for index and non-index members could be sub-ject to further analysis, which was not possible here since the necessary data samples have to be larger than the ones used. The presented event study covers a period of two years and 425 observations, which is a relatively large data basis compared to former intraday analy-ses (e.g. Barclay and Litzenberger 1988; Carter and Soo 1999; Patell and Wolfson 1982).

Therefore, long-term intraday data series covering a number of more years would provide the opportunity to explore highly specialized forecasting models. Furthermore, the existing forecasting approaches, i.e. text mining, explanatory model, and time series model could be integrated into multi-methodic forecasting approaches.

Another valuable extension of the existing approaches can be self-adjusting, i.e. learning model approaches. Currently, the forecasting models are econometrically and manually estimated, i.e. these models do not automatically consider changes in market conditions and market behavior. Therefore, further attention should be given to the development and evaluation of self-learning forecasting models.

- Selection of optimal communication channels

The *MoFin DSS* IT artifact provides support for three push message services SMS, MMS and WAP Push. In the current artifact design, users need to define manually the preferred communication channel, which opens up opportunities for further research. Selection of optimal communication channels for message-based user-to-user communication has been addressed by Muntermann and Milic Frayling (2006) with the design science research approach. Their IT artifact design and the underlying model for selecting the most appropriate communication channel take into account a set of characteristics such as message characteristics, reachability and user preferences. Furthermore, it provides the functionality to estimate the communication costs involved when sending a message via a communication channel. While their proposed artifact is flexible regarding different communication channels, it was designed for supporting user-to-user communication (Muntermann and Milic Frayling 2006). The problem of choosing an optimal communication channel for service-to-user communication is far from settled and will be subject to further research. Besides utilizing the design science research paradigm, research in this field can be based on media richness theory, exploring which communication channels would be preferred by customers, e.g. depending on the message contents or the personal situation (Daft and Lengel 1986).

- Addressing security requirements with novel security mechanisms and technologies

The security analysis presented in section 4.3.5.3 provided insights into as yet unsolved protection goals such as integrity, availability, and accountability. These are closely connected with the communication channels used, i.e. mobile messaging services, which do not provide corresponding security mechanism (Muntermann and Roßnagel 2006). Therefore, further research is required in this field providing novel security mechanisms providing better security features combined with high usability.

On the other hand, in the field of financial information and transaction services, different parties are involved, such as content providers, banks, and customers. All these parties can have different, possibly contradicting interests. The problem of respecting these individual interests can be addressed with the multilateral security paradigm, e.g. by balancing the different security requirements (Rannenberg 2000b). Such research approaches could help to increase adoption rates of mobile financial services since security concerns are one of the major inhibiting factors in this domain (Luarn and Lin 2005).

- Analysis of the IT artifact's influence on the trading behavior of private investors

The design science research paradigm is applied in this work in order to extend the boundaries of capabilities of both investors and service providers. This is addressed with the design of an IT artifact that provides utility. In contrast, behavioral research aims to observe and explain the impact of information systems within an organizational context (Alter 2003). In this context, future behavioral science research could focus on the impact of the IT artifact designed and implemented in this work on the artifact's context, i.e. on the behavior of investors using a corresponding system. Behavioral science research is based on theoretical foundations such as the technology acceptance model, which, for example, could be applied in order to analyze perceived usefulness and how perceived ease of use affects customers' intention to use such a system (Davis 1989). From another perspective, research could be based on Rogers' innovation diffusion theory in order to analyze how different factors, such as technical compatibility or relative advantage, would influence the adoption of the presented IT artifact (Rogers 2003). These examples show that future behavioral research could contribute to the understanding of the artifact's usage and its effects, for example, by conducting case and field studies in order to explore the behavior of the parties involved.

- Development of a generalized simulation-based customer values' evaluation methodology

The business value of IT evaluation methodology presented in Chapter 5 represents a novel approach for assessing the customers' value provided by IT innovations. The approach addresses limitations of existing IT business value evaluation approaches that do not provide the functionality to evaluate new products and services for which no or limited historical empirical data, such as profitability, productivity, or customer demand datasets, is available. The presented simulation-based evaluation methodology (Section 5.3) bridges this gap and provides the functionality to perform *ex ante* customers' value evaluations needed for the assessment of IT innovations such as the presented *MoFin DSS* IT artifact. The developed evaluation methodology is based on defined performance criteria (Section 5.2), which were specifically defined for the evaluation of the *MoFin DSS* IT artifact. Future research in this field is desirable, especially towards a generalized simulation-based evaluation methodology, which enables researchers to estimate quantitatively the customers' value provided by IT innovations. A corresponding generalized methodology for assessing the IT business value provided could be used by design science researchers as a standard methodology for evaluating IT artifacts designed. So far, there exists no standardized evaluation approach, which impedes the comparison and verification of different competing innovations.

These further research directions and questions show that research in the mobile financial service domain is far from settled and that more interdisciplinary research (e.g. including financial research, information systems research and computer science) is needed in this field. This also includes the different research paradigms such as behavioral and design science.

References

Abramowitz, M. (1972) Handbook of Mathematical Functions with Formulas, Graphs, and Mathematical Tables, 9th ed., Dover Publications, New York, NY, USA.

Aharony, J. and Swary, I. (1980) Quarterly Dividend and Earnings Announcements and Stockholders' Returns: An Empirical Analysis, *Journal of Finance* (35:1), pp. 1-12.

Aitken, M. J.; Frino, A.; McCorry, M. S. and Swan, P. L. (1998) Short Sales Are Almost Instantaneously Bad News: Evidence from the Australian Stock Exchange, *Journal of Finance* (53:6), pp. 2205-2223.

Alter, S. (1977) A Taxonomy of Decision Support Systems, *Sloan Management Review* (19:1), pp. 39-56.

Alter, S. (1980) Decision Support Systems: Current Practice and Continuing Challenges, Addison-Wesley, Reading, MA, USA.

Alter, S. (2003) 18 Reasons Why IT-Reliant Work Systems Should Replace "The IT Artifact" as the Core Subject Matter of the IS Field, *Communications of the AIS* (12:23), pp. 365-394.

Anthony, R. N. (1965) Planning and Control Systems: A Framework for Analysis, Harvard Univ. Press, Boston, MA, USA.

Anthony, R. N. and Dearden, J. (1972) Management Control Systems, Irwin, Homewood, IL, USA.

Armitage, S. (1995) Event Study Methods and Evidence on Their Performance, *Journal of Economic Surveys* (8:4), pp. 25-52.

Ashley, J. W. (1962) Stock Prices and Changes in Earnings and Dividends: Some Empirical Results, *Journal of Political Economy* (70:1), pp. 82-85.

Au, Y. A. (2001) Design Science I: The Role of Design Science in Electronic Commerce Research, *Communications of the AIS* (7:1).

Awad, E. M. (2000) The Structure of E-Commerce in the Banking Industry: An Empirical Investigation, in: J. Prasad and W. Nance (Eds.), *Proceedings of the 2000 ACM SIGCPR Conference on Computer Personnel Research,* ACM Press, New York, NY, USA, pp. 144-150.

Ba, S.; Kalakota, R. and Whinston, A. B. (1997) Using Client-Broker-Server Architecture for Intranet Decision Support, *Decision Support Systems* (19:3), pp. 171-192.

BaFin (2002) Ad-hoc-Tatsachen sind unabhängig von Börsenhandelszeiten – unverzüglich - zu veröffentlichen, *www.bafin.de/presse/pm02/020212_wa.htm,* accessed 2003-11-18.

Ball, R. and Brown, P. (1968) An Empirical Evaluation of Accounting Income Numbers, *Journal of Accounting Research* (6:2), pp. 159-178.

Banker, R. D. and Kauffman, R. J. (2004) The Evolution of Research on Information Systems: A Fiftieth-Year Survey of the Literature in Management Science, *Management Science* (50:3), pp. 281-298.

Barclay, M. J. and Litzenberger, R. H. (1988) Announcement Effects of New Equity Issues and the Use of Intraday Price Data, *Journal of Financial Economics* (22:1), pp. 71-99.

Barnes, S. J. and Corbitt, B. (2003) Mobile Banking: Concept and Potential, *International Journal of Mobile Communications* (1:3), pp. 273-288.

Barua, A.; Kriebel, C. H. and Mukhopadhyay, T. (1995) Information Technologies and Business Value: An Analytic and Empirical Investigation, *Information Systems Research* (6:1), pp. 3-23.

Basole, R. C. and Chao, R. O. (2004) Location-Based Mobile Decision Support Systems and Their Effect On User Performance, in: C. Bullen and E. Stohr (Eds.), *Proceedings of the 10th American Conference on Information Systems*, New York, NY, USA, pp. 2870-2874.

Beale, R. and Jackson T. (1990) Neural Computing: An Introduction, Institute of Physics Publishing, York, UK.

Beck, R.; Wigand, R. T. and König, W. (2003) Creating Value in E-Banking: Efficient Usage of E-Commerce Applications and Technologies, in: M. Hillier; D. Falconer; J. Hanisch and S. Horrocks (Eds.), *Proceeding of the 7th Pacific Asia Conference on Information Systems*, Adelaide, Australia, pp. 775-785.

Beckett, A.; Hewer, P. and Howcroft, B. (2000) An Exposition of Consumer Behaviour in the Financial Services Industry, *International Journal of Bank Marketing* (18:1), pp. 15-26.

Benbasat, I. and Zmud, R. W. (1999) Empirical Research in Information Systems: The Practice of Relevance, *MIS Quarterly* (23:1), pp. 3-16.

Berry, M. A.; Gallinger, G. W. and Henderson, G. V. (1990) Using Daily Stock Returns in Event Studies and the Choice of Parametric and Nonparametric test Statistics, *Quarterly Journal of Business & Economics* (29:1), pp. 70-85.

Bhargava, H. K. and Power, D. J. (2001) Decision Support Systems and Web Technologies: A Status Report, in: D. Strong; D. Straub and J. DeGross (Eds.), *Proceedings of the 7th American Conference on Information Systems*, Boston, MA, USA, pp. 229-335.

Binder, J. (1998) The Event Study Methodology Since 1969, *Review of Quantitative Finance and Accounting* (11:2), pp. 111-137.

Birch, D. G. (1999) Mobile Financial Services: The Internet isn't the only Digital Channel to Consumers, *Journal of Internet Banking and Commerce* (4:1).

Bishop, C. (2004) Neural Networks for Pattern Recognition, Oxford University Press, Oxford, UK.

Bishop, M. (2004) Introduction to Computer Security, Addison-Wesley, Boston, MA, USA.

Bodie, Z. and Merton, R. C. (2000) Finance, Prentice Hall, Upper Saddle River, NJ, USA.

Bonczek, R. H.; Holsapple, C. W. and Whinston, A. B. (1981) Foundations of Decision Support Systems, Academic Press, New York, NY, USA.

Booch, G.; Rumbaugh, J. and Jacobson, I. (2005) The Unified Modeling Language User Guide, 2nd ed., Addison-Wesley, Boston, MA, USA.

Boockholdt, J. L. (1989) Implementing Security and Integrity in Micro-Mainframe Networks, *MIS Quarterly* (13:2), pp. 134-144.

Bowman, R. G. (1983) Understanding and Conducting Event Studies, *Journal of Business Finance and Accounting* (10:4), pp. 561-584.

Bresnahan, T. F. (1986) Measuring the Spillovers from Technical Advance: Mainframe Computers in Financial Services, *The American Economic Review* (76:4), pp. 742-755.

Brown, A.; Blaber, G. and Bouchard, J. (2006) Struggle for Handset Differentiation: European Mobile Phone Market Analysis, 4Q05, IDC, Framingham, MA, USA.

Brown, I.; Cajee, Z.; Davies, D. and Stroebel, S. (2003) Cell Phone Banking: Predictors of Adoption in South Africa - Exploratory Study, *International Journal of Information Management* (23:5), pp. 381-394.

Brown, K. C.; Lockwood, L. J. and Lummer, S. L. (1985) An Examination of Event Dependency and Structural Change in Security Pricing Models, *Journal of Financial and Quantitative Analysis* (20:3), pp. 315-334.

Brown, S. J. and Warner, J. B. (1980) Measuring Security Price Performance, *Journal of Financial Economics* (8:3), pp. 205-258.

Brown, S. J. and Warner, J. B. (1985) Using Daily Stock Returns: The Case of Event Studies, *Journal of Financial Economics* (14:1), pp. 3-31.

Brynjolfsson, E. (1993) The Productivity Paradox of Information Technology, Communications of the ACM (36:12), pp. 66-77.

Brynjolfsson, E. (1996) The Contribution of Information Technology to Consumer Welfare, *Information Systems Research* (7:3), pp. 281-300.

Brynjolfsson, E. and Hitt, L. M. (1993) Is Information Systems Spending Productive? New Evidence and New Results, in: J. I. DeGross; R. P. Bostrom and D. Robey (Eds.), *Proceedings of the Fourteenth International Conference on Information Systems,* Orlando, FL, USA, pp. 47-64.

Brynjolfsson, E. and Hitt, L. M. (1996) The Customer Counts, *Information Week* (September 8), pp. 38-43.

Brynjolfsson, E. and Hitt, L. M. (1996a) Paradox Lost? Firm-level Evidence on the Returns to Information Systems Spending, *Management Science* (42:4), pp. 541-558.

Brynjolfsson, E. and Hitt, L. M. (2003) Computing Productivity: Firm-Level Evidence, *Review of Economics and Statistics* (85:4), pp. 793-808.

Brynjolfsson, E.; Hu, Y. and Smith, M. D. (2003) Consumer Surplus in the Digital Economy: Estimating the Value of Increased Product Variety at Online Booksellers, *Management Science* (49:11), pp. 1580-1596.

Bundesaufsichtsamt für den Wertpapierhandel (1998) Gesetz über den Wertpapierhandel (Wertpapierhandelsgesetz - WpHG), *Bundesgesetzblatt* (62), pp. 2708-2725.

Bundesnetzagentur (2006) Jahresbericht 2005, Druckteam Berlin, Bonn, Germany.

Campbell, C. J. and Wasley, C. E. (1993) Measuring Security Price Performance Using Daily NASDAQ Returns, *Journal of Financial Economics* (33:1), pp. 73-92.

Campbell, J. Y.; Lo, A. W. and MacKinlay, A. C. (1997) The Econometrics of Financial Markets, 2nd ed., Princeton Univ. Press, Princeton, NJ, USA.

Carter, M. and Soo, B. (1999) The Relevance of Form 8-K Reports, *Journal of Accounting Journal of Accounting Research* (37:1), pp. 119-132.

Chan, Y. E. (2000) IT Value: The Great Divide Between Qualitative and Quantitative and Individual and Organizational Measures, *Journal of Management Information Systems* (16:4), pp. 225-261.

Chatterjee, D.; Richardson, V. J. and Zmud, R. W. (2001) Examining the Shareholder Wealth Effects of Announcements of Newly Created CIO Positions, *MIS Quarterly* (25:3), pp. 43-70.

Chen, P. P. (1976) The Entity-Relationship Model - Toward a Unified View of Data, *ACM Transactions on Database Systems* (1:1), pp. 9-36.

Chen, P. and Hitt, L. M. (2002) Measuring Switching Costs and the Determinants of Customer Retention in Internet-Enabled Businesses: A Study of the Online Brokerage Industry, *Information Systems Research* (3:13), pp. 255-274.

Chircu, A. M. and Kauffman, R. (2000) Limits to Value in Electronic Commerce-Related IT Investments, *Journal of Management Information Systems* (17:2), pp. 59-80.

Chowdhury, A. (2003) Information Technology and Productivity Payoff in the Banking Industry: Evidence from the Emerging Markets, *Journal of International Development* (15:6), pp. 693-708.

Clemons, E. K. (1991) Evaluation of Strategic Investments in Information Technology, *Communications of the ACM* (34:1), pp. 22-36.

Cobb, C. W. and Douglas, P. H. (1928) A Theory of Production, *The American Economic Review* (18:1 (Supplement)), pp. 139-165.

Comdirect Bank (2005) Preis- und Leistungsverzeichnis, *www.comdirect.de,* accessed 2005-04-01.

Corrado, C. J. (1989) A Nonparametric Test for Abnormal Security-Price Performance in Event Studies, *Journal of Financial Economics* (23:2), pp. 385-395.

Crane, D. B. and Bodie, Z. (1996) Form Follows Function: The Transformation of Banking, *Harvard Business Review* (74:2), pp. 109-117.

Dacorogna, M. M.; Gençay, R.; Müller, U. A.; Olsen, R. B. and Pictet, O. V. (2001) An Introduction to High-Frequency Finance, Academic Press, San Diego, CA, USA.

Daft, R. L. and Lengel, R. H. (1986) Organizational Information Requirements, Media Richness and Structural Design, *Management Science* (32:5), pp. 554-571.

Daniel, W. W. (1978) Applied Nonparametric Statistics, Houghton Mifflin, Boston, MA, USA.

Davern, M. J. and Kauffman, R. J. (2000) Discovering Potential and Realizing Value from Information Technology Investments, *Journal of Management Information Systems* (16:4), pp. 121-143.

Davis, F. D. (1989) Perceived Usefulness, Perceived Ease of Use, and User Acceptance of Information Technology, *MIS Quarterly* (13:3), pp. 319-340.

Denning, P. J. (1997) A New Social Contract for Research - The Science of Future Technology, *Communications of the ACM* (40:2), pp. 132-134.

Deutsche Börse Group (2002) One+ Minimum Lot Size, *www.deutsche-boerse.com*, accessed 2003-01-12.

Deutsche Börse Group (2003) Xetra - The Electronic Trading Platform, *www.xetra.com*, accessed 2004-10-04.

Deutsche Börse Group (2005) Overview Equity Indices, *www.deutscheboerse.com*, accessed 2006-01-05.

Deutsche Gesellschaft für Ad-hoc-Publizität (2002) One-Source Financial Market Communication, Frankfurt am Main, Germany.

Dhar, V. and Stein, R. (1997) Intelligent Decision Support Methods, Prentice Hall, Upper Saddle River, NJ, USA.

Diebold, F. X. (2001) Elements of Forecasting, 2nd ed., South-Western, Cincinnati, OH, USA.

Dodd, P. and Warner, J. (1983) On Corporate Governance, *Journal of Financial Economics* (11:1-4), pp. 401-438.

Dolley, J. C. (1933) Characteristics and Procedure of Common Stock Split-Ups, *Harvard Business Review* (11), pp. 316-326.

Dos Santos, B. L.; Peffers, K. and Mauer, D. C. (1993) The Impact of Information Technology Invest Announcements on the Market Value of the Firm, *Information Systems Research* (4:1), pp. 1-23.

European Commission (2005) Working Document ESC/20/2005 REV1 - Transparency and Admission to Trading, Brussels, Belgium.

European Telecommunications Standards Institute (1992) GSM 3.40 - Technical Realization of the Short Message Service - Point-to-Point, Valbonne Cedex, France.

European Telecommunications Standards Institute (1998) GSM 07.05 - Specification 5.5.0, Valbonne Cedex, France.

Fama, E. F. (1970) Efficient Capital Markets: A Review of Theory and Empirical Work, *Journal of Finance* (25:2), pp. 383-417.

Fama, E. F. (1991) Efficient Capital Markets: II, *Journal of Finance* (46:5), pp. 1575-1617.

Fama, E. F.; Fisher, L.; Jensen, M. C. and Roll, R. (1969) The Adjustment of Stock Prices to New Information, *International Economic Review* (10:1), pp. 1-21.

Fandel, G. (1991) Theory of Production and Cost, Springer, Berlin, Germany.

Field, A. (2005) Discovering Statistics Using SPSS for Windows, 2nd ed., Sage Publications, London, UK.

Flynt, C. (1999) Tcl/Tk for Real Programmers, Morgan Kaufmann, San Diego, CA, USA.

Franke, R. H. (1987) Technological Revolution and Productivity Decline: Computer Introduction in the Financial Industry, *Technological Forecasting and Social Change* (31), pp. 143-154.

Ginzberg, M. J. and Stohr, E. A. (1982) Decision Support Systems: Issues and Perspectives, in: M. Ginzberg; W. Reitman and E. Stohr (Eds.), Decision Support Systems, North-Holland, The Netherlands, pp. 9-32.

Glaser, M. and Weber, M. (2004) Overconfidence and Trading Volume, *CEPR Discussion Paper DP 3941,* Mannheim, Germany.

Gollmann, D. (2005) Computer Security, 2nd ed., Wiley & Sons Ltd., Chichester, UK.

Gorry, G. A. and Scott Morton, M. S. (1971) A Framework for Management Information Systems, *Sloan Management Review* (13:1), pp. 55-70.

Gray, P. (2002) Relevance as "Unfulfilled Promise", in: N. Kock; P. Gray; R. Hoving; H. Klein; M. D. Myers and J. Rockart (Eds.) IS Research Relevance Revisited: Subtle Accomplishment, Unfulfilled Promise, or Serial Hypocrisy?, *Communications of the AIS* (8:23), pp. 336-339.

Grenci, R. T. and Todd, P. A. (2002) Solutions-Driven Marketing, *Communications of the ACM* (45:3), pp. 64-71.

Groebner, D.; Shannon, P.; Fry, P. and Smith, K. (2001) Business Statistics, 5th ed., Prentice Hall, Upper Saddle River, NJ, USA.

Hackathorn, R. D. and Keen, P. G. W. (1981) Organizational Strategies for Personal Computing in Decision Support Systems, *MIS Quarterly* (5:3), pp. 21-27.

Harris, R. I. D. and Sollis, R. (2003) Applied Time Series Modelling and Forecasting, Wiley, New York, NY, USA.

Healy, P. M. and Palepu, K. G. (1993) The Effect of Firms' Financial Disclosure Strategies on Stock Prices, *Accounting Horizons* (7:1), pp. 1-11.

Herzberg, A. (2003) Payments and Banking with Mobile Personal Devices, *Communications of the ACM* (46:5), pp. 53-58.

Hevner, A. R. and March, S. T. (2003) The Information Systems Research Cycle, *IEEE Computer* (36:11), pp. 111-113.

Hevner, A. R.; March, S. T. and Park, J. (2004) Design Science in Information Systems Research, *MIS Quarterly* (28:1), pp. 75-105.

Heymann, H. G. and Bloom, R. (1988) Decision Support Systems in Finance and Accounting, Quorum Books, New York, NY, USA.

Hitt, L. M. and Brynjolfsson, E. (1996) Productivity, Business Profitability, and Consumer Surplus: Three Different Measures of Information Technology Value, *MIS Quarterly* (20:2), pp. 121-142.

Holland, C. P. and Westwood, J. B. (2001) Product-Market and Technology Strategies in Banking, *Communications of the ACM* (44:5), pp. 53-57.

Holland, C. P.; Lockett, A. G. and Blackman, I. D. (1997) The Impact of Globalisation and Information Technology on the Strategy and Profitability of the Banking Industry, in: R. H. Sprague (Eds.), *Proceedings of the 30th Hawaii International Conference on System Sciences,* IEEE Computer Society, Los Alamitos, CA, USA, pp. 418-427.

Howcroft, B.; Hamilton, R. and Hewer, P. (2002) Consumer Attitude and the Usage and Adoption of Home-Based Banking in the United Kingdom, *International Journal of Bank Marketing* (20:3), pp. 111-121.

ISO/IEC (1991) Software Product Evaluation – Quality Characteristics and Guidelines for their Use, ISO/IEC 9216:1991(E).

Jennings, R. and Starks, L. (1985) Information Content and the Speed of Stock Price Adjustment, *Journal of Accounting Research* (23:1), pp. 336-350.

Jennings, R. and Starks, L. (1986) Earnings Announcements, Stock Price Adjustments, and the Existence of Option Markets, *Journal of Finance* (41:1), pp. 107-125.

Jensen, M. C. (1978) Some Anomalous Evidence Regarding Market Efficiency, *Journal of Financial Economics* (6:2), pp. 95-101.

Johnson, R. A. (2000) The Ups and Downs of Object-Oriented Systems Development, *Communications of the ACM* (43:10), pp. 68-73.

Kalay, A. and Lowenstein, U. (1986) Predictable Events and Excess Returns: The Case of Dividend Announcements, *Journal of Financial Economics* (14:2), pp. 423-450.

Karjaluoto, H. (2002) Selection Criteria for a Mode of Bill Payment: Empirical Investigation among Finnish Bank Customers, *International Journal of Retail & Distribution Management* (30:6), pp. 331-339.

Kaserer, C. and Nowak, E. (2001) Die Anwendung von Ereignisstudien bei Ad-hoc-Mitteilungen, *Zeitschrift für Betriebswirtschaft* (70:11), pp. 1353-1356.

Keen, P. G. and Scott Morton, M. S. (1978) Decision Support Systems: An Organizational Perspective, Addison-Wesley, Reading, MA, USA.

Kirs, P. J.; Sanders, G. L.; Cerveny, R. P. and Robey, D. (1989) An Experimental Validation of the Gorry and Scott Morton Framework, *MIS Quarterly* (13:2), pp. 183-197.

Klein, A. and Rosenfeld, J. (1987) The Influence of Market Conditions on Event-Study Residuals, *Journal of Financial and Quantitative Analysis* (22:3), pp. 345-351.

Kock, N.; Gray, P.; Hoving, R.; Klein, H.; Myers, M. D. and Rockart, J. (2002) IS Research Relevance Revisited: Subtle Accomplishment, Unfulfilled Promise, or Serial Hypocrisy? *Communications of the AIS* (8:23).

Kohli, R. and Devaraj, S. (2003) Measuring Information Technology Payoff: A Meta-Analysis of Structural Variables in Firm-Level Empirical Research, *Information Systems Research* (14:2), pp. 127-145.

Krammer, A. (2002) Internet Brokerage - Fragen des (internationalen) Verbraucher- und Anlegerschutzes, Shaker, Aachen, Germany.

Lanedri, A. (2002) Mobile Financial Services, in: R. W. Watson; Y. Murakami and T. Davenport (Eds.), *Proceedings of the 6th Pacific-Asia Conference on Information Systems*, Tokyo, Japan, pp. 1073-1077.

Laudon, K. C. and Laudon, J. P. (2006) Management Information Systems: Managing the Digital Firm, 9th ed., Pearson Prentice Hall, Upper Saddle River, NJ, USA.

Laukkanen, T. and Lauronen, J. (2005) Consumer Value Creation in Mobile Banking Services, *International Journal of Mobile Communications* (3:4), pp. 325-338.

Lee, A. S. (1999) Rigor and Relevance in MIS Research: Beyond the Approach of Positivism Alone, *MIS Quarterly* (23:1), pp. 29-33.

Lee, C. M. C.; Ready, M. J. and Seguin, P. J. (1994) Volume, Volatility, and New York Stock Exchange Trading Halts, *Journal of Finance* (49:1), pp. 183-213.

Lee, M. S.; McGoldrick, P. J.; Keeling, K. A. and Doherty, J. (2003) Using ZMET to Explore Barriers to the Adoption of 3G Mobile Banking Services, *International Journal of Retail & Distribution Management* (31:6), pp. 340-348.

Lee, S. C. (2001) Modeling the Business Value of Information Technology, *Information & Management* (39:3), pp. 191-210.

Leis, J. and Nowak, E. (2001) Ad-hoc-Publizität nach 15 WpHG, Schäffer-Poeschel, Stuttgart, Germany.

Lichtenberg, F. R. (1995) The Output Contributions of Computer Equipment and Personnel: A Firm Level Analysis, *Economics of Innovation and New Technology* (3-4:3), pp. 201-217.

Looney, C. A. and Chatterjee, D. (2002) Web-Enabled Transformation of the Brokerage Industry, *Communications of the ACM* (45:8), pp. 75-81.

Loveman, G. W. (1994) An Assessment of the Productivity Impact on Information Technologies, in: T. J. Allen and M. S. Scott Morton (Eds.), *Information Technology and the Corporation of the 1990s: Research Studies,* Oxford University Press, Cambridge, U.K., pp. 84-110.

Luarn, P. and Lin, H. (2005) Toward an Understanding of the Behavioral Intention to Use Mobile Banking, *Computers in Human Behavior* (21:6), pp. 873-891.

MacKinlay, A. C. (1997) Event Studies in Economics and Finance, *Journal of Economic Literature* (35:1), pp. 13-39.

Makridakis, S. G.; Wheelwright, S. C. and Hyndman, R. J. (1998) Forecasting: Methods and Applications, 3rd ed., Wiley, New York, NY, USA.

Mallat, N.; Rossi, M. and Tuunainen, V. K. (2004) Mobile Banking Services, *Communications of the ACM* (47:5), pp. 42-46.

Mallick, M. (2003) Mobile and Wireless Design Essentials, Wiley, New York, NY, USA.

Mandelker, G. (1974) Risk and Return: The Case of Merging Firms, *Journal of Financial Economics* (1:4), pp. 303-336.

Mang, F. and Georgi, F. (2006) Elektronische mobile Bankdienstleistungen werden hoffähig, *Wirtschaftsinformatik* (48:6), pp. 467-468.

Mankiw, N. G. (2004) Essentials of Economics, 3rd ed., South-Western, Mason, OH, USA.

Marakas, G. M. (2002) Decision Support Systems in the 21st Century, 2nd ed., Prentice Hall, Upper Saddle River, NJ, USA.

March, S. T. and Smith, G. F. (1995) Design and Natural Science Research on Information Technology, *Decision Support Systems* (15:4), pp. 251-266.

March, S. T. and Storey, V. C. (2006) Call for Papers MISQ Special Issue on Design Science Research, *MIS Quarterly*.

Markus, M. L.; Majchrzak, A. and Gasser, L. (2002) A Design Theory for Systems that Support Emergent Knowledge Processes, MIS Quarterly (3:26), pp. 179-212.

Martin, M. C.; Bradbard, D. A. and Peter, C. (2005) Customer Decision Support Systems: Online Tools for Consumer Decision Making, *Journal of E-Business* (1:5).

Mattila, M. (2003) Factors Affecting The Adoption of Mobile Banking Services, *Journal of Internet Banking and Commerce* (8:1).

McCrickard, D. S.; Catrambone, R.; Chewar, C. M. and Stasko, J. T. (2003) Establishing Tradeoffs that Leverage Attention for Utility: Empirically Evaluating Information Display in Notification Systems, *International Journal of Human-Computer Studies* (58:5), pp. 547-582.

McKenney, J. L.; Mason, R. O. and Copeland, D. G. (1997) Bank of America: The Crest and Trough of Technological Leadership, *MIS Quarterly* (21:3), pp. 321-353.

McWilliams, A. and Siegel, D. (1997) Event Studies in Management Research: Theoretical and Empirical Issues, *Academy of Management Journal* (40:3), pp. 626-657.

McWilliams, V. B. (1990) Managerial Share Ownership and the Stock Price Effects of Anti-takeover Amendment Proposals, *Journal of Finance* (45:5), pp. 1627-1640.

Meyer, T. (2006) Online Banking: What We Learn from the Differences in Europe, *www.dbresearch.com,* accessed 2006-03-20.

Minz, R.; Möllenkamp, H.; Dreischmeier, R. and Felden, F. (2004) IT Costs in Banks: Revisit Your Beliefs!, The Boston Consulting Group (Eds.), Munich, Germany.

Mittermayer, M. (2004) Forecasting Intraday Stock Price Trends with Text Mining Techniques, in: R. H. Sprague (Eds.), *Proceedings of the 37th Annual Hawaii International Conference on System Sciences,* Computer Society Press, Los Alamitos, CA, USA.

Morrison, C. J. and Berndt, E. R. (1991) Assessing the Productivity of Information Technology Equipment in U.S. Manufacturing Industries, in: National Bureau of Economic Research (Eds.), *NBER Working Paper No. W3582.*

Muntermann, J. (2004) Notifying Investors in Time - A Mobile Information System Approach, in: C. Bullen and E. Stohr (Eds.), *Proceedings of the 10th American Conference on Information Systems*, New York, NY, USA, pp. 2825-2833.

Muntermann, J. (2005) Automated ANN Alerts: One Step Ahead with Mobile Support, *Hochschulschriften der Johann Wolfgang Goethe-Universität,* publikationen.ub.uni-frankfurt.de/volltexte/2006/2393/, accessed 2006-01-18.

Muntermann, J. and Janssen, L. (2005) Assessing Customers' Value of Mobile Financial Information Services: Empirical-Based Measures, in: D. Avison; D. Galletta and J. I. DeGross (Eds.), *Proceedings of the 26th International Conference,* Las Vegas, NV, USA, pp. 617-628.

Muntermann, J. and Güttler, A. (2004) Mobile Financial Information Services: Capabilities of Suitable Push Services, in: C. Wei (Ed.), *Proceedings of the 8th Pacific-Asia Conference on Information Systems,* Shanghai, China, pp. 648-658.

Muntermann, J. and Güttler, A. (2005) Intraday Stock Price Effects of Ad Hoc Disclosures: The German Case, *Working Paper Series: Finance and Accounting* (145), Department of Finance, Goethe University Frankfurt am Main, Germany.

Muntermann, J. and Güttler, A. (2007) Intraday Stock Price Effects of Ad Hoc Disclosures: The German Case, *Journal of International Financial Markets, Institutions and Money* (17:1), pp. 1-24.

Muntermann, J. and Milic Frayling, N. (2006) Enhancing Asynchronous User Communication with Cross Platform and Channel Agnostic Messaging Services, in: N. Romano (Ed.), *Proceedings of the 12th Americas Conference on Information Systems,* Acapulco, Mexico, pp. 2024-2035.

Muntermann, J. and Roßnagel, H. (2006) Security Issues and Capabilities of Mobile Brokerage Services and Infrastructures, *Journal of Information System Security* (2:1), pp. 27-43.

Muntermann, J.; Roßnagel, H. and Rannenberg, K. (2005) Mobile Brokerage Infrastructures: Capabilities and Security Requirements, in: D. Bartmann; F. Rajola; J. Kallinikos; D. Avison; R. Winter; P. Ein-Dor; J. Becker; F. Bodendorf and C. Weinhardt (Eds.), *Proceedings of the 13th European Conference on Information Systems,* Regensburg, Germany.

Myers John H.; Bakay Archie J. (1948) Influence of Stock Split-ups on Market Price, *Harvard Business Review* pp. 251-255.

Nehmzow, C. (1997) The Internet Will Shake Banking's Medieval Foundations, *Journal of Internet Banking and Commerce* (2:2).

Newell, A. and Simon, H. A. (1976) Computer Science as Empirical Inquiry: Symbols and Search, *Communications of the ACM* (19:3), pp. 113-126.

Nowak, E. (2001) Eignung von Sachverhalten in Ad-hoc-Mitteilungen zur erheblichen Kursbeeinflussung, *Zeitschrift für Bankrecht und Bankwirtschaft* (13:6), pp. 449-524.

Nunamaker, J. F.; Chen, M. and Purdin, T. D. (1991) Systems Development in Information Systems Research, *Journal of Management Information Systems* (7:3), pp. 89-106.

O'Keefe, R. M. and McEachern, T. (1998) Web-based Customer Decision Support Systems, *Communications of the ACM* (41:3), pp. 71-78.

OMG Group (2005) Unified Modeling Language: Superstructure Version 2.0, *www.omg.org/cgi-bin/doc?formal/05-07-04*, accessed 2005-12-04.

Oerke, M. (1999) Ad-hoc-Mitteilungen und deutscher Aktienmarkt: Marktreaktion auf Informationen, Gabler, Wiesbaden, Germany.

Olivier, M. S. (2004) Information Technology Research, 2nd ed., Van Schaik Publishers, Hatfield, Pretoria, South Africa.

Open Mobile Alliance (2004) Multimedia Messaging Service Encapsulation Protocol, *www.openmobilealliance.org*, accessed 2005-12-01.

Orlikowski, W. J. and Iacono, C. S. (2001) Research Commentary: Desperately Seeking the 'IT' in IT Research - A Call to Theorizing the IT Artifact, *Information Systems Research* (12:2), pp. 121-134.

Padmanabhan, N.; Burstein, F.; Churilov, L.; Wassertheil, J.; Hornblower, B. and Parker, N. (2006) A Mobile Emergency Triage Decision Support System Evaluation, in: R. H. Sprague (Ed.), *Proceedings of the 36th Annual Hawaii International Conference on System Sciences,* Computer Society Press, Los Alamitos, CA, USA.

Parsons, D.; Gotlieb, C. C. and Denny, M. (1993) Productivity and Computers in Canadian Banking, *Journal of Productivity Analysis* (4:1), pp. 95-113.

Patell, J. M. (1976) Corporate Forecasts of Earnings per Share and Stock Price Behavior: Empirical Test, *Journal of Accounting Research* (14:2), pp. 246-276.

Patell, J. M. and Wolfson, M. A. (1982) Good News, Bad News, and the Intraday Timing of Corporate Disclosures, *Accounting Review* (57:3), pp. 509-527.

Patell, J. M. and Wolfson, M. A. (1984) The Intraday Speed of Adjustment of Stock Prices to Earnings and Dividend Announcements, *Journal of Financial Economics* (13:2), pp. 223-252.

Pavich, B. (2004) The Importance of Being Alert, *US Banker* (114:8), pp. 58-59.

Peterson, P. P. (1989) Event Studies: A Review of Issues and Methodology, *Quarterly Journal of Business and Economics* (3:28), pp. 36-66.

Philip, G.; Gopalakrishnan, M. and Mawalkar, S. R. (1995) Technology Management and Information Technology Strategy: Preliminary Results of an Empirical Study of Canadian Organizations, *International Journal of Information Management* (15:4), pp. 303-315.

Pikkarainen, T.; Pikkarainen, K.; Karjaluoto, H. and Pahnila, S. (2004) Consumer Acceptance of Online Banking: An Extension of the Technology Acceptance Model, *Internet Research: Electronic Networking and Applications* (14:3), pp. 224-235.

Poddig, T.; Dichtl, H. and Petersmeier, K. (2003) Statistik, Ökonometrie, Optimierung, 3rd ed., Uhlenbruch, Bad Soden, Germany.

Polatoglu, V. N. and Ekin, S. (2001) An Empirical Investigation of the Turkish Consumers' Acceptance of Internet Banking Services, *International Journal of Bank Marketing* (19:4), pp. 156-165.

Porter, M. E. (1980) Competitive Strategy, 16th ed., Free Press, New York, NY, USA.

Pousttchi, K. and Schurig, M. (2004) Assessment of Today's Mobile Banking Applications from the View of Customer Requirements, in: R. H. Sprague (Ed.), *Proceedings of the Proceedings of the 37th Annual Hawaii International Conference on System Sciences,* Computer Society Press, Los Alamitos, CA, USA.

Power, D. J. (2000) Web-Based and Model-Driven Decision Support Systems: Concepts and Issues, in: M. Chung (Ed.), *Proceedings of the 6th Americas Conference on Information Systems,* Long Beach, CA, USA, pp. 352-355.

Power, D. J. (2001) Supporting Decision-Makers: An Expanded Framework, in: E. Boyd (Eds.), *Proceedings of the 2001 Informing Science Conference,* Krakow, Poland.

Power, D. J. (2002) Decision Support Systems: Concepts and Resources for Managers, Greenwood Publishing, Westport, CT, USA.

Power, D. J. (2004) Specifying an Expanded Framework for Classifying and Describing Decision Support Systems, *Communications of the AIS* (13), pp. 158-166.

Rannenberg, K. (2000a) How Much Negotiation and Detail Can Users Handle? Experiences with Security Negotiation and the Granularity of Access Control in Communications, in: F. Cuppens; Y. Deswarte; D. Gollmann and M. Waidner (Eds.), *Proceedings of the 6th European Symposium on Research in Computer Security,* Toulouse, France, pp. 37-54.

Rannenberg, K. (2000b) Mehrseitige Sicherheit - Schutz für Unternehmen und ihre Partner im Internet, *Wirtschaftsinformatik* (42:6), pp. 489-497.

Rannenberg, K.; Pfitzmann, A. and Mueller, G. (1999) IT Security and Multilateral Security, in: G. Müller and K. Rannenberg (Eds.), *Multilateral Security in Communications - Technology, Infrastructure, Economy,* Addison-Wesley-Longman, Reading, MA, USA, pp. 21-29.

Rogers, E. M. (2003) Diffusion of Innovations, 5th ed., Free Press, New York, NY, USA.

Röder, K. (1999) Kurswirkungen von Meldungen deutscher Aktiengesellschaften, Eul, Köln, Germany.

Röder, K. (2000) Intraday Kurswirkungen bei Ad hoc-Meldungen, *Arbeitspapiere zur Mathematischen Wirtschaftsforschung* (175).

Röder, K. (2000b) Ad hoc-Meldungen und Intraday Kurse, in: H. Locarek-Junge and B. Walter (Eds.), *Banken im Wandel; Directbanken und Direct Banking, Neue Betriebswirtschaftliche Studienbücher*, Berlin, Germany, pp. 303-316.

Röder, K. (2002) Intraday-Umsätze bei Ad hoc-Meldungen, *Finanz-Betrieb* (4:12), pp. 728-735.

Salerno, L. M. (1985) What Happened to the Computer Revolution? *Harvard Business Review* (63:6), pp. 129-138.

Salinger, M. (1992) Value Event Studies, *Review of Economics & Statistics* (74:4), pp. 671-677.

Sanger, G. C. and Peterson, J. D. (1990) An Empirical Analysis of Common Stock Delistings, *Journal of Financial and Quantitative Analysis* (25:2), pp. 261-272.

Sawhney, N. and Schmandt, C. (2000) Nomadic Radio: Speech and Audio Interaction for Contextual Messaging in Nomadic Environments, *ACM Transactions on Computer-Human Interaction* (7:3), pp. 353-383.

Schiller, J. H. (2003) Mobile Communications, 2nd ed., Addison-Wesley, Boston, MA, USA.

Schulz, A.; Spiliopoulou, M. and Winkler, K. (2003) Kursrelevanzprognose von Ad-hoc-Meldungen: Text Mining wider die Informationsüberlastung im Mobile Banking, in: W. Uhr; W. Esswein and E. Schoop (Eds.), *Wirtschaftsinformatik 2003: Medien, Märkte, Mobilität, Band II*, Physika, Heidelberg, Germany, pp. 181-200.

Scott Morton, M. S. (1971) Management Decision Systems: Computerbased Support for Decision Making, Harvard Univ. Press, Boston, MA, USA.

Shen, S.; Pittet, S.; Milanesi, C.; Ingelbrecht, N.; Hart, T. J.; Desai, K.; Nguyen, T. H. and Basso, M. (2006) Overview of Consumer Mobile Applications, Gartner Research, Stamford, CT, USA.

Sheshunoff, A. (2000) Internet Banking - An Update from the Frontlines, *ABA Banking Journal* (92:1), pp. 51-53.

Sheskin, D. J. (2004) Handbook of Parametric and Nonparametric Statistical Procedures, 3rd ed., Chapman & Hall, Boca Raton, FL, USA.

Shim, J.; Warkentin, M.; Courtney, J. F.; Power, D. J.; Sharda, R. and Carlsson, C. (2002) Past, Present, and Future of Decision Support Technology, *Decision Support Systems* (33:2), pp. 111-126.

Short, M. (2006) One of Us Must Know, Netsize SA, *The Netsize Guide 2006*, Paris, France, pp. 12-14.

Simon, H. A. (1960) The New Sciences of Management Decision, Harper & Row, New York, NY, USA.

Simon, H. A. (1969) The Sciences of the Artificial, 1st ed., MIT Press, Cambridge, MA, USA.

Simon, H. A. (1996) The Sciences of the Artificial, 3rd ed., MIT Press, Cambridge, MA, USA.

Sircar, S.; Turnbow, J. L. and Bordoloi, B. (2000) A Framework for Assessing the Relationship Between Information Technology Investments and Firm Performance, *Journal of Management Information Systems* (16:4), pp. 69-97.

Smith, B. F.; White, R.; Robinson, M. and Nason, R. (1997) Intraday Volatility and Trading Volume After Takeover Announcements, *Journal of Banking & Finance* (21:3), pp. 337-368.

Smith, P. F. (1978) Money and Financial Intermediation, Prentice-Hall, Englewood Cliffs, NJ, USA.

Southard, P. B. and Siau, K. (2004) A Survey of Online E-Banking Retail Initiatives, *Communications of the ACM* (47:10), pp. 99-102.

Spiliopoulou, M.; Schulz, A. and Winkler, K. (2003) Text Mining an der Börse: Einfluss von Ad-hoc-Mitteilungen auf die Kursentwicklung, in: C. Becker and H. Redlich (Eds.), *Proceedings der 7. Konferenz der SAS-Anwender in Forschung und Entwicklung (KSFE)*, Shaker Verlag, Aachen, Germany, pp. 215-228.

Sprague, R. H. (1980) A Framework for the Development of Decision Support Systems, *MIS Quarterly* (4:4), pp. 1-26.

Sprague, R. H. and Watson, H. J. (1979) Bit by Bit: Toward Decision Support Systems, *California Management Review,* (22:1), pp. 60-68.

Sprague, R. H. and Watson, H. J. (1996) Decision Support for Management, Prentice-Hall, Upper Saddle River, NJ, USA.

Sprent, P. (1996) Applied Nonparametric Statistical Methods, 2nd ed., Chapman & Hall, London, UK.

Srinivasan, A.; March, S. and Saunders, C. (2005) Information Technology and Organizational Contexts: Orienting Our Work along Key Dimensions, in: D. Avison; D. Galletta and J. I. DeGross (Eds.), *Proceedings of the 26th International Conference on Information Systems,* Las Vegas, NV, USA, pp. 991-1001.

Ståhlberg, M. (2000) Radio Jamming Attacks Against Two Popular Mobile Networks, in: H. Lipmaa and H. Pehu-Lehtonen (Eds.), Proceedings of the Helsinki University of Technology - Seminar on Network Security Fall 2000, Mobile Security, Helsinki, Finland.

Stevens, P. and Pooley, R. (2006) Using UML: Software Engineering with Objects and Components, 2nd ed., Addison-Wesley, Boston, MA, USA.

Studenmund, A. H. (2006) Using Econometrics: A practical Guide, 5th ed., Pearson Addison Wesley, Boston, MA, USA.

Subramanyam, R. and Krishnan, M. S. (2001) Business Value of IT-Enabled Call Centers: An Empirical Analysis, in: V. Storey; S. Sarkar and J. I. DeGross (Eds.), *Proceedings of the 22nd International Conference on Information Systems,* New Orleans, LA, USA, pp. 55-64.

Sun, S.; Su, C. and Ju, T. (2005) A study of Consumer Value-added Services in Mobile Commerce: Focusing on Domestic Cellular Phone Companies in Taiwan, China, in: Q. Li and T. Liang (Eds.), *Proceedings of the 7th International Conference on Electronic Commerce,* ACM Press, New York, NY, USA, pp. 597-606.

Swanson, E. B. and Culnan, M. J. (1978) Document-Based Systems for Management Planning and Control: A Classification, Survey, and Assessment, *MIS Quarterly* (2:4), pp. 31-46.

Tiwana, A. and Ramesh, B. (2001) A Design Knowledge Management System to Support Collaborative Information Product Evolution, *Decision Support Systems* (31:2), pp. 241-262.

Turban, E.; Aronson, J. E. and Liang, T. (2005) Decision Support Systems and Intelligent Systems, 7th ed., Pearson Prentice Hall, Upper Saddle River, NJ, USA.

Vahidov, R. (2006) Design Researcher's IS Artifact: a Representational Framework, in: H. Chen; L. Olfman; A. Hevner and S. Chatterjee (Eds.), *Proceedings of the First International Conference on Design Science Research in Information Systems and Technology,* Claremont, CA, USA, pp. 20-33.

van Eyden, R. J. (1996) The Application of Neural Networks in the Forecasting of Share Prices, Finance & Technology Publishing, Haymarket, VA, USA.

van Veen, N.; Reitsma, R.; Carini, A. v. V. N.; Reitsma, R. and Carini, A. (2006) The European Mobile Landscape 2006: European Consumer Technology Adoption Study, Cambridge, MA, USA.

Venable, J. (2006) The Role of Theory and Theorizing in Design Science Research, in: H. Chen; L. Olfman; A. Hevner and S. Chatterjee (Eds.), *Proceedings of the First International Conference on Design Science Research in Information Systems and Technology,* Claremont, CA, USA, pp. 1-18.

von Rosen, R. (2004) DAI Factbook, Deutsches Aktieninstitut, Frankfurt am Main, Germany.

W3C (2004) Extensible Markup Language (XML) 1.1: W3C Recommendation 04 February 2004, *www.w3.org,* accessed 2005-10-23.

WAP Forum (2001a) WAP Push Architectural Overview: Version 03-July-2001, *www.wmlclub.com,* accessed 2004-08-03.

WAP Forum (2001b) MMS Architecture Overview, *www.wmlclub.com,* accessed 2004-10-20.

WAP Forum (2001c) Push OTA Protocol: Version 25-April-2001, *www.openmobilealliance.org,* accessed 2004-03-15.

Wang, Y.; Wang, Y.; Lin, H. and Tang, T. (2003) Determinants of User Acceptance of Internet Banking: An Empirical Study, *International Journal of Service Industry Management* (14:5), pp. 501-519.

Weiers, R. M. (2005) Introduction to Business Statistics, 5th ed., Thomson Brooks/Cole, Belmont, CA, USA.

Whitehorn, M. and Marklyn, B. (2001) Inside Relational Databases, 2nd ed., Springer, London, UK.

Wilcoxon, F. (1945) Individual Comparisons by Ranking Methods, *Biometrics Bulletin* (1:6), pp. 80-83.

Woodruff, C. S. and Senchak, A. (1988) Intradaily Price-Volume Adjustments of NYSE Stocks to Unexpected Earnings, *Journal of Finance* (43:2), pp. 467-491.

Appendix: Realizable Return Distributions

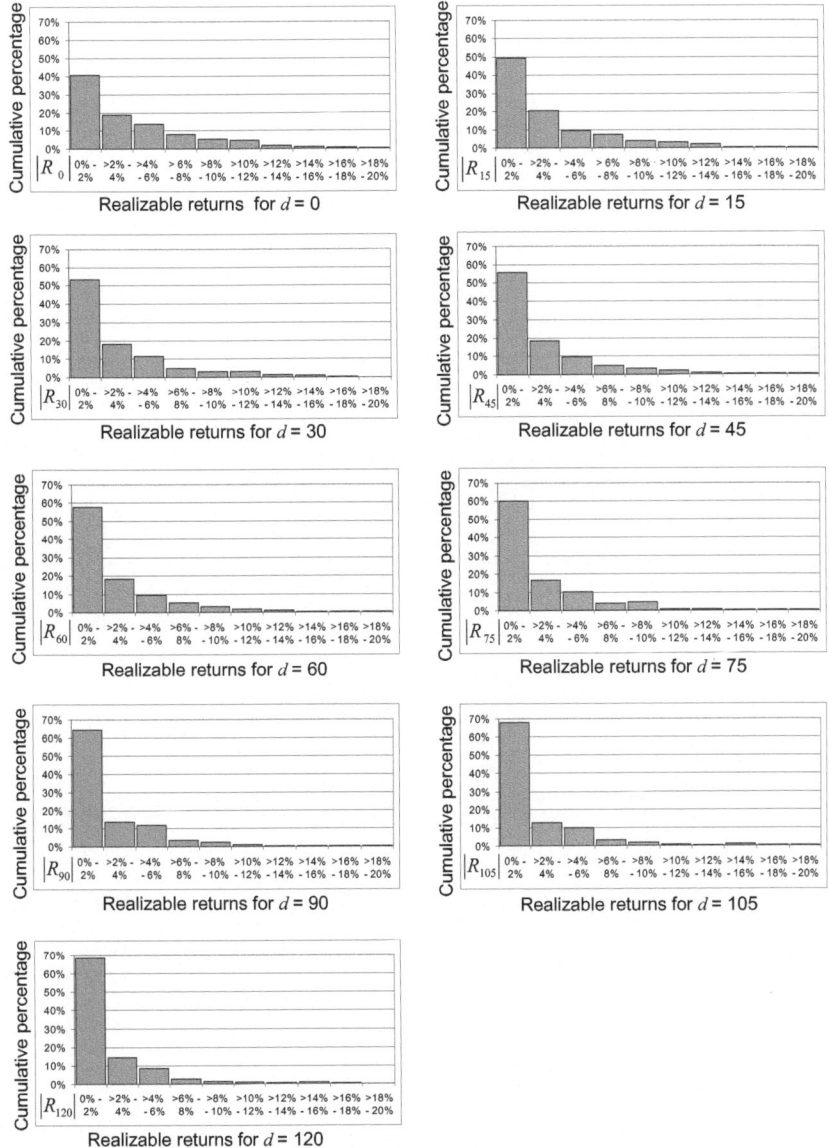

Realizable Return Distributions for all Events (I = 425)

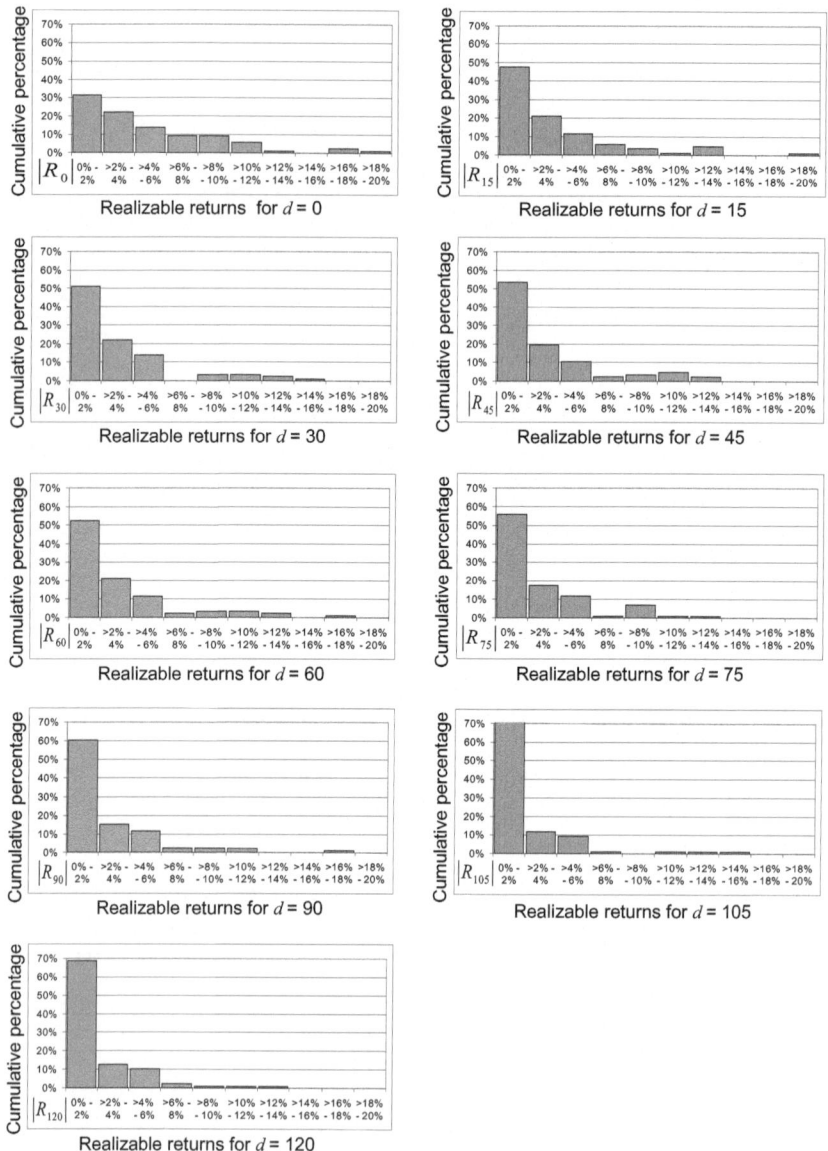

Realizable Return Distributions for all Forecasted *Relevant* Events (*I* = 86)

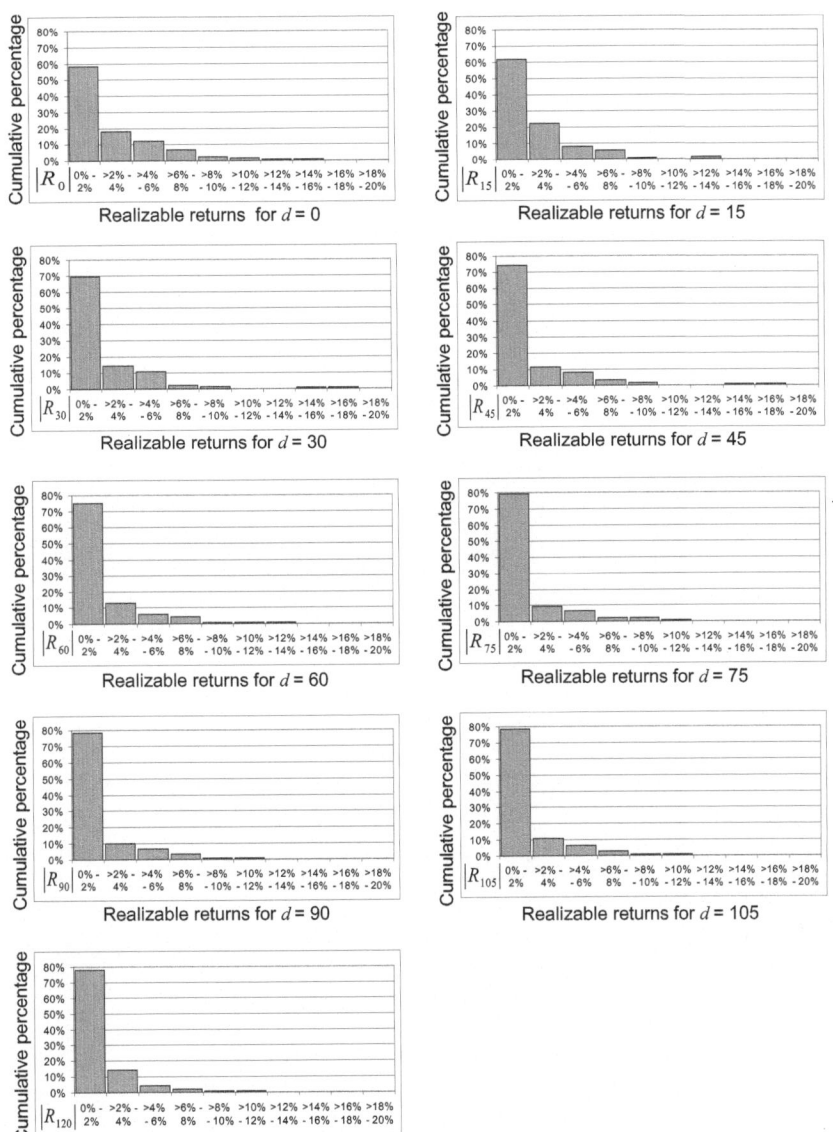

Realizable Return Distributions for all Forecasted *Irrelevant* Events (*I* = 139)